PAT BROWN, MBA

Financial Literacy For Nurses

"Caring for Patients, Now Care for Your Finances: A Nurse's Guide to Financial Confidence."

ABRAM 47 BROWN

First published by AbramBrown47 2025

First edition

ISBN: 978-1-967737-34-5

This book was professionally typeset on Reedsy.
Find out more at reedsy.com

Contents

Author's Preface

I didn't write this book because I had extra time. I wrote it because I kept seeing a pattern I couldn't ignore. It started with one nurse—overworked, overwhelmed, and wondering how she could be so good at caring for others and still feel lost when it came to money.

Then it was another.

Then another.

Before long, it was clear that what I was seeing wasn't rare—it was the norm.

Nurses are everywhere. You are the heart of hospitals, the first face patients see in clinics, the steady hand during emergencies, and the voice of calm when families are breaking down. You advocate, educate, organize, assess, and show up—again and again and again.

But who's advocating for *you*?

Who's walking you through your 403(b) enrollment? Who's explaining student loan repayment options, or helping you plan for the day when you hang up your scrubs for good? Who's teaching you what to do with a travel nurse paycheck, or how to set boundaries when you're earning more than your spouse but still expected to do it all at home?

Who's writing the financial playbook for *you*?

That's what this book is for.

It's not just about numbers. It's about power, clarity, and options. It's about giving you the knowledge and confidence to say "yes" to the things you love—and "no" to what no longer serves you. It's about reclaiming your time, protecting your energy, and creating a financial future that doesn't rely on working double shifts into your sixties.

You Heal Others—But What About Your Own Financial Health?

I've worked in finance for over two decades. I've had clients from every walk of life. But there's a specific type of client that keeps me up at night: the nurse who's amazing at everything except money.

She's got a big heart and a small emergency fund.

She's organized at work but chaotic with her bills.

She earns a solid paycheck—but feels like she's always broke.

She gives and gives and gives—until there's nothing left for her.

I've met her in cities and small towns. I've met him in ICU breakrooms and conference halls. I've worked with nurse educators, LPNs, RNs, CRNAs, NPs, travel nurses, military nurses, and brand-new grads trying to figure out if it's worth it to take the employer match in their 401(k) or pay off their loans faster.

Every one of them had one thing in common: they were never taught the rules of money. Not in nursing school. Not at work. Not by their families. And not by the financial services industry.

So this book is here to fix that.

What This Book Is (And Isn't)

This book is not a financial textbook. It's not filled with graphs, charts, or lectures. It's not going to scold you for past mistakes or guilt you into giving up coffee.

It's a conversation. A roadmap. A guide written in plain English by someone who respects your time and understands your world.

It will help you:

- Understand what's actually in your paycheck and how to read it
- Build a budget that works on rotating shifts and inconsistent hours
- Manage student loans without losing your mind
- Choose the right benefits—without the HR jargon
- Understand 403(b), 457, Roth IRA, and other retirement tools

- Start investing—yes, even if you think it's "too late" or you don't "have enough"
- Buy a home or travel without wrecking your finances
- Say "no" to draining financial relationships and lifestyle pressure
- Avoid common nurse-specific financial traps, scams, and burnout
- Build a plan for financial independence—on your terms

It is *not* a magic fix. But it *is* the financial foundation you never got in nursing school. It's the "clinicals" you wish someone had included in your training.

Why I Wrote This Book

You deserve more than survival mode. You deserve structure, freedom, and peace.

I was raised in a home where we didn't talk about money. In college, I was a student-athlete who learned about finance the hard way—through mistakes and embarrassment. That shame became fuel. I didn't want others to feel what I felt. So I became a financial educator, advisor, and advocate.

Over the years, I've written books for doctors, attorneys, student-athletes, and other professionals. But the more I worked with nurses, the more I realized: *This book needed to exist.*

Because no one teaches you what to do with your first travel nursing contract.

No one breaks down how to stack shifts and still save for retirement.

No one shows you how to protect your income with disability insurance if your back gives out after 20 years on the floor.

No one tells you how to walk away from toxic financial patterns—even when they come from the people you love.

But I will.

I've sat with nurses who were single moms trying to plan for their kid's future.

I've helped nurse practitioners set up solo 401(k)s after going out on their own.

I've shown burnt-out ICU nurses how to use their PTO not just for rest, but for a reset—financially and emotionally.

And now I want to give you the tools I've given them.

What Makes Nurses Financially Unique

You work hard—but your income may vary based on shift differentials, overtime, or per diem.

You're in a helping profession—but you may overextend yourself with family and friends.

You have job security—but you're often underpaid compared to the responsibilities you carry.

You're used to making life-or-death decisions—but no one prepared you for navigating life insurance, estate plans, or tax planning.

You're excellent at documentation—but how many of us are actually documenting our *financial* game plan?

Nurses often give too much—emotionally, physically, financially—and then have little left to invest in themselves. I want this book to change that. Not overnight. Not all at once. But chapter by chapter. Decision by decision.

How This Book Is Structured

Think of this book like a nursing program.

Part 1: Financial Foundations

This is your pre-reqs. Budgeting, credit scores, debt management, bank accounts, and building your emergency fund.

Part 2: Your Career and Cash Flow

Your paycheck anatomy. Your benefits. Negotiating your worth. Choosing jobs that align with your values and lifestyle.

Part 3: Investing and Retirement

Understand investing basics, employer plans, Roth IRAs, compound interest, risk, and how to start—even if you're "late."

Part 4: Protection and Planning

Insurance, estate planning, power of attorney, long-term care, and making sure your family doesn't have to guess.

Part 5: Lifestyle and Legacy

Planning for major purchases, travel, kids, college savings, and financial independence. This is about vision, not just survival.

Every chapter will have real-life examples, plain explanations, and actionable steps you can take—even if you only have 15 minutes between shifts.

This isn't theory. This is practical, nurse-specific, life-saving financial education.

The Emotional Side of Money

Let's talk truth: money isn't just math. It's emotional.

You might feel guilt for earning more than your parents.

You might feel shame from past mistakes.

You might feel pressure to financially support others—even when it hurts you.

You might avoid money because it feels overwhelming, complicated, or just plain boring.

But here's the reality: ignoring money doesn't make the anxiety go away. Learning about it, even just a little at a time, gives you power.

And financial literacy doesn't mean you do everything perfectly. It means you understand what you're doing—and why.

What You Can Expect

Throughout this book, you'll hear one consistent message:

You are capable. You are worthy. You can do this.

I will break things down with respect, not condescension.

I will give you action steps—not vague advice.

I will challenge you to think long-term—even when you're exhausted from the short term.

You will not be alone in this journey.

If you've ever felt behind, broke, or overwhelmed—this book is your permission slip to start fresh.

One Last Thing

You don't have to get it perfect. You just have to get started.

That's what this book is: your start.

Because you've already mastered compassion. Now it's time to master cash flow.

You've already mastered triage. Now let's do taxes.

You've already handled emergencies. Now let's build stability.

You've poured into everyone else. Now it's time to pour into *you*.

This book is for the nurse in school and the nurse approaching retirement.

It's for the nurse who's thriving and the one barely holding it together.

It's for the travel nurse, the staff nurse, the nurse practitioner, and the nurse educator.

It's for you.

Let's change the financial conversation in nursing—starting now.

With deep respect and gratitude,

Patrick Brown, MBA

Author | Financial Educator | Advocate for Healthcare Heroes

Why This Book Matters—Especially for Nurses

From the breakroom to your bank account, the financial health of nurses deserves more attention.

There's a quiet financial crisis happening in the nursing profession. It's not always visible on the surface, but it's real—and it's affecting lives, careers, families, and futures.

Let's talk about it.

Nurses are some of the most trusted professionals in the world. You care for strangers with compassion, keep hospitals running, and make life-or-death decisions daily. But while you're taking care of everyone else, who's helping you take care of *your money*?

You didn't get financial training in nursing school. You didn't have a course on budgeting, credit scores, taxes, or retirement planning alongside pharmacology or pathophysiology. And once you entered the workforce, no one pulled you aside and said, "Hey, here's how to make sure your hard-earned money works *for* you—not just *because of* you."

That's a problem. And it's a common one.

Here's why this book matters:

1. Because Nurses Are Financially Underserved

You may have great job security and decent income—but you've likely never been taught how to manage it strategically. You might be carrying heavy student loan debt, living paycheck to paycheck, or feeling unsure about whether you're saving "enough." The financial industry hasn't exactly rolled out the red carpet for nurses either—advice is often aimed at doctors or high-net-worth individuals, not the backbone of the healthcare system.

This book is designed *specifically* for you. Your schedule. Your lifestyle. Your career arc. Your reality.

2. Because Your Work Is Too Valuable to Be Undervalued

Let's be honest: you didn't get into nursing for the money. But that doesn't mean you shouldn't be financially respected and compensated accordingly. You give too much—emotionally, physically, mentally—to walk through life with money stress constantly tapping on your shoulder.

You deserve peace of mind. And peace of mind often starts with financial confidence.

3. Because You Deserve More Than Just Overtime and Burnout

So many nurses default to "just picking up another shift" when money gets tight. But what if your financial plan didn't rely on working more hours? What if it relied on working *smarter* with the money you already have?

This book isn't about hustling harder. It's about creating a system that works *without* burning you out.

4. Because Nurses Are Often the Financial Anchor of Their Families

Whether you're a single parent, the primary earner, or supporting aging parents, nurses often carry financial responsibilities far beyond the hospital walls. This book helps you set boundaries, build safety nets, and grow generational wealth—not just survive month-to-month.

You've got big responsibilities. You need big clarity.

5. Because You're Already Doing the Impossible—Money Shouldn't Be Another Mystery

If you can handle code blues, irate patients, understaffed units, broken systems, and back-to-back twelve-hour shifts—you can absolutely handle your money. You just need someone to translate the financial world into something that makes sense for *your* world.

That's what this book does.

6. Because Your Career Has a Clock—and So Does Your Retirement

You might love your job, but nursing is physically and emotionally demanding. You may not be able (or want) to do this work forever. And guess what? You *shouldn't* have to.

Whether you retire at 55, 65, or pivot into something new, your money should support that choice—not dictate it. The earlier you learn how to plan for the long-term, the more freedom you'll have in the future.

7. Because No One Should Work This Hard and Still Feel Broke

You work holidays, nights, weekends, and in the middle of pandemics. You skip meals and bathroom breaks, and still show up with empathy.

You should not be Googling "how to pay off credit card debt fast" after a 14-hour shift.

You should not feel embarrassed asking what a Roth IRA is.

You should not be afraid to look at your bank account.

You should feel *empowered.*

8. Because Financial Stress Impacts Mental Health—And Nurses Deserve Better

The connection between money and mental health is real. Nurses already face high rates of anxiety, depression, and burnout. Financial pressure only makes that worse.

This book isn't just about dollars and cents—it's about your well-being. It's about giving you breathing room. Margin. Options. Rest.

9. Because You're Often the Only One Holding It All Together

At work, you're the calm in the storm. At home, you're the rock. At school, at church, in your community—you're the helper. The doer. The reliable one.

But even rocks need a plan. And even helpers need help.

This book gives you that support. In clear language. With real examples. And no judgment.

10. Because Nurses Deserve to Retire With Dignity, Not Fear

You shouldn't be guessing at your retirement numbers. You shouldn't be crossing your fingers that your pension or Social Security is enough. You deserve a clear, tailored plan. One that factors in your goals, your timeline, and your life.

Whether you're just starting your career or preparing to hang up your badge—*this book is for you.*

Final Word: Why It's Personal

This isn't just a project for me. It's personal.

I've seen the stress in your eyes. I've heard the "I should've started sooner" regrets. I've watched amazing nurses pour into patients and have nothing left for themselves at the end of the month.

I've also seen the transformation when they learn to take control of their finances—*and their futures.*

I believe with everything in me that when nurses are financially empowered, families get stronger, healthcare systems benefit, and communities thrive.

That's why this book matters.

That's why you matter.

That's why now is the time.

Let's get started.

How to Use This Book

Bit by Bit. No Shame. No Jargon. Just Progress.

This book wasn't written for you to read in one sitting. It's not a novel, and it's not a textbook. It's more like a friend who pulls up a chair, leans in, and says, "Let's figure this out—together."

If you're feeling overwhelmed by finances, that's okay. If you've made some mistakes, welcome to the club. If you're starting from scratch, you're in exactly the right place.

There's no test at the end. No gold star for finishing first. No shame if it takes you a while to get through it. In fact, you're encouraged to go slow. Take breaks. Reread chapters. Highlight, dog-ear, journal. Talk to a trusted friend. Apply what makes sense *now*—and come back to the rest when you're ready.

Here's how to get the most out of this book, without burnout or guilt:

1. Start Where You Are, Not Where You "Should Be"

This book follows the arc of a nursing career, but your financial journey might not be in sync. Maybe you're a new nurse still figuring out how to read your pay stub. Maybe you're 20 years in and thinking about retirement. Maybe you're in a reset phase after divorce, a career break, or burnout.

Wherever you are, *that's* the right place to begin.

Flip to the section that feels most urgent, most confusing, or most painful. Read that first. Don't worry about being "out of order." This isn't a lecture—it's a resource.

2. Take It One Chapter at a Time

Don't try to digest it all at once. Money is emotional. It brings up old wounds, family stories, insecurities, and fears. One chapter might inspire you. Another might challenge you. That's normal.

Pace yourself.

You might read a chapter a day.

Or a chapter a week.

Or a chapter a month.

What matters is that you keep coming back.

Even one small change—a budget tweak, a Roth IRA contribution, setting up automatic transfers—can shift your whole trajectory over time.

3. Use the Reflection Prompts and Action Steps

At the end of most chapters, you'll find practical exercises, reflection questions, and action steps. This is your chance to apply what you've learned—no fancy degrees required.

You can write your answers in a journal, type them in your notes app, or say them out loud on a walk.

These aren't busywork—they're anchors. They help turn concepts into real-life changes.

Don't skip them. That's where the magic happens.

4. Don't Worry About Getting It Perfect

This book isn't about perfection. It's about progress. You don't have to budget flawlessly, invest like Warren Buffett, or master tax codes. You just have to move forward, one decision at a time.

Mess up your budget this month? You'll get another shot next month.

Forgot to enroll in your 403(b) on time? Do it now.

Still using a high-interest credit card? We'll build a plan to change that.

You are not behind. You are not broken. You are learning. That's what matters.

5. Use the Table of Contents Like a Menu

Think of this book like a restaurant. You don't have to eat everything at once.

If you're hungry for investment basics, go straight to the investing section.

If you're drowning in debt, go straight to the chapters on credit, loans, and repayment.

If you're changing jobs, skip to the section on benefits, contracts, and transitions.

The table of contents isn't just an index—it's a choose-your-own-adventure map.

6. Speak the Words Out Loud (Seriously)

Some of this financial language may be new. That's okay. One trick that helps? *Say it out loud.*

Say:

"Compound interest helps my money grow while I sleep."

"My credit score is a tool, not a grade."

"I deserve financial peace."

"I am learning. I am allowed to ask questions."

The more you say these things, the more comfortable they become. Financial language should not belong to bankers and brokers alone. It belongs to *you*, too.

7. No Jargon Allowed

I made a promise to write this book without the nonsense.

No industry lingo.

No condescending tone.

No charts that make your eyes glaze over.

When we do introduce financial terms (like HSA, Roth IRA, FICO, etc.), I'll break them down like you're learning it for the first time—because you might be. And that's okay.

If you hit a chapter that still feels too technical, mark it and come back later. This book should never feel like a test.

8. Bring Your Whole Self to the Process

Money isn't separate from your values, your family, your trauma, or your dreams. So don't try to approach this like a robot.

If a chapter brings up big feelings, honor that.

If a memory comes up about your parents and how they handled money, explore it.

If you feel proud for saving your first $500—*celebrate it.*

Financial literacy isn't just about spreadsheets. It's about healing. Ownership. And creating a future that reflects who you are—not just what you earn.

9. Share the Journey

You don't have to do this alone. Read it with a friend, a partner, a co-worker, or your nursing crew. Use it as a book club at work. Talk about it over coffee or on break.

You'll be surprised how many nurses are quietly struggling with the same questions. Shame shrinks in the presence of shared stories.

You've supported each other through heartbreak and horror—support each other through this, too.

10. Revisit Often—Your Life Will Change

The beauty of this book is that it will grow with you.

What feels overwhelming today will feel second nature a year from now. And what doesn't apply now may become crucial later.

Keep this book on your shelf. Revisit it when:

- You start a new job
- You move
- You get married or divorced
- You have a child
- You're considering travel nursing
- You're burned out and need a plan
- You're ready to retire

Think of it as your financial companion through the phases of your nursing life.

And Finally...

This is a *safe place.*

This is a *shame-free zone.*

This is a book that believes in *you.*

I didn't write this to impress anyone. I wrote it to serve you. Because you've spent your life showing up for everyone else. It's time someone showed up for you.

Take a deep breath.

Turn the page.

Let's begin—bit by bit, with heart and with hope.

You've got this.

About the Author

Pat Brown, MBA is a financial educator, advisor, and lifelong advocate for clear, empowering conversations about money. A former Division I football player at the University of Kansas and briefly a professional athlete in the Canadian Football League, Pat traded in playbooks for financial plans—carrying with him the discipline of an athlete, the strategy of a coach, and the empathy of someone who's had to learn the hard way.

For more than 20 years, Pat has helped hundreds of professionals—from doctors and pilots to coaches and business owners—navigate budgeting, investing, insurance, and legacy planning with clarity and confidence. His mission is simple: replace guilt and confusion with structure and power.

What makes Pat different is how he teaches. There's no judgment. No jargon. Just relatable stories, real-world tools, and practical steps that meet people exactly where they are. Whether he's guiding a nurse through their first 403(b) or helping a family plan for long-term care, Pat shows up like a teammate—not a salesperson.

He's the founder of multiple financial literacy platforms, including:

- FinancialLiteracyForNIL.com
- FinancialLiteracyForDoctors.com
- FinancialLiteracyForCollegeCoaches.com
- FinancialLiteracyForAttorneys.com
- FinancialLiteracyForDentists.com
- and now, *Financial Literacy For Nurses*—a heartfelt resource for the caretakers who spend their lives supporting others, but may not have had anyone supporting them financially.

Pat is a husband, father of two daughters, and a passionate speaker who's presented to hospital boards, retirement associations, nursing organizations, and university teams. He currently serves as a wealth manager and sits on several community and hospital boards.

Whether you're working night shifts, managing burnout, or preparing for retirement, Pat's message is clear:

You have what it takes to lead in your financial life—just like you lead in every other part of it.

Nurses are some of the most capable, compassionate, and hard-working professionals in the world.

You spend years mastering patient care, pharmacology, emergency protocols, communication, and leadership under pressure. You train longer and work harder than most people ever see—and then you show up, shift after shift, managing lives, emotions, and unpredictability in some of the most demanding environments imaginable.

But here's the truth that rarely gets spoken in staff meetings or during orientation rounds:

Too many nurses are financially unprepared.

Not because you're reckless.

Not because you don't care.

But because no one ever taught you how this stuff works.

You didn't learn financial planning in nursing school. You didn't get a course on investing when you passed the NCLEX. There's no "Money Management 101" on your EHR dashboard. Yet the decisions you make about your finances will determine whether you can retire on time, care for your loved ones, go part-time without stress, or step into your next chapter with peace of mind.

This book—and this chapter—is about calling out that gap. Not to judge you. Not to overwhelm you. But to help you stop *charting blind* when it comes to your money.

What Do We Mean by Financial Literacy?

Financial literacy doesn't mean you need to become a financial advisor, stock trader, or insurance broker. It doesn't mean tracking every dollar on a spreadsheet or reading tax code in your free time.

It means being able to answer questions like:

- Am I building net worth—or just making it to the next pay period?
- What would happen if I got injured and couldn't work?
- Do I know the difference between my 403(b), Roth IRA, and pension options?
- Am I prepared for retirement—or just hoping it'll work out?
- Do I have the right insurance—or am I overpaying for the wrong kind?
- Am I letting burnout or "I deserve it" spending drain my future?

Financial literacy is about understanding how money moves through your life—so you can direct it, not just react to it.

It's knowing how to:

- Read your net worth statement
- Create a spending plan that reflects your actual priorities
- Understand the real cost of debt, taxes, and under-saving
- Protect your income, your health, and your legacy
- Make money decisions with structure—not shame

Above all: It's about using your income to create stability and freedom—not just more stuff.

Why Nurses Are Uniquely Vulnerable

There are specific reasons why nurses—especially full-time, rotating-shift, and mid-career professionals—are uniquely exposed to financial stress and missed opportunities.

1. High Stress, Variable Pay

Some nurses earn strong incomes through overtime, night differentials, travel contracts, or agency work—but it comes with exhaustion and inconsistency. One year might be flush, the next might be cut in half. And when you're emotionally spent, it's easy to spend money emotionally.

2. Physical and Emotional Toll

You can't always count on working until 65. Your back, your knees, your nervous system—nursing wears on your body. And unlike many office jobs, nursing doesn't always offer the luxury of easing into retirement. If you don't plan ahead, you might be forced to exit before you're financially ready.

3. Identity = Nurse

This career becomes part of who you are. And when your identity is tied to the job, it's easy to delay planning for what comes after. You say, "I'll think about it after this shift," "after the kids grow up," "after I get through this season."

But someday comes fast. Don't let yourself arrive there financially unready.

4. Complex Benefits

You may have access to a pension, 403(b), health insurance, disability coverage, or union-negotiated perks. But if you don't understand how they work—or how they *fit together*—you could be leaving thousands on the table.

5. Caregiver Guilt and Time Poverty

You spend your life caring for others. So when someone talks about "paying yourself first," it can feel selfish—or unrealistic. Add in shift work, family responsibilities, and mental fatigue, and money management gets pushed to the bottom of your to-do list.

What the Gap Looks Like in Real Life

These are real stories from real nurses:

- The 58-year-old nurse manager who's been working for 30 years—but only just realized her pension doesn't cover healthcare in retirement.
- The 42-year-old ER nurse with a solid paycheck but no emergency fund, and credit card balances that never seem to go down.
- The nurse couple who each thought the *other* was taking care of retirement planning—and now aren't sure if they're behind.
- The travel nurse who earned six figures last year—but owes a huge tax bill because they didn't plan for self-employment income.
- The nurse who took time off to care for a parent—and had no idea what it would do to her vesting, benefits, or long-term savings.

This book exists so your story doesn't end up like one of those.

Why This Isn't Taught (And Why It Should Be)

We don't expect nurses to guess their way through triage. We train. We prep. We use protocols.

But when it comes to money? The message is often:

- "Just save what you can."
- "Get a Roth IRA if you qualify."
- "Buy a house early."
- "Don't spend too much."

That's not a plan. That's advice disguised as wisdom.

Financial literacy should be part of every nursing education. Until it is, this book is here to close that gap.

What Happens When Nurses Gain Financial Clarity

When you know how money works—and how it works *for* you—everything shifts.

You make better career decisions because you're not trapped by finances

You create boundaries and options for your future

You invest with purpose—not fear

You stop *reacting* to life—and start *designing* it

Nurses don't walk into a shift without a plan. You shouldn't walk into retirement—or life—with wishful thinking either.

What This Book Will Help You Do

This isn't about turning you into a financial expert. It's about giving you:

- Plain-language breakdowns of your 403(b), pension, Roth IRA, and health benefits
- Tools to budget, save, and invest—even during chaotic months
- Guidance for insurance, taxes, estate planning, and debt
- Ways to protect your income, family, and future
- Red flags to avoid—like MLMs, payday lenders, or overpriced products
- Scripts and questions to ask any financial advisor or HR rep
- The confidence to build a plan that honors *your* values—not someone else's opinions

Closing the Gap—One Nurse at a Time

I've spent more than 20 years helping professionals—including many nurses—take control of their financial lives. I've seen the pressure, the burnout, the late starts—and the breakthroughs.

When a nurse takes control of their finances, it's not just about numbers.

It's about peace.

It's about agency.

It's about the ability to say "no" to exhaustion and "yes" to rest, stability, and legacy.

That's why this book exists.

To replace confusion with clarity.

To help you scrub into your own financial life—with the same courage you bring to every patient.

Let's build your plan. Not just for now. But for the life you deserve beyond the badge.

Welcome to *Financial Literacy For Nurses*.

Let's begin.

Part I: From Scrubs to Security – Foundations in School and Early Career

Laying the groundwork for a financially empowered nursing journey.

Part I is where it all begins.

Whether you're a nursing student fresh off your first clinical rotation, a new grad figuring out how to navigate your first paycheck, or a couple years into the job and still wondering why money feels so confusing—this section is your starting line.

This part of the book focuses on the **foundational financial skills** every nurse needs to feel secure and confident from day one. It's not about becoming rich overnight or learning to time the stock market. It's about building the habits, mindset, and systems that will carry you from your school years into a steady, sustainable financial life.

We'll cover topics like:

- How to **budget on a nurse's income**—even with student loans and irregular shifts
- Understanding **your financial aid**, **loan repayment options**, and how to avoid long-term debt traps
- The essentials of **credit scores, banking**, and choosing the right **credit cards** or accounts early on
- How to **read your paycheck**, evaluate your **benefits package**, and avoid the most common money mistakes new nurses make
- The emotional side of money—including financial guilt, shame, im-

poster syndrome, and pressure to support others financially as you begin earning

This section meets you where you are—maybe in scrubs, maybe in debt, maybe unsure what a Roth IRA even is. And that's okay. No judgment, no jargon, no assumptions. Just clear, compassionate guidance from someone who's seen how powerful early financial decisions can be—especially in a profession where burnout is real, debt is common, and long-term planning is often delayed.

By the end of Part I, you'll have a solid grip on your income, your spending, your credit, and your mindset. You'll begin to shift from just "making it through the month" to actually planning your financial life with confidence.

Because financial peace isn't just for later in your career. It starts now—with the right foundation.

Chapter 1: The Cost of Becoming a Nurse

You didn't get into nursing for the money—but that doesn't mean the money isn't real. If you've been through it, you know: becoming a nurse comes at a cost. And not just emotionally or physically. We're talking about cold, hard dollars.

Tuition. Textbooks. Scrubs. NCLEX prep. Testing fees. Transportation to clinicals. Lost wages from working less—or not at all—during nursing school. Every one of those things adds up. And for many nurses, it adds up to tens of thousands of dollars in student loan debt, credit card balances, or savings wiped out before the first paycheck ever hits.

This chapter isn't here to scare you. It's here to lay it out, clean and clear, like a solid shift report. If you're already a nurse, it will help you understand where your financial foundation began. If you're a student or considering nursing, this will show you what to prepare for—without the sugarcoating.

We're going to talk numbers, choices, trade-offs, and strategies. Because once you understand the true cost of becoming a nurse, you can stop feeling behind—and start building forward.

The Real Price Tag of Nursing School

Let's start with tuition. Nursing school isn't cheap, and the cost depends heavily on the type of program:

- **Associate Degree in Nursing (ADN):** $8,000 to $30,000 total at a community college
- **Bachelor of Science in Nursing (BSN):** $30,000 to $100,000+ at public or private universities
- **Accelerated BSN (for second-degree students):** $40,000 to $80,000+
- **Master of Science in Nursing (MSN):** $35,000 to $70,000+
- **Doctor of Nursing Practice (DNP):** $40,000 to $100,000+

That's just the tuition. Add in books, uniforms, lab fees, and equipment—and the total climbs fast.

Then factor in the opportunity cost. Most nursing programs are full-time. That means many students cut back work hours—or quit working entirely. You're not just *spending* money during nursing school. You're also *not earning* it.

The Hidden Costs Nobody Talks About

Beyond tuition, here are the often-overlooked expenses that sneak up on aspiring nurses:

- **NCLEX Prep Courses:** $300–$600 (some optional, some essential)
- **NCLEX Registration and Licensing Fees:** $200–$400
- **Background Checks and Fingerprinting:** $50–$100
- **CPR/BLS Certification:** $60–$100 (and renewing it every two years)
- **Clinical Supplies:** stethoscope ($50–$200), penlight, shears, badge reel, nursing shoes
- **Scrubs and Uniforms:** $200–$500 (plus replacements over time)
- **Commuting to Clinicals:** gas, public transit, parking, wear and tear on your car
- **Unpaid Clinical Hours:** hundreds of hours spent working for free as part of your education
- **Mental Health Costs:** therapy, counseling, or stress-related health issues during school

It's not just one big check—it's death by a thousand swipes. And many nurses use credit cards, loans, or savings to keep up.

Real Talk: What This Means for New Grads

Let's say you graduate with $65,000 in student loan debt. You start your first job at $31/hour in a hospital. That's around $64,000/year before taxes. It feels like good money—until the deductions hit:

- Taxes
- Health insurance premiums
- Retirement plan contributions (hopefully)
- Union dues or parking fees (depending on your facility)

Suddenly your take-home pay is $45,000–$50,000/year. Add in rent, car payments, groceries, and now that loan payment? It's tight. And that's assuming you pass the NCLEX on the first try and find a job right away.

Certification and Continuing Ed: The Costs Don't Stop After Graduation

Welcome to lifelong learning. Nursing is a constantly evolving profession. That means you'll be:

- Renewing your license (typically every 2 years, $100–$200)
- Completing continuing education (CEU) credits (sometimes free, sometimes $15–$50 per course)
- Getting additional certifications (ACLS, PALS, CCRN, etc.) which can range from $150 to $500 each

Some employers cover these costs—but not all. If you're a travel nurse or work for a smaller facility, you may be paying out of pocket.

Pros and Cons: The Education Route You Choose

Let's break it down in real-world terms:

ADN (2-Year Program):

- **Pros:** Cheaper upfront, faster path to RN license, often leads to hospital job
- **Cons:** May limit long-term advancement, may need to "bridge" to BSN later (which costs more)

BSN (4-Year Program):

- **Pros:** Preferred by many hospitals, stronger career growth, foundation for advanced degrees
- **Cons:** Higher cost, more time before you earn a full RN paycheck

Accelerated BSN:

- **Pros:** Ideal for second-career students, condensed timeline
- **Cons:** Intense pace, high tuition, can't work much (if at all) during program

MSN/DNP/Nurse Practitioner Tracks:

- **Pros:** Higher earning potential, leadership roles, autonomy
- **Cons:** Even more debt, more responsibility, often no employer coverage

There's no right answer. Only the right answer *for you*. But whatever path you choose, you need to run the numbers like you would a drip calculation—accurate, honest, and with patient safety (in this case, *your* financial safety) in mind.

Action Steps to Take Now

- **Know your current student loan total.** Log in to your loan servicer and get the real number—not just a guess.
- **Estimate your full program cost.** Tuition + supplies + licensing + living expenses + loss of income.
- **Start a "nursing cost" savings account.** Even $50/month helps cover those NCLEX or CEU surprises.
- **Price shop NCLEX prep options.** Don't default to the most expensive course. Ask grads what worked.
- **Keep receipts for work-related expenses.** Some may be deductible or reimbursable.
- **Understand your hospital's education benefits.** Do they reimburse CEUs? Pay for certifications?

Plain-Language Money Terms You'll See in This Journey

- **Loan servicer:** The company that manages your student loan payments
- **Deferment:** Pausing payments on your loans (interest may still grow)
- **Grace period:** Time after graduation before your first loan payment is due (usually 6 months)
- **Subsidized loan:** Government pays interest while you're in school
- **Unsubsidized loan:** Interest grows while you're in school
- **Forgiveness:** Some or all of your loan may be canceled after years of qualifying payments
- **Income-driven repayment:** Your monthly loan payment is based on your income

You don't have to memorize all of this now—but recognize these as real pieces of your financial puzzle.

A Word About Guilt and Comparison

You may be looking around wondering, "Why did I spend so much to become a nurse?" Or, "Why do other nurses seem to be ahead of me financially?"

Let that go.

No two paths are the same. Some people had help from parents. Others worked three jobs. Some graduated without debt, others with six figures. This book isn't about comparison—it's about *clarity*. You did what you had to do to get here. Now let's build from here.

You're Not Behind. You're Just Beginning.

Understanding the cost of becoming a nurse isn't about blaming the system or regretting your choices. It's about being informed, equipped, and *ready* to move forward.

Because here's the truth: nursing can still be a financially powerful profession. You can pay off your loans. You can build wealth. You can buy a home, retire early, support your family, and fund the life you deserve.

But it starts with seeing the full picture.

You're already smart. You're already resilient. You've already handled way harder things than a student loan statement.

Now it's time to bring that same strength to your money.

One Financial Move Before Your Next Shift

Look up your student loan balance. Not the scary, round estimate. The *real* number. Write it down. Own it. Then make a plan—just one small step. Because the only thing worse than paying that balance is never knowing what it is.

This is where financial clarity begins. Right here. Right now. You've got this.

Next up: Let's build your financial foundation—starting with the budget that actually fits a nurse's life.

Chapter 2: Should You Work While in Nursing School?

Let's have a real conversation—nurse to nurse. Nursing school isn't just hard. It's relentless. The coursework is demanding, the clinicals are exhausting, and the emotional toll? Heavy. Add work into that mix and it can feel like you're choosing between two bad options: financial stress or full-blown burnout.

So let's dig into it: *Should you work while in nursing school?* Not a hypothetical. Not what "they" say. But what makes sense for you—financially, emotionally, academically, and physically. Because this decision isn't just about money. It's about energy. It's about longevity. And it's about making strategic moves so you don't burn out before you even get your license.

This chapter is for the students trying to keep their lights on, the parents balancing diapers and textbooks, and the second-career switchers trying to survive on one income. There's no shame in asking. There's power in knowing what you're signing up for—and how to make it work if you do decide to clock in while studying for NCLEX.

The Financial Pressure Is Real

Let's be honest: the idea of *not* working during nursing school is a luxury not everyone has. Rent still needs to be paid. Groceries still need to be bought. Some students are single parents, some are supporting aging parents, and others just don't have a financial safety net. Scholarships help, but they don't cover everything.

Working during nursing school is often not a choice. It's a necessity. But that doesn't mean it's easy—or smart in every situation.

The Pros of Working While in Nursing School

1. Income to Stay Afloat

Even a part-time paycheck can help cover living expenses, textbooks, scrubs, NCLEX prep, or childcare. Working helps you avoid taking on high-interest credit card debt or maxing out student loans unnecessarily.

2. Less Loan Burden

Every dollar you earn now is a dollar you don't have to borrow—and repay with interest later. Cutting your loan burden by just $5,000 could mean thousands in interest saved over your career.

3. Builds Time Management and Discipline

Balancing school and work requires scheduling, prioritizing, and structure—skills that translate directly into being a nurse. You'll learn how to juggle multiple responsibilities, which comes in handy on the floor.

4. Real-World Experience (If You Work in Healthcare)

Working as a CNA, tech, scribe, EMT, or unit secretary can give you exposure to clinical settings, workflows, and medical terminology before you ever hit the floor as an RN. That familiarity boosts confidence and competence.

5. Networking and Job Offers

Many students who work in a hospital or clinic during school get job offers immediately after graduation. Employers love hiring people they've already trained.

The Cons of Working While in Nursing School

1. Time Starvation

Nursing school is already a full-time job. Add work hours, and you may find yourself with no time left to study, sleep, or breathe. That's a recipe for exhaustion—and academic trouble.

2. Increased Stress

Working while in school can impact your grades, your mental health, and your relationships. It's not just about hours—it's about capacity.

3. Risk of Burnout Before You Even Begin

If you start your nursing career already exhausted, you'll be more prone to mistakes, missed opportunities, and long-term disillusionment with the profession.

4. Less Flexibility with Clinicals

Clinical rotations can vary wildly—days, nights, weekends. If you're working a job with rigid hours, it can be hard to meet clinical requirements.

5. Poor Academic Performance = Delayed Graduation

Failing a class or having to retake courses because you couldn't keep up? That's costly—in time and tuition.

Real-Life Scenarios

Lena, 24, Single with No Kids

Lena works two 8-hour shifts a week as a patient transporter. She lives with roommates, doesn't own a car, and uses her job to pay rent and buy groceries. She studies on breaks and uses her hospital job to get clinical advice from nurses.

Jordan, 35, Parent of Two

Jordan tried to work weekends during an accelerated BSN program but had to quit after his grades tanked and his health suffered. He took out an extra loan but focused full-time on school and graduated with honors. Now working in pediatrics, he's aggressively paying off debt.

Tanya, 29, Second-Career Student

Tanya works PRN as a CNA. Her hours are flexible, and her supervisor is a former nurse who supports her schedule. She's getting experience and income without overloading herself.

Action Steps

- **Run the Numbers:** What's your monthly income gap without working? Can it be covered with loans, savings, or family support?
- **Explore On-Campus or Hospital Jobs:** Look for jobs that are flexible and related to healthcare—unit clerk, CNA, lab tech, etc.
- **Negotiate a Reduced Class Load (If Possible):** If you must work full-time, consider extending your program to avoid overload.
- **Get Real About Your Budget:** Cut what you can. Share expenses. Delay major purchases. Every dollar saved reduces the pressure to work.
- **Set Boundaries:** No 60-hour work weeks and full-time school. It's not sustainable.

What Nobody Tells You

Per diem work sounds great—but it can be inconsistent.

You might not get the shifts you need. Don't count on every week being the same.

PRN jobs often don't come with benefits.

You might earn more hourly, but lose out on healthcare or retirement savings.

Night shift work during school can crush your energy.

Unless you're a night owl and very disciplined, night shifts can ruin your academic focus.

Your clinical schedule owns you.

You can't "move it around" to accommodate your job. The program comes first.

Loans aren't evil—but they need a strategy.

Sometimes taking out a little more now prevents financial and academic disaster later. Just make sure you have a repayment plan.

Educate, Empower, Engage

Let's put the guilt aside. Working while in nursing school is a highly personal decision. You don't get extra points for doing it all. You don't lose credibility for needing a break.

Your job is to get through nursing school—*in one piece.* Your job is to graduate, pass the NCLEX, and enter the profession healthy and ready. Not to crash and burn because you tried to prove something.

You can work. You just need to do it *strategically.*

Remember: the money you earn now matters—but the *license* you're working toward is what will really change your financial life. Don't sacrifice the long-term for the short-term.

One Financial Move Before Your Next Shift

Pull up your class schedule, your work hours, and your budget. Look for red flags. Are you doing too much? Where can you cut, shift, or delegate?

Then ask yourself honestly: *Can I sustain this for another semester?*

Make the move that supports both your wallet *and* your well-being.

Chapter 3: Credit Cards in Nursing School – Friend or Foe?

Let's talk about credit cards.

Not the flashy commercials. Not the points programs. Not the TikTok influencer showing off their upgraded hotel room while you're eating ramen between shifts.

We're going to talk about *your* reality. Because if you're a nursing student—or a new nurse fresh out of school—you've probably asked yourself at some point:

"Should I use a credit card to stay afloat?"

Or maybe:

"Am I digging a financial hole I won't be able to climb out of?"

This chapter doesn't come with judgment. Just truth, tools, and strategy. Because credit cards aren't inherently good or bad. They're tools—like a syringe. In the right hands, with the right dosage and knowledge, they can be helpful. In the wrong hands—or without training—they can cause real damage.

So let's break it down. Clear. Honest. No fluff. Just like you'd want a preceptor to explain a complex med interaction.

Why So Many Nursing Students Lean on Credit Cards

It's no secret: nursing school is expensive, and life doesn't stop just because you're pursuing a better career.

Rent still comes due. Textbooks still cost a small fortune. Car repairs don't wait. And if you're not working—or working less—during school, the gap between income and expenses gets real.

Credit cards can feel like a lifeline. Swipe now, deal with it later.

And sometimes, they *are* a lifeline.

Used strategically, credit can:

- Cover essential short-term expenses when cash flow is tight
- Help you build a credit history, which you'll need for future big moves like renting an apartment or buying a home
- Provide fraud protection and purchase security

But credit cards can also:

- Create long-term debt that outlives your student loans
- Destroy your credit score with one late payment
- Feed a lifestyle you can't afford and trap you in shame cycles

Let's explore both sides.

Credit Cards as a Tool: The Strategic Approach

1. Establishing Credit History

If you've never had a credit card before, opening one and using it responsibly can help you build a credit score. That score affects everything—your ability to rent, get a cell phone plan, qualify for an apartment, or eventually buy a home.

2. Emergency Buffer

If you don't have savings yet, a credit card *can* be a temporary fallback for true emergencies. Think: car breaks down, you need textbooks, you're short on rent. But that's a *backup,* not a budget.

3. Purchase Protection and Rewards

Many cards offer fraud protection, extended warranties, and even cash back or points. But these benefits only matter if you pay the balance in full.

4. Leverage Introductory Offers (Carefully)

Some student cards offer 0% interest for 12–18 months. That can be a smart tool *if* you create a repayment plan to clear the balance before interest kicks in.

Credit Cards as a Trap: The Danger Zones

1. High Interest Rates

Most student and entry-level cards carry interest rates of 20% or more. That $300 textbook you put on your card? If you only make minimum payments, you'll pay double or triple by the time it's gone.

2. Lifestyle Inflation

Credit cards can trick you into thinking you can afford more than you can. One swipe at Target turns into $500 of stress two months later.

3. Minimum Payment Mindset

Making the minimum payment isn't "keeping up." It's treading water while the balance grows. That strategy leaves you broke and exhausted.

4. Missed Payments = Credit Score Crash

One missed payment can drop your score by 50–100 points. That can impact your job applications, car loan rates, housing opportunities, and more.

Real-Life Nurse Scenarios

Ashley, 22, BSN Student

Ashley uses one credit card to buy gas and groceries and pays it off in full each month. Her credit score jumped from 620 to 740 in under two years. She's never carried a balance and only uses 10% of her limit.

Marcus, 27, Accelerated Program Student

Marcus lost hours at his part-time job and used credit cards to cover rent and food. The balance hit $8,000 before he realized he couldn't keep up. Now he's in a debt repayment program and paying $300/month just in interest.

Clara, 34, Second-Career Nurse

Clara took out a 0% interest card to cover NCLEX prep and uniforms. She set up auto-payments and cleared the balance in 10 months. She used the points to buy groceries during her final semester.

The Math of Credit Card Debt

Let's say you charge $1,000 on a card with 22% interest. You only make minimum payments ($35/month).

- It will take 4 years to pay it off
- You'll pay over $700 in interest

That's one small balance. Now imagine carrying $3,000 or more—which many students do.

That's a trap. And it steals future options.

Credit Score 101: The Basics You Were Never Taught

Your credit score is made up of:

- **35% Payment history** (pay on time—every time)
- **30% Amounts owed** (use less than 30% of your total credit limit)
- **15% Length of credit history** (older is better)
- **10% Credit mix** (a combo of loans and credit is ideal)
- **10% New credit** (opening lots of cards at once = red flag)

You don't need a perfect score. But you want a *strong* score—above 700.

That opens doors and lowers borrowing costs.

Action Steps: How to Use Credit Like a Pro

- **Start with one card.** Don't get multiple cards "just because." One solid card with no annual fee is enough to build your credit.
- **Use it for *planned* purchases only.** Not impulse buys.
- **Pay it off *in full* every month.** Avoid interest like you avoid C. diff.
- **Set up auto-pay.** One missed payment can undo a year of good behavior.
- **Keep utilization low.** Stay under 30% of your limit. Under 10% is even better.
- **Don't close old cards.** Length of credit history matters.
- **Check your score regularly.** Credit Karma and many banks offer free tools.

What If You're Already in Over Your Head?

Step 1: Stop the bleeding.

Put the card away. Unlink it from your phone. Stop charging new purchases.

Step 2: Create a debt snapshot.

List every card: balance, interest rate, minimum payment.

Step 3: Call the companies.

Ask for a lower interest rate or hardship program.

Step 4: Choose a repayment strategy.

- **Avalanche method:** Pay off highest interest rate first
- **Snowball method:** Pay off smallest balance first for quick wins

Step 5: Consider a balance transfer or consolidation loan.

ONLY if you commit to a strict payoff plan.

Credit and Mental Health

Credit card debt doesn't just hurt your wallet. It weighs on your mind.

It can cause anxiety, shame, relationship tension, and avoidance.

But here's the truth: you're not lazy. You're not irresponsible. You're not broken.

You're just human. And the system wasn't designed to teach you any of this.

But now you know. And now you can choose differently.

One Financial Move Before Your Next Shift

Pull up your credit card balance. All of them. Write down the total. Breathe. Then:

- If you have no credit yet: apply for one solid card and use it responsibly.
- If you're carrying a balance: choose a repayment strategy. Make a plan.
- If you're using credit wisely: raise your auto-pay amount by $20 this month.

Small moves = big shifts. Start today.

Chapter 4: Understanding Financial Aid, Grants, and Scholarships for Nurses

You want to become a nurse—but between tuition, clinical supplies, and keeping the lights on, it can feel like the deck is stacked against you financially before you ever touch a stethoscope.

This chapter is about unlocking the money already out there with your name on it.

Yes, *your* name. Not just the 4.0 GPA students. Not just the people with perfectly curated essays. Not just the folks who have a parent in the alumni association. There is money out there for future nurses, current students, working RNs going back to school, and even seasoned nurses pursuing advanced degrees.

But the system is confusing. And messy. And full of acronyms. FAFSA. Pell. SEOG. TEACH. HRSA. It can feel like you're decoding another language on top of everything else you're already studying.

This chapter is here to simplify it, humanize it, and help you move confidently toward funding your education—*without drowning in debt.*

Let's Start with the Big Picture

There are three primary ways students get help paying for nursing school:

1. **Financial Aid** – Need-based assistance, primarily from federal and state governments

2. **Grants and Scholarships** – Free money that doesn't need to be paid back
3. **Loan Forgiveness Programs** – Aid tied to working in specific fields or areas after graduation

Most nurses don't use all three. But *you should know about all three.* Because layering them together is how you reduce debt and build a financial foundation from day one.

Let's walk through each.

Understanding Financial Aid – FAFSA Is the First Step

You can't talk financial aid without talking FAFSA.

FAFSA = Free Application for Federal Student Aid.

It's not just for loans. It's how you access *all* federal aid—including grants, subsidized loans, and work-study.

You fill out the FAFSA every year you're in school. It's free to submit. And it's your ticket to unlocking needs-based aid.

The FAFSA determines your **EFC**—Expected Family Contribution (though this term is being phased out in favor of SAI: Student Aid Index). The lower your number, the more aid you're eligible for.

Types of Federal Financial Aid:

- **Pell Grants** – Up to ~$7,000/year. Free money. Based on financial need.
- **FSEOG Grants** – Supplemental grant of ~$100–$4,000/year. Schools distribute this on a first-come basis.
- **Subsidized Loans** – Government pays your interest while you're in school.
- **Unsubsidized Loans** – You're responsible for interest immediately.
- **Work-Study** – Part-time jobs through your school. You earn money while enrolled.

Pro Tip: Fill out the FAFSA *as early as possible* every year. Aid is often awarded on a rolling basis.

Scholarships – Free Money, Real Opportunity

There are scholarships for nurses everywhere. You just have to know where to look.

Types of Scholarships:

1. **Merit-Based:** Based on academic performance, leadership, or achievements
2. **Need-Based:** Based on financial hardship
3. **Identity-Based:** Tied to race, ethnicity, gender, religion, veteran status, LGBTQ+ identity
4. **Career-Focused:** For those pursuing specific specialties like pediatrics, oncology, geriatrics, etc.
5. **Local/Community-Based:** Offered by hospitals, local businesses, or regional foundations

Where to Look:

- Your school's financial aid office
- Your nursing program or department
- Local hospitals or healthcare systems
- National and state nursing associations (like ANA, NSNA, ENA)
- Scholarship search engines (Fastweb, Cappex, Scholarships.com, etc.)
- HRSA (Health Resources & Services Administration)

Real-World Tip: Apply even if you don't meet *every* qualification. Many scholarships go unclaimed because people self-disqualify.

Grants – Another Source of Free Money

Grants work like scholarships—but are often tied to income, life situation, or specific career goals.

Popular Nursing Grants:

- **HRSA Nursing Scholarship Program:** Pays tuition, fees, and provides a stipend in exchange for 2 years of service in a critical shortage facility
- **State-Based Grants:** Many states offer grants for nurses—especially if you commit to working in rural or underserved communities
- **Military & VA Grants:** For active duty, veterans, and their families

Grant Strategy: Pair grants *with* scholarships *with* subsidized loans. It's not either-or. It's both-and.

Loan Forgiveness Programs

What if you *do* need to take loans? Is there a way to make those disappear?

Sometimes, yes.

Nurse Corps Loan Repayment Program (NCLRP):

- Pays off 60% of your loans in 2 years, with an optional 3rd year for 25% more
- You must work in a high-need area at a qualifying facility

Public Service Loan Forgiveness (PSLF):

- Available if you work full-time for a nonprofit or government facility
- Make 120 qualifying monthly payments, and your remaining balance may be forgiven tax-free

State Forgiveness Programs:

- Vary by location but often target rural or shortage areas

Real-Life Nurse Scenarios

Nina, 21, BSN Student in Texas

Nina's family income qualified her for a full Pell Grant and state-level nursing scholarship. Between that and a local hospital foundation grant, she'll graduate with less than $10,000 in debt.

Jason, 34, Accelerated Program Student in California

Jason applied late for FAFSA but still received a small SEOG grant. He supplemented it with work-study and a specialty scholarship for male nurses in mental health. Total aid covered over 50% of his tuition.

Danielle, 45, RN-to-BSN Student in Ohio

Danielle works at a nonprofit hospital. She's making qualifying payments toward Public Service Loan Forgiveness while completing her degree online. She expects $38,000 of debt forgiven after 10 years.

Plain-Language Breakdown: FAFSA to Forgiveness in 5 Steps

1. **File FAFSA** – Every year, as early as possible
2. **Apply for Scholarships and Grants** – Treat it like a part-time job
3. **Understand Your Loan Terms** – Know what's subsidized vs. unsubsidized
4. **Use Free Money Wisely** – Prioritize tuition and required costs. Avoid lifestyle creep.
5. **Plan for Forgiveness** – Keep documentation. Know the criteria. Stay on track.

Strategic Mistakes to Avoid

- **Missing FAFSA Deadlines:** You lose access to free aid
- **Leaving Scholarships on the Table:** Don't assume you won't qualify
- **Borrowing More Than You Need:** Just because it's offered doesn't

mean you take it

- **Ignoring Loan Forgiveness Options:** Especially if you work in public health or a nonprofit hospital
- **Using Grant Money for Vacations or Shopping Sprees:** This isn't free play money—it's a career-launching asset

Action Steps

- **Schedule 1 hour this week to research scholarships.** Start local.
- **Set a calendar reminder for FAFSA each year.** Early = more options.
- **Talk to your school's financial aid office.** Don't go it alone.
- **Create a spreadsheet of every grant, scholarship, and loan you apply for.** Stay organized.
- **Write one solid personal statement.** You can repurpose it for multiple applications.

Mindset Shift: You Deserve Help

Let's be clear: applying for aid isn't begging. It's not weakness. It's smart.

Nursing is a service profession. You are choosing to spend your career helping others—often at the expense of your own body, sleep, and sanity. The system *should* support that. And when it doesn't, you owe it to yourself to fight for the help that *does* exist.

You're not just applying for aid. You're investing in your future.

One Financial Move Before Your Next Shift

Search for one scholarship today. Just one. Write down the deadline. Set a reminder. Apply before the next shift cycle is over.

Your future self will thank you.

Chapter 5: Student Loans – Borrowing Smart, Not Just Easy

Let's be real: student loans are a part of most nurses' origin stories. You don't hear it on Instagram. You don't see it on the badge. But behind that clean uniform and the confident RN title? There's often a five-digit—or six-digit—debt story.

This chapter is not here to judge you for borrowing. It's here to help you understand what you borrowed, how it works, and how to take back control before that debt starts running the show.

Nursing school isn't cheap. You may have had no choice but to take out loans to get through it—and that's okay. The problem isn't that you borrowed. The problem is when you borrow without understanding the *rules of the game.*

Let's break it all down—slow, honest, steady. Like a solid report at shift change.

What Are Student Loans, Really?

A student loan is money you borrow to pay for school—tuition, fees, books, living expenses—and agree to pay back, usually with interest.

There are two major types of loans:

- **Federal Loans** – Issued by the government. Better terms, more flexible options.

- **Private Loans** – Issued by banks or lenders. Riskier. Less flexible.

Within federal loans, there are two key types:

- **Subsidized Loans:** The government pays the interest while you're in school at least half-time, during grace periods, and deferment.
- **Unsubsidized Loans:** Interest accrues the moment the loan is disbursed—even while you're in school.

Subsidized vs. Unsubsidized: What's the Difference?

Let's say you borrow $5,000 in a subsidized loan and $5,000 in an unsubsidized loan.

- **Subsidized:** You owe $5,000 when you graduate.
- **Unsubsidized:** That $5,000 grows every month you're in school. After four years, you could owe $6,000+.

Subsidized = less cost long-term. But it's only available to undergrads and based on financial need.

Private Loans – When to Be Cautious

Private loans are issued by banks or credit unions. You apply based on credit score, not need.

Pros:

- May help fill gaps when federal aid isn't enough
- Can be used for any school expenses

Cons:

- Variable interest rates (can skyrocket)

- No income-driven repayment
- No loan forgiveness or deferment protections
- Often need a co-signer

Plain truth: Private loans should be your *last resort.* Exhaust all federal aid, scholarships, grants, and work-study first.

How Much Is Too Much to Borrow?

This is where it gets real. Here's a general rule of thumb:

Don't borrow more than your expected *first year* nursing salary.

If new grads in your area make around $65,000, then ideally you don't want to graduate with more than $65,000 in total loans.

Why? Because that number gives you a fighting chance to pay it off within 10 years *without* wrecking your life.

More than that? It's not impossible. But you'll need a strategy.

Borrowing Smart in Nursing School

- **Know exactly what you're borrowing.** Don't just accept whatever is offered. Look at the breakdown.
- **Decline unnecessary loan amounts.** Just because they *offer* $20,000 doesn't mean you *need* it.
- **Use loans for needs, not lifestyle.** Tuition, books, rent. Not spring break or Uber Eats every night.
- **Keep track of your total balance every semester.** Don't be surprised at graduation.

Understanding Repayment Plans

Federal loans offer several repayment options. Here's the breakdown:

1. **Standard Repayment:**

- Fixed payments over 10 years
- You pay less interest—but higher monthly payments

2. Graduated Repayment:

- Payments start low and increase every two years
- Good if you expect your income to rise quickly

3. Extended Repayment:

- Up to 25 years of payments
- Lower monthly payments, but much more interest overall

4. Income-Driven Repayment (IDR):

- Payments based on a percentage of your income
- Usually 10–20% of discretionary income
- Forgiveness possible after 20–25 years

Loan Forgiveness for Nurses

Nurse Corps Loan Repayment Program:

- Work in a high-need area
- 60% of loans forgiven after 2 years
- Up to 85% with a third year

Public Service Loan Forgiveness (PSLF):

- Work full-time at a nonprofit or government facility
- Make 120 qualifying payments (10 years)
- Remaining balance forgiven tax-free

State-Based Forgiveness Programs:

- Some states offer programs for rural, underserved, or specialty nursing

Pro Tip: These programs have strict documentation requirements. Keep every record. Every paycheck stub. Every communication.

The Truth About Deferment and Forbearance

It sounds good—pause your loans. But there's a cost.

- **Deferment:** You may not accrue interest if loans are subsidized
- **Forbearance:** Interest *always* accrues

Avoid if possible. It's like putting your loans in the breakroom fridge and forgetting them—they'll rot with time.

Loan Consolidation vs. Refinancing

Consolidation (Federal):

- Combines all your federal loans into one
- Single payment, eligibility for forgiveness programs remains

Refinancing (Private):

- New private loan pays off old ones
- May lower interest, but kills access to federal protections

Caution: Don't refinance federal loans unless you are 100% sure you won't need forgiveness, deferment, or IDR options.

Real-Life Scenarios

Emily, 26, New Grad with $84K in Loans

Emily works at a nonprofit hospital. She enrolled in an IDR plan and is tracking PSLF. She pays $420/month and expects the rest to be forgiven in 10 years.

David, 39, RN Returning for BSN

David took private loans for an accelerated program. He refinanced to a lower interest rate but lost forgiveness options. He's paying aggressively to avoid ballooning interest.

Maria, 31, ER Nurse in Rural Kansas

Maria applied for the Nurse Corps program. Her loans were cut in half within 2 years.

Action Steps

- **Log in to studentaid.gov** and find your loan breakdown.
- **Track your total debt.** Know what you owe, the interest rates, and your servicer.
- **Research forgiveness programs in your state.** Use HRSA.gov as a resource.
- **Start a payoff plan—even if you're still in school.**
- **Avoid capitalized interest.** Pay interest on unsubsidized loans while in school if you can.

Plain Language Terms You Need to Know

- **Capitalization:** When unpaid interest gets added to your loan principal (you pay interest on interest)
- **Disbursement:** When your loan money is sent to your school
- **Grace Period:** Time after school ends before repayment starts (usually 6 months)
- **Default:** Failing to make payments for 270 days. It wrecks your credit.

- **Servicer:** The company that handles your loan payments. You don't pick them—but you do have to deal with them.

Your Mindset Matters

This isn't just about math. It's about emotions. Many nurses feel guilt, regret, or even shame around student debt.

Let that go.

You invested in your education. You entered a profession that's about service, not just salary. You did what you had to do to get here.

Now it's time to work smarter. Build a plan. Own the numbers. And stop letting fear or avoidance cost you more over time.

One Financial Move Before Your Next Shift

Log in to your loan servicer today. Write down:

- Total loan balance
- Interest rate
- Monthly payment

Then take one action:

- Switch to autopay (you might get an interest discount)
- Make an extra $25 payment this month
- Call your HR team and ask if your facility qualifies for PSLF

Just one move. That's how momentum starts.

Chapter 6: Building Credit Without Breaking the Bank

Let's talk credit.

Not in a scary, bank-lender-jargon kind of way. In a real-world, nurse-on-the-floor, late-night charting with a bag of trail mix kind of way.

Because here's the truth: building credit is one of the most powerful financial moves you can make during nursing school—and one of the least understood. Done well, your credit score becomes your financial IV line. It gives you access, stability, and protection when you need it most. Done poorly? It becomes a silent saboteur, blocking your goals, draining your paycheck, and keeping you stuck in a loop.

But this chapter isn't about fear. It's about *skill.* And just like mastering a new piece of equipment or learning how to talk a patient through a scary moment, building credit is something you can absolutely learn. Even if no one ever taught you. Even if you've made mistakes. Even if your current score is a number you're embarrassed to say out loud.

This chapter will walk you through everything—from what your credit score actually *means,* to how to build it wisely, protect it fiercely, and use it as a springboard toward financial security. No shame. Just structure. No confusion. Just clarity.

Let's scrub in.

Why Your Credit Score Matters—Even in Nursing School

You may not be thinking about home ownership, car loans, or personal loans right now. But trust me—those things come faster than you think.

Here's why your credit score matters *now*:

- It determines your **interest rates** on loans (lower score = higher cost to borrow)
- It affects your ability to **rent an apartment** or pass a landlord background check
- Some employers—including hospitals—**check credit** before hiring
- It influences **insurance premiums** in many states
- It impacts your **stress levels** when you need financial help in an emergency

Credit doesn't just reflect your past. It shapes your future.

The Five Ingredients of a Credit Score

FICO scores (the most common type) range from 300–850. Here's how that score is built:

1. **Payment History (35%)** – Do you pay on time?
2. **Amounts Owed (30%)** – How much of your available credit are you using?
3. **Length of Credit History (15%)** – How long have your accounts been open?
4. **Credit Mix (10%)** – Do you have a variety of accounts (credit card, student loan, etc.)?
5. **New Credit (10%)** – Have you opened lots of accounts recently?

You don't need to memorize that. Just understand the big three:

- Pay on time
- Keep balances low
- Build slowly and steadily

How to Build Credit in Nursing School (Without Breaking the Bank)

1. Start with a Student Credit Card

Look for a no-annual-fee card with a low limit ($300–$1,000). Use it for one recurring charge—like gas or your phone bill—and pay it off in full each month.

2. Pay Every Bill On Time

Late payments hurt. Even one 30-day-late mark can drop your score by 50–100 points. Use autopay. Set reminders. Treat due dates like clinical start times.

3. Keep Credit Utilization Low

Credit utilization is the % of your available credit you're using. Keep it below 30%—and ideally under 10%. If your limit is $1,000, stay under $100–$300.

4. Don't Apply for Every Card You See

Each new application triggers a "hard inquiry" that can slightly lower your score. More importantly, it looks risky if you're opening too many accounts.

5. Ask for Credit Line Increases (Responsibly)

After 6–12 months of on-time payments, you can ask for a credit limit increase. This lowers your utilization *without* needing to open a new card.

6. Keep Old Cards Open

Unless there's a steep annual fee, keep older cards open to boost your average account age.

Real-Life Nurse Scenarios

Taylor, 22, Nursing Student

Taylor opens a student credit card with a $500 limit. She sets it to autopay her Spotify subscription and pays it off in full every month. In one year, her score jumps from 610 to 735.

James, 28, Accelerated BSN Program

James used a credit card for groceries and emergencies but didn't realize how interest added up. After carrying a balance for six months, he owed $1,200 on a $1,000 limit. He entered a debt repayment plan, got back on track, and now uses his card strictly for needs—with a strict budget.

Alicia, 35, RN Going Back for MSN

Alicia used a secured credit card to rebuild credit after bankruptcy. She put down a $200 deposit, used the card responsibly, and saw her score grow steadily. She now qualifies for a rewards card and is applying for a home loan.

Common Credit Pitfalls to Avoid

- **Carrying a balance just to "build credit"** – False. You don't need to carry a balance. Just use and pay off.
- **Paying late "just once"** – It sticks. Avoid at all costs.
- **Co-signing for a friend or family member** – You're 100% responsible if they miss payments.
- **Closing your oldest account** – Hurts your credit history length.
- **Ignoring your credit report** – Mistakes happen. Monitor it regularly.

Plain-Language Breakdowns of Jargon

- **APR:** Annual Percentage Rate. The interest you'll pay if you carry a balance.
- **Credit Limit:** The max amount you're allowed to charge on a card.
- **Minimum Payment:** The smallest amount due each month. Paying

only this means high interest costs.

- **Hard Inquiry:** A credit check that can lower your score temporarily.
- **Secured Card:** A credit card backed by a cash deposit. Great for building credit from scratch.

Action Steps for Nurses Building Credit

- **Check your credit score today.** Use a free tool like Credit Karma or your bank.
- **Open one credit card if you don't have one.** Start small. Use wisely.
- **Set up autopay or calendar reminders.** Avoid late payments at all costs.
- **Keep utilization under 30%.** Under 10% is even better.
- **Don't open multiple cards at once.** Build slowly.
- **Don't close old accounts.** Keep the credit age strong.
- **Check your credit reports annually.** Use annualcreditreport.com

Mindset Check: Building Credit Is a Long Game

There's no rush. No trophy for hitting 800 before graduation. This isn't a sprint—it's a marathon. And you're building *trust* with lenders. That takes time, consistency, and integrity.

There's also no shame in starting late. Or fixing what's broken. Credit is *fluid.* It can be rebuilt. It can be shaped. It can be used to move your life forward—not hold you back.

You don't need to be a financial expert. You just need a game plan.

One Financial Move Before Your Next Shift

Check your current credit score. Just check it. Write it down. No judgment.

Then pick one habit to start:

- Open a credit card (if you don't have one)

- Pay your bill in full (if you've been carrying a balance)
- Set a reminder for your due date (if you've been paying late)

Just one move. Start where you are. Build from there.

Chapter 7: Opening Your First Bank and Investment Accounts

Let's start with this: if no one ever taught you how to open a bank account—or even what kind to open—you are not behind. You are not bad with money. You are not alone.

Most nurses were trained to take care of other people, not to build wealth for themselves. So when it comes time to set up a basic checking account, open a high-yield savings account, or even dip a toe into the world of investing, it can feel like you're faking it. Smiling and nodding. Hoping no one notices that you've been using the same student checking account since undergrad and still don't know the difference between a Roth IRA and a brokerage account.

This chapter is here to fix that.

No shame. Just strategy. No over-complicated jargon. Just real talk about how to get your money *organized, working,* and *protected*—starting with the very accounts that hold it.

Let's scrub in.

First Things First: You Need a Banking System

A good financial setup for a nurse—student or seasoned—starts with three core accounts:

1. **A checking account** – for bills and everyday spending

2. **A savings account** – for your emergency fund and short-term goals
3. **A high-yield savings or money market account** – to actually *earn* interest on your savings

And eventually, if you want to build long-term wealth:

1. **An investment account** – to grow your money beyond the bedside

Let's take these one at a time.

1. Checking Accounts: Your Money's Home Base

Think of your checking account like the nurse's station. Everything flows through it—your paycheck, your rent, your groceries, your utilities.

What to look for in a checking account:

- No monthly fees (or easy ways to waive them)
- No minimum balance requirement
- Free ATM access or wide ATM network
- Mobile banking app
- Direct deposit capability

Avoid overdraft fees like you avoid expired meds. Set up alerts. Keep a cushion ($50–$100) to prevent bounced payments.

Pro tip: Use one checking account for spending and another for bills. This makes it easier to see where your money's going.

2. Savings Accounts: Your Financial Crash Cart

This is where your emergency fund lives.

- Start with a goal of $500 if you're still in school
- Build to 1 month of expenses once you're working

- Eventually aim for 3–6 months of expenses

A traditional savings account is fine for quick access, but interest rates are usually trash (think 0.01%). That's why we also want...

3. High-Yield Savings Accounts (HYSAs): Your Passive Income Sidekick

A HYSA is an online savings account that earns 10–20x the interest of a traditional bank account.

As of now, many offer 4%–5% APY.

That means if you stash $10,000, you could earn $400–$500/year in interest—*just for letting it sit there.*

Use it for:

- Your emergency fund (once it's large enough)
- Saving for short-term goals (wedding, vacation, down payment)
- Any money you want to keep safe *and* growing

No fees. No gimmicks. Just solid interest.

4. Investment Accounts: The Future Nurse Fund

Once you've got your bills paid and emergency fund started, it's time to build wealth.

There are two main ways to invest:

1. **Retirement accounts** – 401(k), 403(b), Roth IRA
2. **Brokerage accounts** – for investing money you can access before retirement

We'll dive into retirement accounts in their own chapters later. For now, let's focus on:

Beginner Brokerage Accounts:

- Think of this like your “freestyle” investing account
- You can buy stocks, ETFs, mutual funds
- No penalties for withdrawing (unlike retirement accounts)
- You’ll pay capital gains tax on profits

Use it for:

- Long-term investing (5+ years)
- Extra income you don’t need right away
- Building wealth beyond your 403(b)

Start small. $25–$50 per month is enough to build the habit.

Plain-Language Breakdowns

- **APY:** Annual percentage yield—how much interest you earn on savings
- **ETF:** A bundle of stocks you can invest in, like a nursing union of the stock market
- **Mutual Fund:** A professionally managed collection of investments
- **Capital Gains:** The profit you make from selling investments
- **FDIC Insured:** Your deposits are safe up to $250,000 if the bank fails

Real-Life Nurse Scenarios

Maria, 24, Nursing Student

Maria opened a free student checking account at her local credit union. She set up a high-yield savings account online and auto-transfers $10/week from her checking to savings. She’s up to $700 in her emergency fund.

Jordan, 32, Floor Nurse

Jordan was tired of earning $0.08/month in interest. He opened a high-yield savings account and moved $12,000 into it. It now earns $480/year with zero effort.

Aisha, 40, Nurse Practitioner

Aisha started investing through a beginner brokerage account. She puts $100/month into an ETF. She doesn't try to time the market. She plays the long game.

Choosing Where to Open Accounts

For Checking/Savings:

- Credit unions (low fees, local support)
- Online banks (better tech, higher yields)
- Big banks (convenient, but often more fees)

For HYSAs:

- Ally, Marcus, Discover, SoFi, Capital One (rates change, so shop around)

For Brokerages:

- Fidelity, Schwab, Vanguard (low fees, good support)
- M1 Finance, Betterment, SoFi (more automated or beginner-friendly)

Action Steps

- **Open a high-yield savings account.** Transfer $10 just to get started.
- **Set up direct deposit to checking.** Make sure your paycheck is landing safely.
- **Create automatic transfers to savings.** Start with $5/week. Let it grow.
- **Open a brokerage account (when ready).** Fund it with your first $50. Pick a low-cost ETF.

- **Track all your accounts in one app.** Try Mint, Monarch, or Empower.

Pros and Cons of Different Account Types

Checking

- Pros: Fast access, bill paying
- Cons: No interest, risk of overdraft

Savings

- Pros: Safe, separate from spending
- Cons: Low interest if not high-yield

HYSA

- Pros: Great interest, FDIC insured
- Cons: Limited withdrawals per month

Brokerage

- Pros: Long-term growth, wealth-building
- Cons: Can lose value, taxed on gains

Nurse Money Truth: This Isn't Optional—It's Foundational

You don't need 12 accounts or fancy strategies. But you do need a system.

Because your bank and investment setup is the *bedrock* of your financial life. Without it, everything is harder:

- Saving is inconsistent
- Investing gets delayed

- Money slips through the cracks

But with it? You gain power. You make moves. You sleep better.

And it doesn't take a lot. Just intention.

One Financial Move Before Your Next Shift

Open one new account this week:

- A checking account with no fees
- A high-yield savings account
- A beginner brokerage account (if you're ready)

Fund it with just $25. That's it.

That's how the wealth journey starts—not with complexity. With *clarity.*

Part II: Landing the Job – Financial Transitions After Graduation

Where your paycheck begins—and your financial strategy shifts into high gear.

You graduated. You passed the NCLEX. You got the job.

Now what?

Part II of *Financial Literacy For Nurses* is all about the money moves that matter **after** the scrubs become official. This isn't just about celebrating your first real paycheck—it's about **what you do with it** that sets the tone for everything that comes next: your savings, your lifestyle, your debt, your future.

This section meets you at the exact moment you go from student to full-fledged nurse—and helps you transition your finances with clarity, control, and confidence.

You'll learn how to:

- Read and break down your **first paycheck** (what are all these deductions?)
- Choose **benefits** that actually benefit you—health insurance, retirement plans, disability, and more
- Avoid the trap of **lifestyle inflation** when the money finally starts rolling in
- Handle **relocation expenses**, licensing, and job offers without draining your emergency fund
- Set up your **first budget** as a working professional—with real numbers

- Understand **taxes**, **overtime**, and what those "differentials" really mean
- Navigate **nurse-specific financial red flags**, from burnout-spending to debt-avoidance

This part also includes real-world scenarios from new nurses who made mistakes—and those who made smart early moves that paid off big down the line.

Whether you're entering med-surg, the ICU, a clinic, or travel nursing, **Part II is your bridge** from paycheck to prosperity. It's the financial orientation every new nurse deserves—but never gets.

This is where financial adulting begins. Not with guilt or overwhelm, but with structure, strategy, and the swagger that comes from knowing you've got a plan.

Chapter 8: Your First Paycheck – Don't Blow It

You've made it.

You're officially clocking in, collecting vitals, crushing shift reports—and for the first time, getting paid as a full-fledged nurse.

There's nothing like that first paycheck. It's validation. It's reward. It's the sweet relief of financial oxygen after years of living on loans, ramen, and grind.

But here's the warning label no one hands you during orientation:

Just because your paycheck got bigger doesn't mean your financial problems disappear.

If you don't slow down and understand what's actually *in* that paycheck, you might find yourself just as broke as before—but now with designer scrubs, a new car lease, and a whole lot more financial pressure.

This chapter isn't about guilt. It's about power. It's about clarity.

It's your financial stethoscope for reading your earnings, understanding deductions, and planning like the professional you've become.

Let's break it down.

Your Gross Pay vs. Your Net Pay

Gross pay is what you *think* you're earning.

Net pay is what actually lands in your account.

The difference? Taxes and deductions.

Let's say your job offers you $35/hour as a new grad RN. You're working full-time (36 hours/week on 3 twelves). That's about $65,520/year before taxes.

You're thinking, "That's more money than I've ever seen!"

But here's what you might actually *take home* each month:

- Gross: ~$5,460/month
- After taxes and deductions: $3,500–$4,000/month (depending on your state, benefits, and tax situation)

That's a **$1,500–$2,000/month** haircut you weren't expecting.

Where Did My Money Go?

Let's break down your paycheck line by line.

1. Federal Income Tax

The U.S. uses a progressive tax system. The more you make, the higher your rate *on that portion* of income.

2. State Income Tax

Varies by state. Some (like Texas, Florida, Nevada) have no income tax. Others (like California, New York) take a bigger bite.

3. FICA Taxes

This covers Social Security (6.2%) and Medicare (1.45%). Total: 7.65% of your income.

4. Health Insurance Premiums

If you opted into your hospital's health plan, this comes out pre-tax. Could range from $100 to $300+/month.

5. Retirement Contributions

If you're contributing to a 403(b) or 401(k), that also gets deducted—pre-tax.

6. Union Dues or Miscellaneous Deductions

Some hospitals deduct union dues, parking, uniforms, or disability insurance.

That's why you can earn over $65K/year and still feel like your checking account isn't moving.

Understand Your Paycheck Frequency

Hospitals often pay biweekly (every 2 weeks). Some pay weekly.

- Biweekly = 26 paychecks/year
- Weekly = 52 paychecks/year

If you're budgeting monthly, you'll have two "bonus" checks per year if you're paid biweekly. Plan for them. Don't let them disappear.

Overtime, Shift Differentials, and Taxes

As a nurse, you might earn more through:

- Overtime (time and a half)
- Night shift differential
- Weekend or holiday pay

But here's the trap: these earnings often bump you into higher tax brackets *temporarily*. You may owe more at tax time if you don't adjust your withholdings.

Don't just focus on your *hourly* rate—track your *effective* tax rate and net income.

Real-Life Nurse Scenario

Tasha, 26, New Grad in a Large City

- $34/hour, full-time, night shift
- Overtime once a week

- Total gross pay: $78,000/year
- Net take-home: $51,500/year (~$4,300/month)
- Rent: $2,000/month
- Student loan: $400/month
- Car payment: $500/month
- Leftover: ~$1,400/month for everything else

Tasha was shocked to feel broke even though she was "making bank." Once she created a budget and automated her savings, she started building momentum.

How to Read Your Pay Stub

Every pay stub includes:

- **Gross pay** – your total earnings before deductions
- **Taxes withheld** – federal, state, Social Security, Medicare
- **Pre-tax deductions** – health, dental, vision insurance, retirement
- **Post-tax deductions** – union dues, wage garnishments
- **Net pay** – your take-home amount

Look for errors. Ask HR if something looks off. This is *your* money. Know where it's going.

What to Do With Your First Few Paychecks

1. Celebrate responsibly.
You earned it. Take yourself to dinner. Buy the nice stethoscope. Then get serious.

2. Build a starter emergency fund.
Put your first $500–$1,000 into a high-yield savings account.

3. Create a basic budget.
Track your fixed expenses (rent, car, loans) and variable ones (groceries,

eating out). Give every dollar a job.

4. Set up autopay for bills.

Missed payments hurt your credit. Autopay builds stability.

5. Start saving for the next emergency or goal.

Use automatic transfers to move 10%–15% of your check into savings or investment accounts.

6. Pay down high-interest debt.

If you're carrying credit card balances, make a plan to crush them.

Action Steps

- **Review your pay stub.** Find your net pay, tax withholdings, and deductions.
- **Know your pay frequency.** Budget around it.
- **Track your last 30 days of spending.** Print your statements and highlight your "surprises."
- **Build a simple money plan.** Spend. Save. Invest. Automate.

Mindset Shift: It's Not About What You Earn—It's About What You Keep

You're not just a new nurse. You're a new professional—with new money.

Don't let that money control you.

Take the time to build structure now. Learn what those numbers mean. Avoid lifestyle inflation. Don't buy a new car just because your paycheck got bigger.

This is where financial security begins. Not with big raises or bonuses. But with understanding your *first* dollar.

One Financial Move Before Your Next Shift

Pull up your most recent pay stub. Highlight your gross pay. Circle your net pay.

Then do the math: What % are you actually keeping?

Set a goal: Can you save or invest just 5% of your net pay this month?

Just one move. That's how it begins.

Chapter 9: Budgeting on a New Grad Nurse's Salary

You made it through school. You passed the NCLEX. You're finally earning a real paycheck.

But now comes the part no one taught you: how to *actually manage that money.*

This chapter isn't about guilt, restrictions, or some rigid spreadsheet template. It's about understanding your cash flow, building structure, and giving every dollar a clear purpose—without sucking the joy out of your new career.

Because here's the truth: a budget isn't a punishment. It's a prescription.

Just like you wouldn't wing it on med administration or ignore a patient's vitals, you shouldn't ignore your own financial vitals. A smart budget is how you make sure your money supports your goals—not sabotages them.

Let's walk through how to budget on a new grad nurse's salary. Not hypothetically. Not someday. *Right now.*

What You're Working With

Let's say you make $34/hour. You work 36 hours a week (3 12s). That's around $63,648/year before taxes.

After taxes, benefits, and deductions, your take-home pay might be closer to **$3,800/month**.

Sound like a lot? It can be. But without a plan, it disappears fast.

The #1 Threat: Lifestyle Creep

Lifestyle creep is when your expenses increase every time your income increases.

You get a raise → You upgrade your apartment.

You pick up overtime → You buy a new car.

You get a bonus → You book a trip.

And suddenly, you're making more than you ever have—and still broke.

This chapter is your antidote.

Build Your Nurse Budget: The Simple 50/30/20 Framework (With a Twist)

50% Needs – Rent, groceries, transportation, insurance, student loan minimums

30% Wants – Dining out, travel, subscriptions, self-care

20% Financial Goals – Savings, debt payoff, investing

If your take-home is $3,800/month:

- **Needs = $1,900**
- **Wants = $1,140**
- **Goals = $760**

But here's your *nurse twist* to this model:

Many nurses work inconsistent hours, extra shifts, or differentials. So you'll also want:

- A **base budget** – for your predictable income (2 shifts/week or 72 hours/pay period)
- A **bonus budget** – for extra shifts, overtime, and unexpected windfalls

Use your base budget for needs.

Use your bonus budget for goals (savings, debt payoff) and wants (with boundaries).

Step-by-Step: Build Your Monthly Nurse Budget

Step 1: Know Your Net Pay

Check your pay stub. Write down your net pay per check.

Multiply by 2 (biweekly) or 4 (weekly) to get monthly income.

Step 2: List Fixed Expenses

Rent, car payment, phone bill, insurance, minimum debt payments.

These don't change.

Step 3: Estimate Variable Expenses

Groceries, gas, dining out, coffee, Target runs. These change but can be tracked.

Step 4: Automate Savings Goals First

- Emergency fund? Aim for $500–$1,000 to start.
- Sinking funds for irregular costs? (car repair, holidays, license renewal)
- Roth IRA or 403(b)? Get in the habit *now.*

Step 5: Track Spending Weekly

You don't need an app (though they help).

Just check your transactions every week.

Notice patterns. Adjust without shame.

Step 6: Review & Reset Monthly

Every month, check:

- Did your income change?
- Any unexpected expenses?
- Where did your money feel tight or flow too freely?

Budgeting Scenarios for Real Nurses

Samantha, 25, Lives Alone, $3,900 Take-Home Pay

- Rent: $1,300
- Car + Gas: $550
- Insurance: $300
- Food: $400
- Debt Payments: $400
- Wants: $600
- Savings + Roth IRA: $350

Carlos, 32, Married with One Child

- Dual income, $6,800/month
- Uses joint budget for needs
- Each partner gets $300/month personal spending
- Prioritizes $500/month into savings + $300 toward future house

Tina, 29, Living at Home to Save

- Take-home: $3,500/month
- Rent: $0
- Allocates:
- $1,000/month to student loans
- $500/month to emergency fund
- $300/month to Roth IRA
- Lives on $1,700 and is building wealth fast

Nurse-Specific Budget Tips

1. Budget for Burnout Weeks

Some months, you'll need more for takeout or therapy. That's okay. Budget for real life.

2. Watch for Per Diem Traps

Per diem pay feels like a windfall—but it doesn't come with benefits or job security. Budget accordingly.

3. Build a Sinking Fund for License Fees, CEUs, and Certifications

These sneak up. Save $20–$30/month now.

4. Budget Differentials as Bonuses, Not Baseline

Don't count on night/weekend/overtime pay in your base budget. That way, it becomes extra—not essential.

5. Create a "Wellness Line Item"

Massages, float tanks, therapy, therapy dog grooming—whatever helps you reset. You need it.

The Mental Game: Guilt-Free, Nurse-Smart Budgeting

You are not bad with money.

You are not behind.

You are not irresponsible because you bought something you enjoyed.

But you do need structure.

Because the hospital gives you structure on the floor—but no one's doing it for your wallet.

A budget is your personal preceptorship for every dollar.

What Budgeting Is (and Isn't)

It IS:

- Permission to spend with intention
- A system to build wealth

- A tool for alignment

It ISN'T:

- A spreadsheet jail cell
- A reason to beat yourself up
- A magic fix for systemic financial issues

Action Steps

- Create a base budget today. Use your lowest guaranteed income.
- Add a line for savings, even if it's $20/month.
- Write down every fixed expense.
- Estimate one variable (like food) and track it for 30 days.
- Automate one savings transfer—just $10 if that's what you can do.

Pros and Cons of Budgeting Tools

Spreadsheets:

- Pros: Fully customizable
- Cons: Takes time to maintain

Apps (YNAB, EveryDollar, Monarch):

- Pros: Easy tracking, automation
- Cons: May cost money, learning curve

Pen + Paper:

- Pros: Tactile, mindful
- Cons: Not ideal for tracking trends over time

Mindset Reset: Budgeting is a Muscle

The first few months might feel awkward.

You might overspend.

You might forget to check your account.

You might hate every second of it.

That's okay. You're building a new skill.

Just like you didn't walk into clinicals knowing how to run a code or calculate a drip rate, you won't master money overnight.

Give yourself grace.

Then get back to it.

One Financial Move Before Your Next Shift

Write down your next paycheck amount.

Then:

- Create three spending buckets: Needs, Wants, Goals
- Assign percentages to each—try 50/30/20
- Pick one goal (like saving $50 this month) and automate it

That's it. No guilt. Just structure.

Because the only thing worse than working 12-hour shifts is having nothing to show for it at the end of the month.

You're not just making money now. You're building a life.

Chapter 10: Understanding Offer Letters and Job Benefits

Let's be honest.

You didn't go to nursing school for the paperwork. You went for the purpose, the people, the patient care.

But here's the reality: the moment you get that job offer, you're no longer just a nurse. You're also a *professional employee*—and your offer letter isn't just a welcome note. It's a financial document that determines your income, your benefits, your protections, and your potential.

And if you don't know what to look for, you could end up underpaid, underprotected, and overwhelmed.

This chapter is here to break down every part of an offer letter and nurse benefit package—clearly, calmly, and without the fluff. We'll cover everything from shift differentials and per diem roles to health insurance, overtime, and sign-on bonuses.

Because understanding the *real value* of a job offer is a skill—one that can set you up for financial success far beyond your starting salary.

Let's break it down.

What an Offer Letter Actually Is

An offer letter is a written summary of the job the employer is offering you. It outlines your compensation, your position, and often a brief overview of your benefits.

But here's the key:

Most offer letters are high-level. They don't always include every detail you *need* to make an informed decision. That's why you have to ask follow-up questions.

What to Look For in an Offer Letter

1. Job Title and Status

- Are you full-time, part-time, or per diem?
- Are you salaried or hourly?
- Is this a temporary contract or permanent?

2. Pay Rate and Structure

- Hourly rate: What's your base rate?
- Shift differential: Do you earn more for evenings, nights, weekends, holidays?
- Overtime policy: When does OT kick in? At 40 hours/week? 8 hours/day?

3. Work Schedule

- How many hours per week?
- What shift? Day, night, rotating?
- Is it consistent or variable?

4. Bonuses

- Sign-on bonus: How much, when do you receive it, and what are the conditions? (Read: *Do you have to stay for 1–2 years to keep it?*)
- Retention bonus: Offered after a year or more?
- Referral bonus: Can you earn extra for bringing in other nurses?

5. Benefits Overview

- Health, dental, vision insurance?
- Retirement plans—403(b), 401(k), match?
- PTO: How many hours or days per year?
- Sick leave policy?
- CEU or tuition reimbursement?

6. Union Status

- Are you in a union? What dues are deducted?
- What does the union contract include?

7. Start Date and Orientation

- Is orientation paid?
- How long is the preceptorship?
- Will you be on unit immediately or shadowing first?

Real-World Nurse Scenario

Kelsey, 26, Receives Two Offers

Offer A:

- $32/hour, full-time, day shift
- $4,000 sign-on bonus (paid after 6 months)
- 403(b) with 2% match
- Basic health plan

Offer B:

- $29/hour, full-time, night shift
- $8,000 sign-on bonus (paid up front, must stay 2 years)

- 403(b) with 5% match
- Premium health plan

Kelsey almost took Offer A because the base pay was higher. But after factoring in differentials (+$3/hr for night shift), stronger retirement benefits, and a better health plan, **Offer B actually had higher total compensation**.

This is why you have to do the math.

Understanding Shift Differentials

Shift differentials are additional hourly pay for working less desirable shifts.

Typical ranges:

- Evenings: +$2/hour
- Nights: +$3–5/hour
- Weekends: +$2–6/hour
- Holidays: +Time and a half or double time

Pro tip: Never calculate your salary off your base rate alone. Include average shift differential earnings in your budgeting.

Per Diem vs. Staff: Pros and Cons

Per Diem:

- Pros: Higher hourly pay, flexible schedule
- Cons: No benefits, less job security, inconsistent hours

Staff Nurse:

- Pros: Steady schedule, benefits, PTO, retirement contributions

- Cons: Lower hourly pay, less flexibility

Hybrid strategy: Some nurses work one full-time staff job and pick up per diem shifts elsewhere for extra income.

Sign-On Bonuses: What No One Tells You

- Many bonuses are *taxed heavily* when paid out
- Many require you to stay 1–3 years to keep the full bonus
- Some are paid in installments (e.g., $2,000 at 6 months, $2,000 at 1 year)
- If you leave early, you may have to **pay it back**

Always read the fine print.

Understanding Job Benefits

Health Insurance

- What's the premium? Deductible? Out-of-pocket max?
- Are your doctors in-network?
- What's the ER visit cost?

Dental & Vision

- Often low-cost, but limited coverage—check if it's worth it based on your needs

Retirement Plans

- 403(b) (nonprofit hospitals) or 401(k) (for-profit hospitals)
- What's the match? (e.g., 100% of the first 3%)
- When are you *vested* (fully own the match)?

PTO and Sick Leave

- How is it accrued? Can you carry it over?
- Is there separate sick leave, or is it combined?

Disability Insurance

- Short-term: Pays a % of salary if you're out for weeks/months
- Long-term: Critical protection, especially for nurses

CEU & Tuition Reimbursement

- How much do they cover annually?
- Do you have to work for a period after using it?

Malpractice Insurance

- Most hospitals cover this, but some nurses get additional coverage

Benefits with Hidden Value

- **Employee Assistance Programs (EAP):** Free therapy or counseling
- **Hospital cafeteria discounts:** Saves $100s a year
- **On-site childcare or fitness programs**
- **Loan repayment programs or PSLF-eligible employment**

Action Steps for Evaluating a Job Offer

- List *all* forms of compensation (base, differentials, bonuses)
- Estimate benefits value (health insurance, retirement, PTO)
- Ask about vesting schedules for retirement plans
- Read bonus fine print *before* you sign
- Ask HR for a benefit summary or packet

- Talk to a current nurse at that facility if possible

Red Flags to Watch For

- Huge sign-on bonus but high turnover
- No mention of orientation or preceptorship
- No retirement benefits
- Vague language like "competitive pay" with no details

Mindset Reset: You're Not Just Lucky to Get an Offer—You're a Professional Making a Choice

Yes, the job market is tough in some areas.
Yes, it's exciting to land your first role.
But that doesn't mean you should blindly accept whatever's offered.
You have value.
You have leverage.
And you deserve to know exactly what you're signing up for.

One Financial Move Before Your Next Shift

If you're considering or comparing offers:

- Make a compensation comparison chart
- Ask HR about shift differentials, retirement match, and bonus terms
- Get clarity before you commit

Because the choices you make now will shape your financial health for years to come—not just your schedule for next week.

Chapter 11: Emergency Funds – Start Here Before Investing

Let's talk about the thing no one glamorizes on TikTok or brags about in nurse lounges: **emergency funds.**

They're not flashy. They're not fun. But they are *foundational.*

Before you dive into investing, before you obsess over retirement accounts, before you celebrate your new RN salary with a down payment on a car you may not need—you've got to build your financial seatbelt. That's what your emergency fund is.

Because the question isn't *if* something unexpected will happen. It's *when.*

You know that as a nurse. Life turns fast. One illness, one shift injury, one family emergency, and suddenly your carefully balanced world is upside down.

This chapter is your permission slip and your step-by-step guide to build a buffer between you and burnout. Because nothing makes a hard season harder than being broke while it's happening.

Let's build your emergency fund—the right way, the nurse-smart way.

What Is an Emergency Fund?

An emergency fund is cash set aside in a separate, liquid, *easy-to-access* account to cover life's unexpected expenses.

It's not for shopping.

It's not for vacations.

It's not for routine car maintenance or holiday gifts.

It's for the **"oh crap"** moments:

- You slip a disc during a 12-hour shift and can't work for two weeks
- Your car dies and you need a $2,000 repair
- You lose your job or hours are cut unexpectedly
- You need to fly home suddenly for a family emergency

It's a financial tourniquet. Not the cure—but the thing that keeps you from bleeding out.

Why Nurses Especially Need Emergency Funds

1. We work with our bodies.

Nursing isn't a desk job. One injury can pause your income.

2. Burnout is real.

Sometimes, you need to take a break before your mental health breaks you. An emergency fund gives you options.

3. Our schedules can be unpredictable.

Canceled shifts, hospital cutbacks, changing roles—it's not always stable.

4. We support others.

A lot of nurses are the financial backbones of their families. Emergencies rarely affect just us.

5. We *see* what can happen.

We've witnessed firsthand how quickly life can change—financially and physically.

How Much Should You Save?

Start with this rule of thumb:

- **Step 1:** $500–$1,000 starter fund

- **Step 2:** 1 month of essential expenses
- **Step 3:** 3–6 months of essential expenses

What's "essential"? Rent, food, gas, minimum loan payments, insurance, meds.

Not Spotify, not lash fills, not streaming bundles.

If your essential expenses are $2,800/month, then:

- Starter Fund: $1,000
- Full Emergency Fund: $8,400–$16,800

It sounds like a lot. But you build it in layers—one shift at a time.

Where Should You Keep It?

The ideal emergency fund is:

- **Safe:** Not invested in the stock market
- **Liquid:** You can access it within 1–2 days
- **Separate:** Not in the same account you pay bills from
- **Earning something:** Like a high-yield savings account (HYSA)

Best Options:

- Online HYSAs (Ally, Capital One, Marcus, SoFi, etc.)
- Credit union savings accounts
- Money market accounts

Avoid:

- Cash under the mattress (inflation eats it)
- Checking accounts with no interest
- Investment accounts (too volatile for emergency use)

How to Build It as a Nurse

1. Use part of your sign-on bonus.

Take $500–$1,000 and move it immediately into savings.

2. Set up automatic transfers.

Even $25 per week adds up. Treat it like a bill.

3. Bank your overtime.

Work a weekend? Send half to savings. Build your buffer while you're energized.

4. Pause extra debt payments.

It's okay to make minimum payments temporarily if it helps you build your emergency safety net.

5. Cut one expense.

Cancel a subscription or eat out one less time per week. Re-route that money directly into savings.

6. Use tax refunds wisely.

If you get a refund, pretend it never happened—send it straight to your emergency fund.

Real Nurse Scenarios

Gabby, 24, First-Year Med-Surg RN

Started with $0 saved. Set up a $50/week auto-transfer. Reached $1,000 in 5 months. Used it when her car battery and alternator failed the same week.

Trent, 30, ICU Nurse with $8K Credit Card Debt

Paused extra debt payments to build a $2,000 emergency fund. When his apartment flooded and he had to cover hotel + pet boarding for 4 nights, he didn't use his credit card. Game changer.

Samira, 41, Charge Nurse and Mom of 3

Saved $15,000 in an online HYSA after years of being paycheck to paycheck. When her husband was laid off, they had a 3-month buffer and never missed a mortgage payment.

Emergency Fund Pros and Cons

Pros:

- Peace of mind
- Prevents credit card debt during emergencies
- Allows flexibility in life decisions (taking leave, switching jobs, etc.)

Cons:

- Doesn't grow much (low interest)
- Can feel boring or slow to build
- Tempting to use it for "non-emergencies"

How to Keep It Safe (and Untouched)

- Label it clearly in your bank ("Emergency Only")
- Don't connect it to debit cards or bill pay
- Set rules: "3-day wait rule" before withdrawing
- Tell someone you trust: "Hold me accountable if I try to touch it for concert tickets"

What Counts as a Real Emergency?

ER visit and deductible

- Job loss
- Unexpected medical leave
- Essential car repair
- Emergency travel
- Coachella tickets
- Birthday brunch
- "I just don't want to cook this week"

- Black Friday sales

Emergency funds should feel a little boring. That's the point.

What If You're Living Paycheck to Paycheck?

That's real. Here's your strategy:

- Start with $10/week
- Use cash-back rewards or coin jar apps to stash small amounts
- Cut just one thing this month (maybe it's Starbucks, maybe it's Target)
- Side hustle once a month and save all of it

Slow is still forward.

Mindset Reset: Saving Is Self-Respect, Not Sacrifice

You're not "being good with money." You're being smart with your life.

You're not "missing out." You're building your options.

You're not "behind." You're taking the first step that 70% of Americans *never* take.

This fund is your freedom.

It's your exit plan from burnout.

It's your parachute when life yanks the rug out.

You deserve that safety.

Action Steps

1. Open a separate savings account today
2. Set a goal: $500 by [insert date]
3. Automate a weekly transfer—even if it's just $10
4. Rename the account "Emergency Fund" so you don't forget
5. Write one sentence on a sticky note: "This money is for future me

when life hits hard."

Put it on your mirror, your locker, or your laptop.

One Financial Move Before Your Next Shift

If you don't have an emergency fund yet:

Open the account. Transfer $25. That's it.

If you do:

Raise your auto-transfer by $5/week. Or celebrate your win—because you're doing what most never will.

This is the foundation. The financial bedrock beneath your career.

Before you build wealth, before you invest, before you pay off every loan—**you start here.**

Chapter 12: Retirement Plans 101 – 401(k), 403(b), 457(b), and Pensions

Let's talk about the thing most nurses put off until "someday."

Retirement.

Not the far-off version with rocking chairs and Florida condos. But the real financial plan you build *now* so that 30 years from now, you're not forced to work when you're exhausted, injured, or just ready to be done.

This chapter isn't about guilt. It's not about telling you you're behind.

It's about structure.

Because whether you're a 26-year-old nurse still figuring out your paycheck—or a 59-year-old manager wondering if you've done enough—understanding your employer's retirement plan can unlock freedom, reduce anxiety, and put real money to work behind the scenes.

Let's break down the options: 401(k), 403(b), 457(b), pensions, and how to make the most of them as a nurse.

What Retirement Planning Actually Means

It means creating future income for yourself.

So that someday, your **money works**—even when you don't.

A solid retirement plan gives you:

- Dignity

- Flexibility
- Time with family
- Choices
- Peace

You don't want to be 68 with bad knees and no savings.

Let's prevent that—starting now.

The Big Four Retirement Plans for Nurses

1. **401(k)** – For nurses at *for-profit* hospitals or clinics
2. **403(b)** – For nurses at *nonprofit* hospitals, public schools, or religious orgs
3. **457(b)** – For nurses working for government or certain nonprofit employers
4. **Pension (Defined Benefit Plan)** – Rare, but still offered in some public hospitals or union positions

401(k) and 403(b): The Core of Retirement for Nurses

What They Are:

- Employer-sponsored retirement accounts
- You contribute pre-tax or Roth (post-tax) money
- Your money grows tax-deferred
- Many employers *match* a portion of your contributions

How It Works:

- You decide how much to contribute (usually a % of your paycheck)
- Your employer may match a % (free money!)
- Money is invested in mutual funds, target-date funds, ETFs, etc.

Example:

You earn $70,000 and contribute 5% = $3,500/year

Your employer matches 3% = $2,100/year

Total = $5,600/year growing toward retirement

Over 30 years? That adds up to hundreds of thousands.

Roth vs. Traditional Contributions:

- **Traditional:** You contribute pre-tax → lower your taxable income now
- **Roth:** You contribute post-tax → money grows tax-free, and withdrawals in retirement are tax-free

If you're early in your career or expect to be in a higher tax bracket later, **Roth often makes sense.**

What Is "Vesting"?

Vesting means *how much of your employer's contributions you own* if you leave the job.

- **Immediate vesting:** You own all contributions right away
- **Graded vesting:** You gain ownership over time (e.g., 20% per year)
- **Cliff vesting:** You own 0% until a certain year—then 100%

Pro tip: Always check your plan's vesting schedule. If you're thinking of leaving, you might want to time your exit right after you become fully vested.

457(b): The Overlooked Option

Who it's for: Nurses working for government or certain nonprofits—especially city/county hospitals or university systems

Why it's powerful:

- Similar to a 403(b), but can be used *in addition* to one
- Can contribute *to both* 403(b) and 457(b) → double savings
- No early withdrawal penalty if you leave the job (though taxes still apply)

Example:

Maria, an ER nurse at a city hospital, contributes $19,500 to her 403(b) *and* $19,500 to her 457(b). That's $39,000/year toward retirement—legally.

Even contributing $5,000 to each gets her ahead faster.

Pensions: The Unicorn

Pensions (defined benefit plans) are becoming rare. But some unionized public hospital nurses still have them.

How they work:

- You earn "credit" each year you work
- At retirement, you receive monthly income for life
- Amount depends on salary and years of service

Example: 2% × 30 years × $70,000 salary = $42,000/year in retirement

If you have one—protect it. Understand how to qualify. Know your "normal retirement age." Don't leave before you're vested.

How Much Should You Contribute?

Here's a simple ladder to climb:

Step 1: Contribute enough to get the full employer match (don't leave free money!)

Step 2: Work toward 10% of your salary

Step 3: Aim for 15–20% if possible, especially if you started later

If you're behind? Don't panic—just start. Every dollar compounds.

Real Nurse Scenarios

Angela, 29, New Grad at a Nonprofit Hospital

- Contributes 6% to her 403(b), gets 3% match
- Chooses Roth contributions
- Her target-date fund does all the investing for her

Mark, 45, ICU Nurse at a County Hospital

- Has both a 403(b) and 457(b)
- Contributes $10K to each annually
- Plans to retire at 60 with a pension and $700K in retirement savings

Lisa, 58, Nurse Manager, No Savings Yet

- Starts contributing 20% of her $90K salary
- Uses catch-up contributions
- Hopes to work until 67 and use Social Security + savings

Investment Options in Your Plan

Most plans offer:

- **Target-date funds** (pick a year, and it auto-adjusts your investments over time)
- **Index funds** (broad, low-cost market exposure)
- **Bond funds, stock funds, blended funds**

Pro tip: If you don't know what to pick, target-date funds are a great one-click solution.

Mistakes to Avoid

- Not contributing at all
- Missing the employer match
- Taking money out early (huge taxes and penalties)
- Forgetting to roll over your retirement when changing jobs
- Over-concentrating in company stock (risky!)

How to Get Started

1. Log in to your HR/benefits portal
2. Find your retirement plan provider (TIAA, Fidelity, Vanguard, Empower, etc.)
3. Choose your contribution %
4. Decide between Roth or Traditional
5. Pick your investment (target-date is fine to start)
6. Save login info and check in every 6 months

What If You're Per Diem or Part-Time?

- Some employers offer access to 403(b)s for all employees—even without benefits
- You can still open a **Roth IRA** (individual retirement account) if you have earned income

Roth IRA contribution limits:

- $7,000/year (as of 2024)
- Income limits apply

If your employer offers nothing, your IRA becomes your retirement engine.

Action Steps

- Check if you're contributing enough to get your match
- Set a goal to increase by 1% every 6 months
- Understand your vesting schedule
- Review your investment fund options
- Open a Roth IRA if you're not eligible for a 403(b) or 401(k)

Mindset Reset: Retirement Isn't a Luxury—It's a Form of Self-Protection

This isn't about being rich.

It's about being ready.

It's about having options when your body says "enough."

You don't have to max everything today.

You just have to begin.

And when you understand your retirement options, you're no longer hoping it'll all work out—you're *making it happen.*

One Financial Move Before Your Next Shift

Log into your HR portal.

Find your retirement plan.

Set your contribution—even 2% to start.

Then schedule a reminder to increase it next quarter.

That's it.

You're not just preparing for retirement.

You're respecting your future self.

Chapter 13: Roth IRA or Traditional IRA? What's Right for Nurses

Let's take a moment and zoom out.

You're working your shifts, maybe overtime. You're investing in your 403(b) or 401(k) through work—or thinking about it. And then someone says: "Hey, you should open an IRA too."

If you're like most nurses, your response is: "What's the difference? And what the heck is a Roth?"

This chapter will break it all down.

No jargon. No shame. Just a clear, confident conversation about one of the most powerful tools you'll ever have to build long-term wealth outside of your employer: the Individual Retirement Account—or IRA.

There are two types: Roth and Traditional.

Each has pros, cons, and ideal use cases depending on where you are in your nursing career.

Let's scrub in.

What Is an IRA?

IRA stands for **Individual Retirement Account**.

It's a retirement savings account you open on your own (not through your employer).

It lets you invest in things like:

- Mutual funds
- Index funds
- ETFs
- Bonds

Why use an IRA if you already have a 403(b)? Because:

- You want to save more for retirement than your employer plan allows
- You want more control over your investments
- You may not have access to an employer retirement plan at all (per diem, part-time, private clinic)

Roth IRA vs. Traditional IRA – What's the Difference?

Roth IRA:

- Contributions are made *after-tax*
- Money grows tax-free
- Withdrawals in retirement are *tax-free*

Traditional IRA:

- Contributions may be *tax-deductible* now
- Money grows tax-deferred
- Withdrawals in retirement are *taxable*

Put simply:

- Roth = Pay taxes now, avoid them later
- Traditional = Skip taxes now, pay them later

Why This Matters for Nurses

As a nurse, your income changes. Your taxes change. Your stress levels change. So your strategy has to adapt.

Here's when each one might be right:

Choose a Roth IRA if:

- You're early in your career and in a lower tax bracket
- You want tax-free income in retirement
- You expect your income (and tax rate) to go up
- You want flexibility: You can withdraw contributions anytime (not gains)

Choose a Traditional IRA if:

- You're mid-career and want a tax break now
- You're close to retirement and need to lower taxable income
- You expect to be in a lower tax bracket in retirement

Income Limits You Should Know (2025)

Roth IRA income limits (2025):

- Full contribution if modified adjusted gross income (MAGI) is under $146,000 (single) or $230,000 (married filing jointly)
- Phase-out range begins above those limits

Traditional IRA:

- Anyone can contribute
- But deduction limits apply if you or your spouse has a workplace plan

How Much Can You Contribute in 2025?

As of 2025:

- $7,500/year ($8,500 if age 50+)
- You can't exceed your earned income

You can't max out both a Roth and Traditional IRA at once. The $7,500 limit applies across both.

Real Nurse Examples

Jasmine, 27, New Grad RN

- Makes $66,000/year
- Contributes 3% to her 403(b)
- Opens a Roth IRA and puts in $100/month
- She's building tax-free retirement income in her lower-income years

Greg, 38, ER Nurse with 2 Kids

- Household income = $155K (married)
- Opens a Traditional IRA to lower taxable income this year
- Gets a $1,000+ tax deduction while still saving for retirement

Carmen, 54, Per Diem with No Employer Plan

- Opens both Traditional and Roth IRAs
- Contributes based on her yearly tax situation
- Keeps control and flexibility over her retirement savings

Pros and Cons

Roth IRA Pros:

- Tax-free growth
- No taxes in retirement
- No required minimum distributions (RMDs)
- Flexibility to withdraw contributions (not earnings)

Roth IRA Cons:

- No immediate tax deduction
- Income limits to contribute

Traditional IRA Pros:

- Possible upfront tax deduction
- Lower taxable income now
- Anyone with earned income can contribute

Traditional IRA Cons:

- Taxes owed on withdrawals
- RMDs start at age 73
- Less flexibility before retirement age

What Happens If You Withdraw Early?

Roth IRA:

- You can take out your contributions any time, no penalty
- Earnings are taxed + 10% penalty if withdrawn before age 59½ (unless qualified exception)

Traditional IRA:

- Tax + 10% penalty on *all* withdrawals before 59½ (with some exceptions)

When to Switch Strategies

You don't have to stick with one forever.

In your 20s–30s: Roth is usually smarter

In your 40s–50s: Consider Traditional if you want to lower taxes now

In your 60s: Start planning withdrawals, backdoor strategies, or Roth conversions

The Backdoor Roth IRA

If you make too much to contribute to a Roth IRA, there's a legal loophole:

1. Contribute to a Traditional IRA (non-deductible)
2. Convert it to a Roth IRA

This is called a **Backdoor Roth IRA**.

Speak to a CPA or advisor before doing this—it can get complex.

Action Steps for Nurses

1. Check your income: Are you eligible for a Roth?
2. Choose a provider (Fidelity, Vanguard, Charles Schwab, etc.)
3. Open your IRA online—it takes 15 minutes
4. Choose automatic contributions—even $50/month
5. Pick a simple fund (like a target-date fund or S&P 500 index)
6. Set a calendar reminder to review every 6 months

What If You Have a 403(b) and an IRA?

Perfect.

You can contribute to both:

- Max your 403(b) with employer match
- Then add to an IRA for tax diversification

This combo gives you flexibility, control, and more retirement security.

Mindset Reset: You Don't Need to Max Out—You Just Need to Start

Even $20/month gets the ball rolling.

You're not just investing in funds. You're investing in your future sanity. Your ability to retire on your terms.

Because the last thing you want at 65 is to be on your feet for 12-hour shifts because you didn't know the difference between a Roth and a Traditional IRA.

Now you know. And now you're ready.

One Financial Move Before Your Next Shift

Open an IRA.

Pick one.

Roth or Traditional—based on where you are.

Fund it with $25.

Automate monthly contributions.

That's it.

This isn't about being perfect. It's about being prepared.

You're not just a nurse. You're a wealth builder.

And this is one of your smartest tools.

Chapter 14: Saving While Paying Down Student Loans – How to Balance Short-Term Debt and Long-Term Savings

You've got your RN license.

You're finally earning a steady income.

And now the bills show up.

Your loan servicer wants a piece.

Your rent wants a bigger piece.

And your future—you know, that thing called retirement—wants you to start thinking about that too.

So how do you juggle it all?

This chapter is for every nurse who has ever asked, "Should I pay off my student loans first or start saving and investing?"

The answer isn't black and white. But this chapter will help you build a balanced, nurse-smart strategy—one that respects your current reality and still moves you toward long-term freedom.

Let's get into it.

The False Choice: It's Not Either/Or

Too many nurses are told: "You have to get out of debt before you even think about saving."

Wrong.

Here's the truth:

You can do both—if you build a smart system.

The goal isn't perfection. The goal is momentum.

And you're going to learn how to split your dollars with intention, so you're not just surviving, but growing.

Step 1: Know Your Numbers

Before you build your plan, you need the truth.

- What's your total student loan balance?
- What's the interest rate on each loan?
- Are they federal or private?
- What's your monthly minimum?
- What's your current income and take-home pay?
- How much are you currently saving—if anything?

This is your financial vital signs. You can't triage your plan without them.

Step 2: Build a Simple Starter Budget

We recommend starting with a 50/30/20 framework:

- **50% Needs** – Rent, groceries, loan minimums, insurance
- **30% Wants** – Dining out, hobbies, travel
- **20% Goals** – Savings, retirement, extra loan payments

If you're tight, adjust. But keep *something* in the "goals" column—even if it's just $20 a paycheck.

Because consistency beats intensity.

Step 3: Prioritize These 3 Financial Moves First

1. **Build a mini emergency fund** ($1,000–$2,000)
   So you don't turn to credit cards when life happens.
2. **Get your employer match** on your 403(b)/401(k)
   This is free money. Don't leave it on the table.
3. **Make all your student loan minimums** on time
   No missed payments. No dings to your credit.

Once those are covered, then you can decide how to split your extra cash.

The Case for Paying Down Loans Faster

You should pay more on your loans if:

- You have high interest rates (over 6–7%)
- You're ineligible for forgiveness
- You hate debt and it's causing stress
- You want to free up future cash flow

Pros:

- You save money on interest
- You reduce risk
- You get peace of mind

Cons:

- You lose liquidity
- You delay investing (and compound growth)

The Case for Saving and Investing Now

You should save more now if:

- You're eligible for Public Service Loan Forgiveness (PSLF)
- Your loans are at low interest (3–5%)
- You're behind on retirement
- You want to build financial resilience

Pros:

- You grow long-term wealth
- You create options and buffers
- You take advantage of compounding

Cons:

- You carry debt longer
- You may pay more in total interest

What About PSLF?

If you work for a nonprofit or government hospital, **you may qualify for Public Service Loan Forgiveness**:

- Make 120 qualifying payments (10 years)
- While working full-time for a qualifying employer
- Under an income-driven repayment (IDR) plan

If this is your path, your goal isn't paying loans off fast.
Your goal is **paying the minimum and maximizing forgiveness.**
In that case: focus on saving and investing.

How to Split the Difference (Sample Plans)

Plan A: Save 10%, Pay Extra 10% Toward Loans

- Great for nurses with moderate loans and moderate incomes

Plan B: Save 5%, Pay Extra 15% Toward Loans

- Great for nurses who hate debt and want to pay off faster

Plan C: Save 15%, Pay Minimum on Loans

- Best for PSLF candidates or low-interest loan holders

Real-Life Nurse Stories

Natalie, 28, Pediatric Nurse, $68K Income, $42K in Loans at 4.5%

- Emergency fund: $1,000
- Contributes 6% to 403(b) for match
- Pays an extra $100/month on loans
- Invests $50/month in Roth IRA

Javier, 33, Travel Nurse, $110K Income, $90K Loans at 6.9%

- No forgiveness eligibility
- Aggressively paying $2,000/month on loans
- Saving $200/month in HYSA for short-term goals

Tina, 40, ICU Nurse, $75K Income, PSLF Candidate

- IDR plan: $220/month loan payment
- Saving $600/month in Roth IRA + 403(b)

- Planning full forgiveness in 6 years

Tips to Make It Easier

- **Automate everything** – payments and savings
- **Celebrate progress** – every $1,000 paid down or saved matters
- **Avoid lifestyle creep** – raises = more savings, not just more spending
- **Refinance carefully** – only if you give up federal protections knowingly

Mental Health Check-In

Debt can mess with your head.

So can saving too aggressively and feeling broke.

Balance is your antidote.

Build a plan that allows you to breathe—then commit to it.

Action Steps

1. Write down your total loan balance, interest rate, and monthly minimum
2. Build a base budget with at least one line for saving—even if it's $10
3. Decide your monthly "split" (savings vs. loans)
4. Automate both
5. Reevaluate every 6 months or after major life changes

One Financial Move Before Your Next Shift

Pick a number: 10%, 15%, 20%.

That's your financial growth number.

Split it between saving and debt payoff.

Stick to it for 3 months.

Because you're not just a nurse with student loans.

You're a nurse building wealth.
And you're doing it with purpose.

Chapter 15: Saving While Paying Down Student Loans – How to Balance Short-Term Debt and Long-Term Savings

You've got your RN license.

You're finally earning a steady income.

And now the bills show up.

Your loan servicer wants a piece.

Your rent wants a bigger piece.

And your future—you know, that thing called retirement—wants you to start thinking about that too.

So how do you juggle it all?

This chapter is for every nurse who has ever asked, "Should I pay off my student loans first or start saving and investing?"

The answer isn't black and white. But this chapter will help you build a balanced, nurse-smart strategy—one that respects your current reality and still moves you toward long-term freedom.

Let's get into it.

The False Choice: It's Not Either/Or

Too many nurses are told: "You have to get out of debt before you even think about saving."

Wrong.

Here's the truth:

You can do both—if you build a smart system.

The goal isn't perfection. The goal is momentum.

And you're going to learn how to split your dollars with intention, so you're not just surviving, but growing.

Step 1: Know Your Numbers

Before you build your plan, you need the truth.

- What's your total student loan balance?
- What's the interest rate on each loan?
- Are they federal or private?
- What's your monthly minimum?
- What's your current income and take-home pay?
- How much are you currently saving—if anything?

This is your financial vital signs. You can't triage your plan without them.

Step 2: Build a Simple Starter Budget

We recommend starting with a 50/30/20 framework:

- **50% Needs** – Rent, groceries, loan minimums, insurance
- **30% Wants** – Dining out, hobbies, travel
- **20% Goals** – Savings, retirement, extra loan payments

If you're tight, adjust. But keep *something* in the "goals" column—even if it's just $20 a paycheck.

Because consistency beats intensity.

Step 3: Prioritize These 3 Financial Moves First

1. **Build a mini emergency fund** ($1,000–$2,000)
So you don't turn to credit cards when life happens.
2. **Get your employer match** on your 403(b)/401(k)
This is free money. Don't leave it on the table.
3. **Make all your student loan minimums** on time
No missed payments. No dings to your credit.
Once those are covered, then you can decide how to split your extra cash.

The Case for Paying Down Loans Faster

You should pay more on your loans if:

- You have high interest rates (over 6–7%)
- You're ineligible for forgiveness
- You hate debt and it's causing stress
- You want to free up future cash flow

Pros:

- You save money on interest
- You reduce risk
- You get peace of mind

Cons:

- You lose liquidity
- You delay investing (and compound growth)

The Case for Saving and Investing Now

You should save more now if:

- You're eligible for Public Service Loan Forgiveness (PSLF)
- Your loans are at low interest (3–5%)
- You're behind on retirement
- You want to build financial resilience

Pros:

- You grow long-term wealth
- You create options and buffers
- You take advantage of compounding

Cons:

- You carry debt longer
- You may pay more in total interest

What About PSLF?

If you work for a nonprofit or government hospital, **you may qualify for Public Service Loan Forgiveness**:

- Make 120 qualifying payments (10 years)
- While working full-time for a qualifying employer
- Under an income-driven repayment (IDR) plan

If this is your path, your goal isn't paying loans off fast.

Your goal is **paying the minimum and maximizing forgiveness.**

In that case: focus on saving and investing.

How to Split the Difference (Sample Plans)

Plan A: Save 10%, Pay Extra 10% Toward Loans

- Great for nurses with moderate loans and moderate incomes

Plan B: Save 5%, Pay Extra 15% Toward Loans

- Great for nurses who hate debt and want to pay off faster

Plan C: Save 15%, Pay Minimum on Loans

- Best for PSLF candidates or low-interest loan holders

Real-Life Nurse Stories

Natalie, 28, Pediatric Nurse, $68K Income, $42K in Loans at 4.5%

- Emergency fund: $1,000
- Contributes 6% to 403(b) for match
- Pays an extra $100/month on loans
- Invests $50/month in Roth IRA

Javier, 33, Travel Nurse, $110K Income, $90K Loans at 6.9%

- No forgiveness eligibility
- Aggressively paying $2,000/month on loans
- Saving $200/month in HYSA for short-term goals

Tina, 40, ICU Nurse, $75K Income, PSLF Candidate

- IDR plan: $220/month loan payment
- Saving $600/month in Roth IRA + 403(b)

- Planning full forgiveness in 6 years

Tips to Make It Easier

- **Automate everything** – payments and savings
- **Celebrate progress** – every $1,000 paid down or saved matters
- **Avoid lifestyle creep** – raises = more savings, not just more spending
- **Refinance carefully** – only if you give up federal protections knowingly

Mental Health Check-In

Debt can mess with your head.

So can saving too aggressively and feeling broke.

Balance is your antidote.

Build a plan that allows you to breathe—then commit to it.

Action Steps

1. Write down your total loan balance, interest rate, and monthly minimum
2. Build a base budget with at least one line for saving—even if it's $10
3. Decide your monthly "split" (savings vs. loans)
4. Automate both
5. Reevaluate every 6 months or after major life changes

One Financial Move Before Your Next Shift

Pick a number: 10%, 15%, 20%.

That's your financial growth number.

Split it between saving and debt payoff.

Stick to it for 3 months.

Because you're not just a nurse with student loans.

You're a nurse building wealth.
And you're doing it with purpose.

Chapter 16: Loan Forgiveness for Nurses – Public Service and Beyond

Let's talk about something few people tell nurses early enough: **you may not have to pay back all your student loans.**

If you work in the right setting, serve the right communities, or follow the right steps, forgiveness is possible.

But here's the catch: forgiveness isn't automatic.

You have to qualify. You have to apply. And you have to understand the rules well enough not to get tripped up by them.

This chapter will walk you through the major loan forgiveness and repayment programs available to nurses in 2025, so you can stop feeling buried—and start building strategy.

What Is Loan Forgiveness?

Loan forgiveness means you are no longer required to repay some or all of your student loan debt—because you met certain service, employment, or payment requirements.

Forgiveness can happen through:

- Federal public service programs
- Employer-sponsored repayment support
- State-based nursing incentives
- Shortage-area service agreements

Let's walk through the big ones.

Public Service Loan Forgiveness (PSLF)

Best for: Nurses working full-time at government or nonprofit hospitals and clinics

Requirements (2025):

- Work full-time for a qualifying employer (government or 501(c)(3) nonprofit)
- Be enrolled in an income-driven repayment (IDR) plan
- Make 120 monthly qualifying payments
- Submit the PSLF Employment Certification Form annually

What gets forgiven: The full remaining balance of your **Direct Loans**, tax-free

Important details:

- You must recertify your income annually
- Parent PLUS Loans are not eligible (unless consolidated)
- Only payments made **after consolidation** count if you consolidate midway

Pro tip: Use the **StudentAid.gov PSLF Help Tool** to track progress and submit forms

Nurse Corps Loan Repayment Program (NCLRP)

Best for: Nurses working in critical shortage facilities (CSFs)

What it offers:

- Repayment of up to 85% of unpaid nursing education debt
- 60% for 2 years of service

- Additional 25% for a third year

Eligibility:

- Licensed RNs, APRNs, or nurse faculty
- Working in a CSF located in a designated Health Professional Shortage Area (HPSA)
- U.S. citizen or permanent resident

Pros:

- Generous repayment amounts
- Doesn't require nonprofit or government employment

Cons:

- Highly competitive
- Must commit to working in underserved areas

Application tips:

- Apply early in the calendar year
- Make your case clear and compelling in your personal statement

NHSC Loan Repayment Program (For APRNs and Nurse Practitioners)

Best for: NPs working in underserved communities

What it offers:

- Up to $50,000 for 2 years of full-time service
- Additional support for extended service

Requirements:

- Work at an NHSC-approved site
- Serve full-time or half-time
- Licensed and certified

State-Specific Nurse Loan Forgiveness Programs

Most states offer their own programs for nurses who:

- Work in rural or high-need areas
- Teach at nursing schools
- Serve in correctional facilities, veterans' homes, or public health

Examples (as of 2025):

- **California**: Bachelor of Science Nursing Loan Repayment (up to $10,000)
- **Texas**: Professional Nursing Student Loan Repayment Program
- **New York**: Regents Nursing Scholarship Forgiveness
- **Kansas**: Rural Opportunity Zones – up to $15,000 over 5 years

How to find your state program:

- Visit your state's Department of Health or Education website
- Search "nurse loan forgiveness [your state]"
- Ask your HR department—they often have state-specific info

Employer-Based Repayment Support

Some hospitals and clinics offer:

- Sign-on bonuses to repay loans

- Monthly student loan contributions
- Annual stipends tied to years of service

Questions to ask your employer:

- Is there a formal loan repayment assistance program?
- Does the bonus require repayment if I leave early?
- Are there tax consequences?

Income-Driven Repayment (IDR) Forgiveness

Even if you don't qualify for PSLF, you may qualify for **IDR forgiveness**:

- Make payments under an IDR plan for **20–25 years**
- Remaining balance is forgiven (taxable)

Plans include:

- SAVE (Saving on a Valuable Education)
- PAYE (Pay As You Earn)
- IBR (Income-Based Repayment)
- ICR (Income-Contingent Repayment)

Important: As of 2025, under the SAVE plan, your forgiven balance is **not taxable** in most cases.

Pros and Cons of Forgiveness

Pros:

- Potential to erase tens of thousands in loans
- Encourages work in meaningful, underserved areas
- Creates breathing room in your budget

Cons:

- Complex rules and paperwork
- Changing legislation can impact programs
- May require years of commitment
- You may owe taxes (depending on program)

Real Nurse Scenarios

Sarah, 31, NICU Nurse at a Nonprofit Hospital

- Enrolled in SAVE plan
- Certifies PSLF employment yearly
- Expects forgiveness after 10 years

James, 35, NP in Rural Alabama

- Works at an NHSC site
- Received $50,000 in loan repayment
- Plans to renew for another two years

Danielle, 41, Nurse Faculty in Chicago

- Received Nurse Corps award
- $22,000 in loans forgiven in two years
- Reapplied for year 3

How to Avoid Common Pitfalls

- **Missing annual certification** (PSLF)
- **Changing jobs without checking employer eligibility**
- **Consolidating loans mid-program**
- **Relying on verbal HR promises—get everything in writing**

Action Steps

1. Check your loan type (Direct Loans, FFEL, Perkins?)
2. Use the PSLF Help Tool at StudentAid.gov
3. Certify your employer annually
4. Review state and national forgiveness options
5. Apply early—many programs have limited funding

One Financial Move Before Your Next Shift

Log into your loan portal.

Check your loan type and current repayment plan.

Then ask: Are you eligible for forgiveness?

If yes—take the first step.

Because you didn't become a nurse to stay in debt forever.

You did it to serve, to heal, to grow.

Now let's make sure your finances reflect that too.

Part III – Life, Lifestyle, and Growing Into the Role

This part of the journey is where the scrubs start to feel familiar, the rhythm of shift work becomes second nature, and you finally exhale just long enough to look around and ask: "Now what?"

Part III of *Financial Literacy For Nurses* isn't just about paychecks and pensions—it's about what you *do* with them. This is the phase where financial growth meets real life. We walk beside you as you balance debt, build savings, and begin making decisions that shape your lifestyle, not just your survival.

Whether you're a new grad learning how to budget on a nurse's salary or a seasoned RN trying to stop lifestyle creep before it wrecks your progress, this section meets you there. We explore how to read offer letters like a contract nurse, how to avoid common traps like spending your first real paycheck too fast, and how to balance investing, emergency funds, and student loan repayment with grace—not guilt.

It's not about being perfect. It's about being prepared. It's about learning to treat your money like your patients—with attention, intention, and consistency.

This section gives you tools to make smart, nurse-friendly decisions around:

- Building an emergency fund that fits your shift life
- Understanding retirement plans that hospitals offer

- Choosing between Roth and Traditional IRAs
- Managing money with both confidence and compassion

You didn't work this hard to feel broke and burned out.

Part III reminds you: financial peace isn't about how much you make—it's about how well you move with what you've got. Let's grow into the role together.

Chapter 17: Housing Decisions – Should Nurses Rent or Buy Early?

You're out of school, working 12s, paying on student loans, and now you're wondering: should I keep renting—or is it time to buy a place of my own?

You've finally got steady income, maybe even some savings. A lender might even pre-approve you. But just because you *can* buy a home early in your nursing career doesn't automatically mean you *should*.

This chapter is about clarity, not pressure. It's about walking through the decision with honesty—acknowledging your lifestyle, your shift schedule, your mental bandwidth, and your long-term goals.

This isn't HGTV. This is real life. Real nurse life.

Let's break it down together.

The Nursing Lifestyle – And Why It Impacts Your Housing Choice

Nursing isn't a 9-to-5 job.

You work weekends, nights, 12-hour shifts, holidays. You may change floors, hospitals, or cities in the early years.

That means flexibility is valuable.

Before buying a home, ask:

- Do I plan to stay in this city for at least 3–5 years?
- Is my current job stable and satisfying?

- Do I have time and energy to maintain a home?
- Can I handle unexpected repairs during a night shift rotation?

Your time isn't just money—it's *capacity.*

Pros of Renting as a Nurse (Especially Early in Your Career)

1. Flexibility

- You can move for better pay, shifts, or hospitals
- Ideal if you're considering travel nursing or relocating

2. Fewer responsibilities

- No repairs, maintenance, or property taxes
- Great if your shifts already leave you emotionally and physically drained

3. Predictable expenses

- Fixed rent vs. fluctuating homeowner costs
- Easier to budget in tight seasons

4. Lower upfront costs

- Security deposit vs. down payment, closing costs, inspections, moving costs

5. Time to build credit and savings

- Renting gives you room to improve your financial position before committing

Cons of Renting

1. No equity

- You're not building ownership over time

2. Rent increases

- Landlords can raise rent annually

3. Less control

- You can't customize, renovate, or sometimes even hang wall art

4. May feel temporary

- Lack of "roots" or long-term investment

Pros of Buying a Home as a Nurse

1. Build equity

- Monthly payments go toward ownership
- Can grow in value over time (especially in strong markets)

2. Stability

- Fixed-rate mortgage = predictable housing costs

3. Tax deductions

- Mortgage interest and property taxes may be deductible (check with a tax advisor)

4. Ownership perks

- Renovate, customize, paint that kitchen purple if you want

5. Long-term wealth

- Homes are a major asset and often a key part of retirement strategies

Cons of Buying a Home

1. Lack of flexibility

- Selling takes time and may incur loss if the market drops

2. Upfront costs

- Down payment, closing costs, inspection, moving, furnishing

3. Ongoing costs

- Maintenance, repairs, property taxes, insurance, HOA fees

4. Emotional bandwidth

- Unexpected roof leak + 3 back-to-back shifts = stress you don't need

5. Hidden risks

- Home values can drop
- You may not recoup your investment if you sell too soon

The 5-Year Rule

A general rule of thumb: **Only buy if you plan to stay in the home for at least 5 years.**

Why?

- Closing costs + market appreciation take time to break even
- Short stays often result in losses, not gains

If you're unsure about your location, specialty, or employer, renting gives you room to move.

What About Travel Nurses?

Buying rarely makes sense unless you:

- Plan to use the home as a rental when on assignment
- Want a "home base" but travel part-time
- Are staying in one region consistently

Most travel nurses rent furnished short-term units, keeping flexibility and minimizing responsibility.

Can You Afford to Buy?

Here's what lenders *might* look at:

- Credit score (620+ for most conventional loans)
- Debt-to-income ratio (under 36% is ideal)
- Stable income history (2+ years preferred)
- Down payment (3%–20%)
- Emergency fund (3–6 months of expenses)

But here's what **you** should look at:

- Will I still be able to save for retirement?
- Will homeownership stretch me too thin?
- Will this create peace—or pressure?

Real-Life Nurse Scenarios

Alex, 26, Med-Surg Nurse

- Renting a 1BR near the hospital
- Saves 15% of income, building credit and emergency fund
- Planning to buy in 2–3 years after she decides on a specialty

Monique, 34, Nurse Manager

- Bought a townhouse after 6 years renting
- Puts extra toward mortgage and maxes 403(b)
- Loves having her own space to unwind post-shift

Carlos, 41, Travel Nurse

- Rents furnished units around the country
- Keeps expenses low, invests heavily, plans to buy later in life

Tanya, 29, ICU RN

- Bought early, then switched hospitals and ended up commuting 45 minutes
- Now feels "stuck" and regrets rushing into homeownership

Action Steps

1. Ask yourself: *Am I buying stability, or am I buying stress?*
2. Run your real budget, not just what the lender approves
3. Save for a down payment **and** maintenance fund
4. Get pre-approved *after* you understand the true monthly cost
5. Talk to a fee-only financial advisor before making a final decision

One Financial Move Before Your Next Shift

Log into your banking app.

Review how much rent (or housing) takes up your monthly budget.

Ask yourself:

- Is this affordable?
- Am I saving alongside it?
- Am I ready to settle—or still exploring?

Where you live is more than a zip code. It's a reflection of your freedom, your goals, and your energy.

Pick the path that keeps you grounded—not just financially, but emotionally.

Because a home should hold your rest—not your regret.

Chapter 18: Buying Your First Home as a Nurse – How Much House Can You Afford, and Nurse-Specific Mortgage Programs

So you've decided you're ready.

Not just dreaming of homeownership, but ready to step into it—with open eyes, a stable income, and a solid strategy.

This chapter is for the nurse who's tired of paying rent and wants to build something of their own. Not a fantasy. Not a flip. But a home.

Whether you're working day shift, night shift, or travel contracts, this chapter will walk you through how to afford your first home responsibly—and how to explore mortgage programs designed specifically with nurses in mind.

Let's walk through the financial, personal, and professional factors that go into buying your first place. And let's do it without shame, stress, or sales pressure.

What's the Right Budget for Your First Home?

Forget what the lender says you can afford.

Ask yourself: what can I afford and still sleep at night?

A smart formula:

- Mortgage + taxes + insurance = no more than 28–30% of your *gross* monthly income
- Total monthly debts (including student loans, car, credit cards) = under 36–40% of your gross income

But ideally?

Keep your mortgage around **25% of your take-home pay** if you want room to save, breathe, and grow.

How Much Should You Have Saved?

Before you buy, aim for:

- Down payment: 3%–20% of purchase price
- Closing costs: 2%–5%
- Moving & setup: $2,000–$5,000 (minimum)
- Emergency fund: 3–6 months of expenses *after* closing

Example:

On a $300,000 home:

- $9,000 to $60,000 down payment
- $6,000 to $15,000 closing costs

Buying is not just about the mortgage—it's about having the cushion to handle life after the keys.

Understand What Goes Into a Mortgage Payment

PITI = Principal + Interest + Taxes + Insurance

What looks affordable in the listing price can become overwhelming when:

- Property taxes spike
- Insurance increases
- HOA dues sneak in
- Maintenance costs pile up

Use a mortgage calculator that includes **all 4 components**.

Don't Forget Lifestyle Alignment

Ask yourself:

- Will my commute stress me out after 3 12s in a row?
- Is this neighborhood safe at 7am when I get off?
- Does this layout allow for recovery and rest?
- Can I afford this without depending on overtime?

A home isn't just shelter. It's your recovery unit.

Nurse-Specific Mortgage and Homebuyer Programs

Some lenders and organizations offer mortgage benefits tailored for healthcare workers. These may include:

1. Nurse Next Door

- Grants and down payment assistance up to $8,000
- Discounted real estate agent and lender fees
- Available to RNs, LPNs, NPs, and other nursing professionals

2. Homes for Heroes

- Cashback savings on real estate services
- No income limits
- Available to all nurses and healthcare staff

3. State & Local Programs

- First-time buyer grants
- Below-market interest rates
- Special programs for frontline workers post-COVID

Pro tip:

Search "first-time homebuyer nurse program [your state]" and check local credit unions or housing authorities.

Real-Life Nurse Buyer Stories

Lily, 29, ER Nurse in Chicago

- Bought a $260K condo using Nurse Next Door
- Put down 5% and received $6,000 in closing cost assistance
- Keeps mortgage under 30% of take-home pay

Marcus, 34, Travel Nurse in Texas

- Bought a duplex using a first-time buyer program
- Lives in one unit, rents the other
- Uses rent to offset his mortgage

Tasha, 42, Nurse Educator in Georgia

- Saved aggressively for 3 years
- Put down 20% on a $325K home to avoid PMI
- Says the peace of mind was worth the wait

Pitfalls to Avoid

1. **Getting emotionally attached too early**

- Always have a walk-away price

1. **Not factoring in hidden costs**

- Appliances, repairs, HOA dues

1. **Skipping the inspection**

- Always get a licensed inspector

1. **Ignoring your own red flags**

- If you're stretching or stressed—it's not the right time

Building Equity Starts on Day One

Equity is your ownership stake in the home. You build it by:

- Paying down the principal
- Benefiting from appreciation
- Making extra principal payments (optional)

But remember: equity isn't liquid.
You can't swipe equity at Target.
So balance your home ownership with accessible savings.

Nurse Schedule = Unique Home Needs

Consider:

- Soundproofing (you'll be sleeping during the day)
- Lighting (blackout curtains are your friend)
- Proximity to work (and if you'll change hospitals)
- Safety if you're coming home at 7am or leaving at 6pm

Action Steps Before You Buy

1. Pull your credit score and check for errors
2. Calculate how much house you can afford—not just qualify for
3. Research nurse-specific buyer programs in your area
4. Interview 2–3 lenders and ask about nurse loan options
5. Talk to other nurse homeowners about what they wish they'd known
6. Build your down payment + emergency fund
7. Get pre-approved *only* when you're ready to seriously look

One Financial Move Before Your Next Shift

Set up a separate savings account labeled: **"First Home Fund."**

Automate a small transfer—$25, $50, $100 per paycheck.

Name it. Watch it grow. Know what it's for.

Because someday you'll sign those papers, hold those keys, and say:

"This house isn't just a place to live.

This is something I *built.*"

Not with shortcuts. Not with guilt.

But with strategy, care, and the steady hand of a nurse who knows how to plan for more than just today.

Chapter 19: Transportation – Lease, Finance, or Drive Until It Dies?

You work hard. You clock 12-hour shifts. You get off at 7am and just want your car to start, run quietly, and get you home.

So when it's time to get a new set of wheels, the question hits hard:

Should I lease? Finance? Or drive this thing until it dies?

Cars aren't just about transportation—they're about lifestyle, identity, convenience, and money. Lots of money. For nurses, who rely heavily on reliable vehicles for early-morning shifts, long commutes, night drives, or unpredictable weather, the decision has real financial impact.

In this chapter, we break down the pros and cons of the major transportation paths—and how to align your car choices with your financial goals.

Not with guilt. Not with judgment. But with clarity.

The Truth About Cars

Cars are not investments. They are **depreciating assets**. That means from the moment you drive it off the lot, it loses value.

But cars *are* essential tools for most nurses—especially in areas with limited public transportation or for those who commute for higher pay or better shifts.

So your job isn't to avoid spending on cars altogether. It's to **make smart**

choices that won't wreck your financial plan.

Option 1: Leasing a Car

How it works:

You're essentially renting the car for 2–4 years. You make monthly payments, but you don't own the car. At the end of the lease, you return it or buy it out.

Pros:

- Lower monthly payments
- New car every few years
- Lower maintenance costs
- Often includes warranty coverage

Cons:

- You don't own the car
- Mileage limits (usually 10k–15k/year)
- Charges for wear and tear
- More expensive long-term

Best for:

- Nurses who want a reliable car with low repair risk
- Nurses who value convenience and always want a newer car
- Short commutes and predictable driving patterns

Worst for:

- Long-distance commuters
- Travel nurses who may drive cross-country
- Anyone who values ownership

Option 2: Financing (Buying With a Loan)

How it works:

You take out a loan to buy the car. You make monthly payments until it's paid off. Then the car is yours.

Pros:

- You build equity (eventually own the car)
- No mileage restrictions
- Can sell or trade in

Cons:

- Monthly payments usually higher than leasing
- Interest charges
- Depreciation means you may owe more than it's worth in early years

Best for:

- Nurses with longer commutes
- Those who want to keep their car 5–10+ years
- Those willing to buy used and save more

Worst for:

- Nurses who tire of cars quickly
- Buyers who don't maintain vehicles properly

Option 3: Buying in Cash

How it works:

You pay for the car outright, no loan.

Pros:

- No monthly payment
- Total ownership from day one
- No interest

Cons:

- Large upfront cost
- May delay other goals if it depletes savings
- Not possible for all buyers early in career

Best for:

- Nurses with strong emergency funds and no debt
- Second or third car purchases later in career

Option 4: Drive It Until It Dies

How it works:

You buy a reliable used car, maintain it, and keep it as long as possible.

Pros:

- Long-term savings
- Lower insurance
- Maximizes every dollar spent

Cons:

- Higher repair costs with age
- May lack newer safety or tech features
- May be less reliable for long commutes or night shifts

Best for:

- Nurses who want to minimize monthly bills
- Those with emergency savings for repairs

Worst for:

- Nurses who drive long hours without time for surprise breakdowns

What Can You Really Afford?

Rules of thumb:

- Car payment = no more than 10% of take-home pay
- Total car expenses (gas, insurance, repairs) = under 15%–20%
- If buying, down payment = at least 10%–20%
- Keep loan terms 36–60 months MAX

Nurse Life and Car Needs

Ask yourself:

- Do I commute long distances?
- Do I work night shift and need reliability in bad weather?
- Do I carpool or need space for kids?
- Do I have time to handle breakdowns?

Your car choice isn't just financial. It's *functional.* A breakdown on the way to your 7am shift isn't just inconvenient—it's job-threatening.

Real Nurse Scenarios

Samantha, 27, Cardiac Nurse

- Leased a new Honda Civic for $310/month

- Values reliability, low maintenance, and a modern commute

Troy, 35, ED Nurse

- Bought a used Toyota Highlander for $18K
- Drives 45 minutes each way, wanted AWD for winter shifts

Maria, 41, Nurse Educator

- Bought a 5-year-old car with cash after saving aggressively
- No payments, low stress, and funds maintenance herself

Action Steps

1. Check your monthly car budget and compare it to income
2. Decide how long you realistically want to keep your car
3. Factor in *total* cost of ownership—not just the sticker price
4. Get pre-approved before going to a dealership
5. Don't buy based on emotion—buy based on use, budget, and your schedule

One Financial Move Before Your Next Shift

Open a "next car fund" savings account.

Start with $25/paycheck—even if your car's still running fine. Because eventually, that check engine light is coming. And when it does, you'll be ready.

Buying a car as a nurse isn't about status.

It's about strength, structure, and strategy.

Keep it steady. Keep it smart.

And if you ever find yourself trying to justify a $700/month car payment with "I work hard, I deserve it"—pause.

Because you deserve freedom. Not another bill.

Chapter 20: Health Insurance, HSA, FSA – Benefits Breakdown

You spend your days helping others navigate health crises—but when it comes to understanding your own health insurance and benefits? It might feel like reading a foreign language in the middle of a 12-hour shift.

This chapter exists to change that.

As a nurse, your health plan isn't just a checkbox during onboarding. It's a tool that protects your paycheck, your physical and mental health, and your long-term financial future.

Let's break down your employer health benefits—clearly, calmly, and in plain language—so you can stop guessing and start optimizing.

Start With What You Have: Understanding Your Coverage Options

Most hospitals and large healthcare employers offer 2–4 medical plan options:

1. PPO (Preferred Provider Organization)

- Higher premiums, but greater flexibility
- You can see specialists without referrals
- Often includes both in-network and out-of-network coverage

2. HMO (Health Maintenance Organization)

- Lower premiums, but more restrictions
- Must choose a Primary Care Physician (PCP)
- Requires referrals for specialists

3. HDHP (High Deductible Health Plan) + HSA

- Lower monthly premiums
- Higher deductibles
- Eligible for Health Savings Account (HSA)

4. EPO (Exclusive Provider Organization)

- Similar to PPO but no out-of-network coverage
- Referrals often required

What's the Right Plan for You?

Ask Yourself:

- Do I go to the doctor often?
- Do I have chronic conditions or dependents with special needs?
- Am I healthy and mainly need protection for big, unexpected events?
- Do I want access to an HSA for long-term tax-free savings?

If you:

- Rarely see a doctor → Consider HDHP + HSA
- See multiple specialists → PPO may be worth the cost
- Want lower premiums and coordinated care → HMO might work

Breaking Down Key Terms

Premium = What you pay from your paycheck, even if you don't use the insurance

Deductible = What you pay out-of-pocket before your insurance starts paying

Copay = A fixed fee for services (like $20 per visit)

Coinsurance = The percentage you pay after the deductible (e.g., 20%)

Out-of-pocket maximum = The most you'll pay in a year before insurance covers 100%

HSAs: A Nurse's Secret Weapon

If your plan includes an HSA (Health Savings Account), **use it.**

Why HSAs rock:

- Contributions are tax-deductible
- Money grows tax-free
- Withdrawals are tax-free for medical expenses
- It's yours forever (unlike FSAs)

Nurse Tip:

Use your HSA as a stealth retirement account by investing the balance and paying out-of-pocket now (if you can).

2025 HSA Limits:

- Individual: $4,150
- Family: $8,300
- Catch-up (age 55+): +$1,000

FSAs: Use It or Lose It

If you don't have an HSA, your employer may offer an FSA (Flexible Spending Account).

Key FSA facts:

- Use pre-tax dollars for medical, dental, vision
- Can also be used for dependent care (with a separate limit)
- Must use funds by year-end or forfeit (some plans allow $640 rollover)

Best For:

- Nurses with predictable yearly healthcare costs (glasses, therapy, prescriptions)

Dependent Care FSA (DC-FSA)

If you have kids under 13 or adult dependents:

- Contribute up to $5,000/year pre-tax
- Can be used for daycare, summer camp, elder care, etc.

Dental and Vision: Don't Skip It

Nurses often overlook this coverage until it's too late.

Dental coverage usually includes:

- Preventive care (100%)
- Basic (fillings, 80%)
- Major (crowns, 50%)

Vision plans typically include:

- One annual eye exam
- Glasses or contacts allowance

You work long hours, often under strain. Protect your eyes and teeth—they're part of your job performance and long-term health.

Disability Insurance: The Benefit Nurses Ignore

If your job offers **short-term or long-term disability**, take it seriously.

- **Short-term** covers you for weeks/months after surgery, injury, or illness
- **Long-term** kicks in for major or chronic disability

Ask:

- Is it employer-paid or optional?
- How long is the elimination (waiting) period?
- What percentage of income does it cover?

Pro tip:

Nurses are more likely to use disability insurance than life insurance. Your hands, back, and mental health are essential. Protect your paycheck.

Mental Health Coverage: It Matters

Most plans now include:

- Therapy visits (copay or coinsurance)
- Virtual counseling options
- Coverage for psychiatric services and medications

Burnout is real. So is compassion fatigue. Use your mental health benefits—

no shame, no guilt.

Nurse-Specific Considerations

Night shift stress? Choose a plan with strong mental health support.

Physically demanding unit? Don't skimp on disability coverage.

Planning a family? Compare maternity and NICU coverage before enrolling.

Action Steps

1. Request a full Summary of Benefits from HR
2. Compare **total cost** (premium + deductible + copays) across plans
3. Contribute to an HSA or FSA, even if just $50/month
4. Confirm who's in-network—your PCP, OB-GYN, therapist, etc.
5. Ask HR about additional wellness perks (step challenges, reimbursements)

One Financial Move Before Your Next Shift

Log into your benefits portal.

Check how much you're contributing to your HSA or FSA.

If it's $0, consider starting with just $25 per paycheck. That's less than a dinner out. But it's a start toward building cushion and coverage for your real life.

Because you can't pour from an empty cup.

And when life happens (because it will), you'll be glad you've got the benefits to back you up.

Chapter 21: Relationship Money Talk – Combining Finances with a Partner

Let's get real.

Talking about money in a relationship can feel harder than a double shift with no tech and three admissions.

But if you're going to build a life with someone—married, partnered, dating seriously—you've got to be able to talk money. Openly. Honestly. Without shame. Without secrecy. And without the silent stress that piles up like unsorted laundry after a long week of shifts.

This chapter is about how to **combine your financial life with another person** in a way that keeps the peace, respects your goals, and builds a future.

Because nurses know how to work as a team on the floor.

Now it's time to build that same teamwork at home.

The First Money Talk

Before combining a single account, credit card, or Amazon order:

Sit down and ask each other:

1. What was money like growing up in your house?
2. How do you feel about debt?
3. What does financial security mean to you?
4. What are your biggest financial fears?

5. What are your top 3 money goals?

This isn't just about numbers—it's about understanding financial *habits, histories, and hopes.*

To Merge or Not to Merge?

There's no one right way. But here are the **common options:**

1. Fully Combined Finances

- One joint account for everything
- All income and bills in the same pot

2. Partially Combined

- Joint account for shared expenses (rent, bills, groceries)
- Separate personal accounts for individual spending

3. Completely Separate

- Each partner handles their own money
- Split shared expenses proportionally or 50/50

What works best for nurses?

It depends on your schedule, trust, communication style, and comfort level with joint planning.

The "Unequal Income" Equation

If one partner earns significantly more (which is common if one is still in school or not in healthcare):

Proportional Contributions May Work Best

- Example: If you earn 60% of the household income, you cover 60% of shared expenses.

This prevents resentment and keeps both partners contributing fairly—even if not equally.

Joint Goals and Budgeting

Sit down once a month for a **Money Huddle.**
Talk about:

- Bills due
- Debt payments
- Short-term goals (vacation, home upgrade)
- Long-term goals (house, retirement, college savings)

Set shared priorities, not just individual wish lists.

Common Landmines (And How to Defuse Them)

1. Secret Spending

- Agree on a "no surprises" policy
- Give each partner a monthly guilt-free personal spending amount

2. Hidden Debt

- Lay it all on the table—credit cards, student loans, collections
- Work on a joint payoff strategy

3. Different Money Styles

- One saver, one spender?

- Use percentages, not fixed dollars, for personal allowances

4. Financial Control

- No one person should dominate money decisions
- Even if one earns more, decisions should be joint

Combining Debt Loads

If both of you have student loans or credit cards:

- Don't rush to pay off your partner's debt unless you're legally married or have a legal agreement
- Prioritize the highest-interest debt first (regardless of whose it is)
- Support each other without becoming financially codependent

Credit Scores in Relationships

You can love someone with a bad credit score.

But you need to **plan together** if you want to buy a home, co-sign, or apply for loans.

Talk about:

- What's on each of your credit reports
- How to improve scores (pay on time, lower balances)
- Whether to apply for things jointly or individually

Planning for Kids (Now or Someday)

Kids add costs, complexity, and importance to financial planning.

Talk through:

- Who handles daycare drop-off vs. overtime shifts

- How much parental leave you get—and how much is paid
- How you'll fund childcare, savings, and healthcare costs

Set a game plan *before* the baby arrives, not while you're changing diapers.

Protecting Each Other

Even if you're not married, consider:

- Term life insurance policies
- Powers of attorney and healthcare directives
- Shared emergency fund
- Updated beneficiaries on accounts

You plan for patient safety on shift—do the same for your partner.

Real Nurse Relationship Stories

Danielle (35, ER Nurse):

"I earn double what my husband does. We split bills 60/40. We each keep our own 'fun money' account, and everything else goes into joint savings."

Marcus & Javier (both ICU Nurses):

"We rotate who covers rent and groceries every other month. We also have a shared spreadsheet to track all our debt payoff goals."

Sabrina (29, L&D Nurse):

"My fiancé had credit card debt I didn't know about. Once we had the talk, we set up a debt snowball together. We call it our 'freedom plan.'"

One Financial Move Before Your Next Shift

Send your partner a text:

"Hey—I'd love to have a no-pressure money talk this weekend. No judgment, just clarity. Let's figure out where we're going as a team."

Then follow through.

You can't afford to ignore money in your relationship. But you *can* afford to face it together.

Because shared goals create shared power.

And in a world where nurses fight so hard for their patients—don't forget to fight just as hard for your peace, partnership, and financial freedom.

Chapter 22: Kids, Daycare, and Career Choices

Let's talk about one of the most beautiful, complicated, exhausting, and expensive parts of a nurse's life: **parenting while working in healthcare.**

This chapter is your financial roadmap for balancing the demands of parenting with the realities of nursing schedules—and how to budget for the big, ever-changing cost of childcare without losing your mind or your financial footing.

Because let's be real: daycare decisions can feel harder than triaging a trauma bay on three hours of sleep.

But we're going to make it make sense.

Parenting as a Nurse: The Real-Life Puzzle

Whether you're a brand-new parent or juggling school drop-offs with night shifts, **the reality of nursing and parenting is unlike any other combo.**

You may have:

- 12-hour shifts that start before daycare opens and end after it closes
- Nights, weekends, and holidays when childcare options are limited
- A partner who also works long or inconsistent hours
- The constant question: "Is this worth it?"

Let's Start With the Numbers: How Much Does Childcare Cost?

On average, full-time center-based care in the U.S. costs:

- **Infants**: $12,000–$21,000/year
- **Toddlers**: $9,000–$16,000/year
- **Preschoolers**: $7,000–$13,000/year

In high-cost-of-living areas, these numbers can **double**.

And for nurses working odd shifts, finding someone you trust who is also available can mean paying even more for flexible or overnight care.

Common Childcare Options for Nurses

1. Traditional Daycare Centers

- Usually open 7 AM–6 PM
- Not ideal for night shifts
- Structured environment, licensed

2. In-Home Daycares

- Smaller settings, often more flexible
- May be willing to work with rotating shifts
- Check licensing and references carefully

3. Nanny or Nanny Share

- In your home or shared with another family
- Pricey, but personalized and schedule-adaptable

4. Family Help

- Parents, siblings, trusted friends
- Affordable, flexible—but may come with emotional costs or inconsistency

5. Hospital-Based Childcare

- Offered at some large hospitals or academic centers
- May include extended hours for staff

Making the Numbers Work: Budgeting for Childcare

Step 1: Get Real About Costs

- Don't guess. Research actual rates in your area.
- Ask other nurses, look on local parent Facebook groups, and tour centers.

Step 2: Compare Cost vs. Take-Home Pay

Ask:

- After taxes, what's your hourly wage?
- How much of that is going to childcare?
- Is there a financial case for adjusting shifts or reducing hours temporarily?

Step 3: Use Your Dependent Care FSA

- Contribute pre-tax dollars (up to $5,000 per household per year)
- Use for daycare, after-school care, even summer camps

Step 4: Build Childcare Into Your Emergency Fund

- Kids get sick. School closes. Backup care is needed.

- Budget a few hundred dollars per year for last-minute childcare solutions

Career Flexibility: When Nursing Has to Bend

At some point, you may feel like nursing has to give way to parenting.

Options nurses consider:

- Per diem shifts (more control, less stability)
- Going part-time
- Taking a break from bedside
- Moving to outpatient or school-based roles
- Remote case management or telephone triage

Each choice has trade-offs:

- Fewer hours = more time but less money and slower retirement savings
- Leaving bedside = fewer differentials and bonuses, but more predictability

The goal? Build a life—not just a paycheck.

Real Nurse Scenarios

Alyssa, 30 (Labor & Delivery):

"I dropped to three 8-hour shifts per week and picked up one night per diem. That way, I'm there for daycare drop-off and pick-up. It meant cutting our budget, but I gained peace."

Marisol, 39 (ICU):

"My mom watches the kids during my weekend shifts. We budget $100/month to send her on a spa day every quarter. It's cheaper than a nanny—and shows appreciation."

Jordan & Sam (dual-nurse couple):

"We split our shifts strategically. I work Mon-Wed, Sam works Fri-Sun. Thursdays are family days. No childcare costs, but we had to budget carefully to make it work."

What to Ask Before Choosing a Childcare Setup

1. Can they accommodate rotating or night shifts?
2. What's their sick policy?
3. Do they charge late pickup fees?
4. Is there a waitlist? (Plan early!)
5. What backup care is available?

Action Steps

1. Add "childcare" as its own category in your monthly budget
2. If planning a baby, build a 3–6 month "maternity leave fund"
3. Review your employee benefits: do they offer backup care stipends?
4. Track your childcare costs for 3 months. Adjust if needed.
5. Explore per diem, outpatient, or hybrid roles to increase family flexibility

One Financial Move Before Your Next Shift

If you're currently paying for childcare, pull your last three paychecks.
Calculate: **How much of your take-home pay is going to care?**
If it's more than 30%, it might be time to:

- Adjust your work schedule
- Reevaluate your provider
- Explore tax-advantaged savings (like DC-FSA)

Final Thought

Nursing is demanding. Parenting is relentless. Doing both at once?

That's Olympic-level multitasking.

But you can do this.

Not by hustling harder.

Not by pushing through burnout.

By **planning smarter**, budgeting better, and choosing the options that support your family, your health, and your legacy.

This chapter isn't just about daycare.

It's about dignity.

It's about structure.

It's about giving yourself permission to define success on your own terms—and build a career and family life that *actually works*.

You've got this. One budget, one shift, one decision at a time.

Chapter 23: Continuing Education and Specialization – Is It Worth It?

You've put in the hours. You've taken vitals, pushed meds, held hands, saved lives, and probably skipped a few meals along the way. Now you're wondering if you should take the next step in your career—become a Nurse Practitioner (NP), a Certified Registered Nurse Anesthetist (CRNA), a Nurse Midwife (CNM), or even pursue a Doctor of Nursing Practice (DNP).

But let's be real.

These degrees are expensive. They demand your time, energy, and often a whole lot of sacrifice. The question becomes: **Will it pay off?**

Let's walk through it—honestly, clearly, and with no sugarcoating. We'll look at costs, expected income, job flexibility, career trajectory, and how to calculate whether it's financially (and emotionally) worth it.

Section 1: What Continuing Education Actually Costs

Before you start dreaming about the "Dr." in front of your name or signing those student loan documents, **run the numbers.**

Typical Tuition Costs in 2025:

- **NP (MSN)**: $20,000–$80,000
- **CRNA**: $60,000–$200,000+
- **CNM**: $30,000–$100,000

- **DNP**: $35,000–$90,000

Now add these hidden costs:

- Lost income if you reduce work or stop altogether
- Books, fees, scrubs, equipment
- Clinical hours (many unpaid)
- Potential relocation or commuting

Real Talk: That DNP that costs $90K might also cost you 2 years of full-time income. That's a total opportunity cost of $180K–$250K+.

Section 2: Income Boosts – What Can You Expect to Make?

Here's a ballpark of 2025 national averages (varies by location):

- **RN (BSN)**: $75,000–$105,000
- **NP**: $110,000–$140,000
- **CRNA**: $180,000–$230,000+
- **CNM**: $105,000–$130,000
- **DNP (as administrator, professor, or NP)**: Varies—can be $120K–$160K

Will you make more? Usually.
Will it be enough to justify the cost? That's the ROI question.

Section 3: The ROI Formula for Nurses

Return on Investment (ROI) = (Increased Earnings - Cost of Education) / Cost of Education
Example:

- $50,000 MSN program cost

- You earn $30,000 more annually after graduation

You break even in 1.67 years. After that, it's pure gain.

Now flip it:

- $200,000 DNP cost
- You earn $20,000 more per year

It takes 10+ years to break even. That might be too long, especially if you're starting at 40 or 50.

Section 4: Non-Financial Factors That Still Matter

This chapter is about financial literacy—but let's not pretend this is all math.

Some reasons nurses pursue advanced degrees:

- Autonomy and expanded practice scope
- Career burnout at the bedside
- Desire to teach, lead, or influence healthcare
- Passion for a specific population (women's health, anesthesia, pediatrics)

If a degree lets you practice in a way that aligns with your values, that's a kind of wealth too.

But you still need to plan for the financial part.

Section 5: Financing Your Degree Without Drowning in Debt

1. Employer Tuition Reimbursement

- Ask your HR rep if your hospital offers partial reimbursement
- Some require you to stay 1–3 years afterward

2. Nurse Corps Scholarship Program

- Covers tuition, fees, stipend, in exchange for working in underserved areas

3. Public Service Loan Forgiveness (PSLF)

- If you work at a qualifying non-profit and make income-driven payments, remaining balance is forgiven after 120 payments

4. Pay-As-You-Go Strategy

- Stretch the program out, pay per class using savings or current income

5. Graduate Assistantships

- Available at some schools, often competitive

Section 6: Choosing the Right Program for Your Budget and Goals

Online vs. In-Person

- Online gives flexibility but may lack networking or mentorship
- In-person often more immersive, sometimes more expensive

Accredited vs. Not

- Always choose an accredited program to avoid issues with licensing or transferring credits

Full-time vs. Part-time

- Part-time lets you keep working but takes longer

- Full-time fast-tracks you, but drains your income faster

Real Nurse Scenarios

Lindsey, 32 – ICU RN → CRNA Student

"I knew it would be brutal. I took out $180K in loans, but I'll make $190K+ after graduation. I've already mapped out a 10-year payoff plan."

Reese, 38 – RN → NP with a newborn

"I did a part-time NP program over 4 years while working and raising my baby. It cost me my social life, but we avoided debt."

Taylor, 41 – Burned out bedside nurse → Educator

"I got a DNP and now teach full time. I don't make much more, but I sleep better. For me, that was worth it."

Action Steps for Nurses Considering More School

1. Run your numbers—actual tuition, fees, lost income
2. Use an ROI calculator—don't guess
3. Talk to 3 nurses *currently* in the job you want
4. Interview the school's alumni. Ask what jobs they got.
5. Don't start school until you know your financial aid options
6. Consider a 2-year post-grad loan payoff plan—make it part of the plan

One Financial Move Before Your Next Shift

Write down the *real* reason you're considering a higher degree. Not just the money—**the "why."**

Then write down the **actual cost.**

Put them side by side. Does the motivation match the investment?

If yes—start building your budget and application strategy.

If no—pause. Rethink. It's okay to change your mind.

Final Note

Advancing your nursing career is powerful.

But power without planning leads to pressure.

You deserve both the **autonomy** and the **abundance** that come from doing this wisely. This chapter doesn't say "don't go back to school." It says:

Don't go back blindly.

Don't go back broke.

Don't go back without a strategy.

Because your brain, your license, and your heart are already worth so much. Let's make sure your next move multiplies—not drains—your long-term wealth.

You've got the skills.

You've got the drive.

Now let's make sure you've got the financial blueprint to match.

Chapter 24: Should You Work PRN, Per Diem, or Travel?

Let's talk shifts—not just the ones you clock into, but the career shifts that could change your money, your sanity, and your future.

PRN. Per diem. Travel nursing. These aren't just schedule preferences—they're financial decisions. They affect your taxes, your time, your burnout risk, and your bank account. And for nurses burned out from rigid staffing ratios or craving something new, they can look like a lifeline—or a trap.

So how do you decide?

You run the numbers. You run the emotional calculus. And you choose what works for your life, not just your badge.

Section 1: Defining the Options

PRN (Pro Re Nata)

- Latin for "as needed"
- You're on-call or scheduled per demand
- Typically no benefits
- Higher hourly wage

Per Diem

- Usually synonymous with PRN, but may refer more broadly to temp-style roles
- Paid a flat rate per day (or high hourly)
- Often zero benefits

Travel Nursing

- You take contracts—usually 8–13 weeks—at facilities across the country
- Paid a base rate + non-taxable housing, travel, and per diem stipends
- May come with benefits if through an agency

Section 2: Pros and Cons – The Real Trade-Offs

PRN Pros:

- High hourly wage
- Flexible schedule
- Can work at multiple facilities

PRN Cons:

- No benefits
- No guaranteed hours
- Must hustle to stay on staff

Per Diem Pros:

- Even higher rates than PRN in some markets
- Freedom to pick and choose days
- Avoids long-term burnout

Per Diem Cons:

- Same as PRN: no job security or retirement match
- No sick leave, paid time off, or health insurance

Travel Nurse Pros:

- Huge pay potential in high-demand locations
- Non-taxed stipends add up fast
- Paid to see the country

Travel Nurse Cons:

- Constant relocation stress
- Higher burnout risk from unfamiliar units
- Difficult to maintain relationships or family routines
- Must manage licensure in multiple states

Section 3: Taxes and Benefits – The Hidden Story

Let's get into what the paychecks don't show:

No Benefits = You Must DIY:

- Health insurance (through ACA marketplace or private broker)
- Retirement (no 401(k)? Open a Roth IRA)
- No PTO = unpaid vacation = plan your budget accordingly

Travel Nursing Taxes:

- You only get tax-free stipends if you maintain a permanent tax home
- Misreporting = IRS nightmares
- Always consult a tax pro before assuming your $4,000/month stipend is "free money"

Self-Employment Taxes (If 1099):

- No employer withholding = you're on the hook for estimated quarterly taxes
- Budget 25–30% for taxes if you're not W-2

Section 4: Burnout Math – The Emotional ROI

You can't talk finances without talking fatigue.

Scenario 1: You make $55/hr PRN.

- But you say yes every time they call
- You pick up weekend shifts even when your body says no
- You have no benefits, no PTO, and you're exhausted

Scenario 2: You make $40/hr staff RN

- You get 4 weeks PTO, health insurance, retirement match
- You have a team that feels like family
- You sleep 7 hours a night

Who's really winning?

Burnout has a cost. It's called ER visits, chronic stress, relationship strain, and the financial mistake of quitting without a plan.

Section 5: Income Potential – Short-Term vs. Long-Term

Short-Term Gain:

- PRN or Travel = more money now
- But can feel unstable
- May not qualify for mortgages or loans (inconsistent W-2 income)

Long-Term Gain:

- Staff roles often include raises, tuition reimbursement, and advancement
- Easier to save consistently with fixed income

Real Nurse Voices

Avery, 29 – Travel Nurse

"I cleared over $180K last year. But I missed 3 weddings, a funeral, and went 7 months without seeing my dog. I'm tired."

Camila, 35 – PRN at Two Hospitals

"I love the flexibility. I'm home for my kids more. But I also stress when the census drops and shifts get canceled."

Marcus, 44 – Staff ICU Nurse

"I stayed for the pension and the people. I get OT when I want it. I know what my week looks like. That stability is wealth to me."

Action Steps – How to Decide What's Right for You

1. List your financial priorities (emergency fund? paying off loans? saving for a house?)
2. Calculate your monthly "bare minimum" income need
3. Estimate how many PRN or per diem shifts it would take to cover that
4. Evaluate your risk tolerance—can you handle inconsistent pay?
5. Talk to 3 nurses working each model. Ask what *they* wish they knew.
6. Look at job postings and compare actual rates + benefits
7. Run a burnout check-in: How much longer can you do *this* schedule?

Final Thoughts – What Working Nurses Need to Hear

You don't have to pick one forever.

You can:

- Be staff now and travel later
- Be PRN while going back to school
- Be a travel nurse for 2 years and use that money to buy a home

Just make sure **your finances and your body** are aligned.

Because no job is worth breaking your back—or your bank account.

Make One Move Before Your Next Shift

Ask HR what your hourly rate would be if you went PRN.

Then ask yourself:

Is the extra cash worth losing my benefits?

If yes—start saving aggressively.

If no—start optimizing your staff benefits now.

Either way, *you're the one in control.* That's the first step to real wealth.

You've got this.

Chapter 25: Nurse Burnout and Financial Consequences

Nursing is a calling—but it's also a career. And while it's full of heart, purpose, and humanity, it's also one of the most emotionally, physically, and mentally demanding professions out there. Shift work, trauma exposure, short staffing, high patient ratios, and moral injury all contribute to burnout. But what rarely gets talked about is the financial stress that's hiding underneath the exhaustion.

Yes, nurse burnout is emotional.

Yes, nurse burnout is physical.

But nurse burnout is also financial.

Let's scrub in.

The Overlap of Financial Stress and Burnout

Burnout doesn't happen in a vacuum. It builds over time. And one of the biggest silent drivers is money—or the lack of clarity around it.

You could be making $75K, $100K, even $150K a year and still feel like you're suffocating. Why?

Because it's not about how much you make. It's about how much clarity, control, and cushion you have.

You can be in the middle of a busy med-surg unit, heart pounding, charting behind, and silently worrying:

- "Did that last car repair just overdraft my account?"
- "How am I going to pay off these student loans if I keep picking up shifts just to breathe?"
- "Is working another double this weekend worth it—or will it break me?"

This is financial stress. And it's a core contributor to burnout.

What Burnout Really Costs You Financially

Let's break it down—because burnout isn't just emotional. It hits your wallet, your long-term goals, and your earning potential hard.

1. Lost Shifts = Lost Pay

Burnout can lead to calling in, reducing hours, or even taking unpaid medical leave. That means real money left on the table—sometimes thousands per month.

2. Increased Healthcare Costs

Stress-related illness, mental health challenges, and physical breakdowns cost you financially—even if you have insurance. Copays. Prescriptions. Missed time. It adds up.

3. Career Changes or Pauses

Burned-out nurses may leave clinical care, switch careers, or go part-time. That decision—while necessary for health—can reduce lifetime earning potential by six figures or more if not planned for.

4. Poor Financial Decisions from Exhaustion

When you're exhausted, it's harder to make smart money choices. You might:

- Spend impulsively to self-soothe
- Forget to pay bills
- Put off saving or retirement planning

5. Increased Dependence on Overtime

If your budget requires you to pick up extra shifts just to make ends meet, you're living in a financial pressure cooker. That's not sustainable.

Burnout Symptoms That Have Financial Side Effects

Burnout shows up in different ways, and some of them hit your finances indirectly:

- **Insomnia** → Lower energy = missed shifts or errors
- **Cynicism and detachment** → Increased risk of disciplinary issues
- **Reduced concentration** → Mistakes that could affect licensure
- **Emotional exhaustion** → Less bandwidth to manage budgets or goals

Burnout blurs the boundary between your work life and your financial life. They're more connected than most nurses are told.

The Real-World Burnout Equation

Let's say you make $90,000/year.

You're overworked and running on empty. You start:

- Missing 2 shifts/month = ~$1,500/month lost income

- Needing therapy and meds = $250/month out-of-pocket
- Losing time to manage your finances = $0 going into savings

That's a $21,000 swing in your financial life in one year due to burnout. Not including the emotional cost.

Now multiply that over 3 years of not making a change.

It's not just burnout.

It's financial bleed.

Better Financial Planning = Burnout Prevention

You can't fix short staffing or hospital politics overnight. But you can strengthen your *financial stability* to reduce the burden of burnout.

Here's how:

1. Build a Real Emergency Fund

Not just a vague savings account. We're talking 3–6 months of living expenses in a high-yield savings account. So if you need to step away, you can do it without panic.

2. Get Clear on Your Fixed Expenses

If you don't know exactly what your bills cost monthly, you're working blind. Track it. Name it. Own it. Then build breathing room.

3. Budget to Not Rely on OT

OT can be a blessing, but it should never be your baseline. Build a budget on base pay and treat OT as bonus or savings fuel.

4. Make Mental Health Part of Your Financial Plan

Yes, therapy is a line item. So is rest. So is saying "no" to one shift a month. If you don't invest in your wellness, you'll be forced to spend on your illness.

5. Use PTO Proactively, Not Just Reactively

Plan recharge time. Don't wait until you're at your breaking point. Budget your time off just like you would your money.

Case Study: Sarah, the Burned-Out ICU Nurse

- **Age:** 34
- **Income:** $110K
- **Student Loans:** $95K
- **Savings:** $3,000
- **Burnout Status:** High

Sarah picked up OT every week to pay down loans fast. But she started:

- Snapping at coworkers
- Waking up in dread
- Skipping meals and appointments

She crashed. Took 2 months off. No short-term disability. Drained her savings. Had to borrow from family. She felt like she failed financially.

But what actually failed her?

The system? Yes.

But also: no financial runway. No stress cushion. No plan for pause.

Now she's rebuilding:

- Budgeting based on base pay only
- Putting 15% of income into an emergency fund

- Scheduling self-care and therapy weekly
- Saying no to OT unless it's voluntary

Her health improved.
Her money stabilized.
Her power returned.

Action Steps for Nurses on the Edge

Here's your "Burnout Prevention Financial Checklist":
Know your monthly number (exact living expenses)

- Build a $1,000 starter emergency fund, then 3–6 months
- Review your benefits—do you have short-term disability?
- Use PTO before you're mentally wrecked
- Invest in mental health (yes, budget for it)
- Say no to guilt-driven OT
- Create a side hustle or savings fund labeled "Burnout Exit Plan"
- You deserve to work hard *and* be well.

You Can't Self-Care Your Way Out of Financial Insecurity

Let's be real: bubble baths won't fix systemic burnout.
But financial clarity? That helps.

- Financial independence gives you options.
- Options give you power.
- Power gives you peace.

When you understand your money, plan your future, and have savings that let you say no—you shift from survival to strategy.

What's at Stake

This isn't about hoarding money.
It's about:

- Saying no to double shifts that break your body
- Saying yes to a job that pays less but treats you better
- Taking 6 months off when life hits hard
- Retiring before 65 with joy instead of resentment

Financial literacy for nurses is not just about retirement accounts and side hustles.
It's about protecting your purpose.

The "Shift Mindset" You Need

Instead of asking:
"How can I survive one more year of this?"
Ask:
"What financial moves can I make now so I'm not stuck in this forever?"
That's the shift.
That's the antidote to burnout.
That's the foundation for your financial comeback.

Your Call to Act

Make one financial move before your next shift.
Just one.
And do another next week.

- Open that high-yield savings account.
- Cancel one subscription you don't use.
- Transfer $50 into your emergency fund.

- Decline that guilt-trip OT shift and rest instead.

Because the only thing worse than working yourself sick is staying stuck when you've got the skills, strength, and smarts to shift into abundance.

You didn't survive nursing school, patient emergencies, or life's chaos just to stay broke and burned out.

You're not here to run on fumes.

You're here to build wealth, rest often, and retire with pride.

Let's make that happen.

Part IV: Building Wealth and Thinking Long-Term – From Stability to Strategy

This part of the journey is about zooming out. You've survived school, landed the job, and learned to manage the basics—but now it's time to build. Not just savings. Not just a cushion. *Wealth.*

This section teaches nurses how to shift from survival mode to wealth-building mode, no matter what stage of their career they're in. Whether you're a new nurse wondering how to invest your first $500, or a seasoned nurse thinking about legacy, this part gives you a financial roadmap that grows with you.

You'll learn how to assess investment options, protect what you've earned with the right types of insurance, plan for retirement with confidence, and understand your long-term goals—not just as a nurse, but as a whole person. We'll talk Roth IRAs, traditional IRAs, 403(b)s, 401(k)s, compound interest, financial independence, and the power of small, consistent decisions over time.

We'll also tackle the tough stuff—burnout, family obligations, major purchases, and navigating career transitions—so you can plan not just for a paycheck, but for a life of purpose, peace, and options.

This is your blueprint for building a financial future that's not just safe, but abundant. Because you didn't become a nurse to stay broke, stressed, or one emergency away from chaos. You became a nurse to help others—and now it's time to help *you.*

Let's build your wealth like you build patient care: intentionally, skillfully, and with the long game in mind.

Chapter 26: Investing Basics – Index Funds, IRAs, and Diversification

Simple Strategies for Busy Nurses

You already know how to handle pressure. You manage patients, shift changes, charting systems, emotional families, and gut-wrenching decisions. So why does investing feel like it's in another universe?

Because no one ever taught you how.

This chapter is for every nurse who has thought: *I make good money now, but I have no idea what to do with it.* Or: *I want to invest but don't have time to learn everything.*

Here's the good news: You don't have to learn *everything*. You just need to know the right things.

Let's start with the foundation and build up from there.

Why You Should Start Investing Now

You're not too late. You're not too early. You're right on time.

And if you've ever said, *I'll start investing once I pay off my loans,* here's a gentle reframe: *Don't wait to invest until you're debt-free. Start investing alongside your debt payoff.*

Why? Because time is the most powerful ingredient in wealth building. It's called compound interest, and it's your best friend.

Plain-Language Breakdown: What Is Investing?

Investing means putting your money into assets that can grow over time. That includes:

- Stocks (ownership in companies)
- Bonds (loans to companies or governments)
- Mutual funds (bundles of stocks or bonds)
- Index funds (automated mutual funds that track the market)
- Real estate

For this chapter, we're focusing on the stock market—especially index funds and retirement accounts.

Let's Talk About IRAs (Traditional and Roth)

An IRA is an Individual Retirement Account. Think of it as a container where your investments grow with tax advantages.

- **Traditional IRA**: You put in pre-tax money now, lower your taxable income, and pay taxes when you take it out later.
- **Roth IRA**: You put in post-tax money now, and it grows tax-free. You never pay taxes on it again.

Which is better for nurses?

- Early-career nurses in lower tax brackets? *Roth IRA is usually the winner.*
- Later-career, high-earning nurses? A *Traditional IRA* might offer better tax savings now.

Contribution limit (as of 2025): $7,000/year if you're under 50; $8,000 if you're over 50.

The Power of Index Funds

Index funds are low-cost, low-effort, high-trust investments.

They track a specific portion of the market. For example:

- **S&P 500 Index Fund**: Tracks the 500 largest companies in the U.S.
- **Total Stock Market Index Fund**: Covers thousands of U.S. companies.
- **International Index Funds**: Track non-U.S. companies.

Benefits:

- Low fees
- Passive (no picking stocks)
- Broad diversification (you're not betting on one company)

You can buy them inside an IRA, a 403(b), or a brokerage account.

Diversification: Don't Put All Your Scrubs in One Hamper

Diversification means not putting all your eggs in one basket.

- Own different *types* of investments: stocks, bonds, real estate, cash.
- Own different *geographies*: U.S., international.
- Own different *sectors*: healthcare, tech, energy, etc.

Why? Because if one thing crashes, the others can help balance it out.

A basic starter mix:

- 80% stock index funds (U.S. + international)
- 20% bond index funds

As you get older, shift more toward bonds for stability.

403(b)s and 401(k)s: Your Workplace Retirement Plans

If you work at a hospital or nonprofit, you probably have a 403(b).

If you're with a private employer, it's likely a 401(k).

These accounts let you invest *before* taxes are taken out—which lowers your taxable income.

- 2025 Contribution Limit: $23,000/year (under 50); $30,500/year (50+)
- Check if your employer offers a match—always contribute at least enough to get the match.

How to Get Started: A Nurse's Simple Investment Plan

1. **Build your emergency fund first.** Three to six months of expenses.
2. **Open a Roth IRA.** Put in $50-$100 per pay period.
3. **Contribute to your 403(b).** At least enough to get the employer match.
4. **Invest in index funds.** Choose a total market or S&P 500 fund.
5. **Automate it.** Make it automatic and let it run while you work your shifts.

Real-Life Scenario: Paige the Pediatric Nurse

Paige makes $78,000/year. She has $40,000 in student loans and rents a 2-bedroom apartment with a roommate.

Her plan:

- Save $300/month toward her emergency fund.
- Invest $250/month into a Roth IRA with a total market index fund.
- Contribute 5% of her salary to her 403(b), which gets her full employer match.

Paige isn't trying to time the market. She's not watching CNBC. But her investments are growing steadily in the background.

Common Myths Nurses Believe About Investing

- *"I need a lot of money to start."* Nope. Many platforms let you start with $10.
- *"The market is too risky."* Over time, the stock market has averaged 7-10% annually.
- *"I'll invest when I have more time."* Waiting costs you the most.

Mistakes to Avoid

- Investing without an emergency fund
- Withdrawing early and paying penalties
- Chasing hot stocks or trends

- Not understanding your risk tolerance

Your Nursing Career Is a Marathon—So Is Investing

You don't have to be a finance nerd. You just have to be consistent.

Set it. Forget it. Review it annually. Adjust as you grow.

And remember: *Your money should work just as hard as you do.*

Call to Act

Before your next shift:

- Open a Roth IRA.
- Set up a $50 monthly contribution.
- Choose a low-cost index fund.

Next week, review your 403(b) and see if you're getting the full employer match.

Financial freedom isn't about earning more shifts. It's about making your money work when *you're* not.

You've stabilized patients under pressure.

You can stabilize your finances.

Let's build wealth—one paycheck, one fund, one confident decision at a time.

Chapter 27: How to Start Investing in Real Estate (Without Losing Sleep or Money)

Real estate investing can sound intimidating. There are shows about flipping homes, friends talking about passive income, and TikToks hyping up "rentals that pay your mortgage." But when you're a nurse working 12-hour shifts, dealing with charting backlogs, and barely remembering your own lunchbox, the idea of becoming a landlord—or even just investing in real estate at all—might feel way out of reach.

This chapter is about changing that perception. Not with fluff or hype. Not with sleepless nights worrying about broken water heaters. But with clarity, calmness, and a clear-eyed plan.

Whether you're a brand-new RN, a mid-career ICU nurse, or a seasoned school nurse thinking about building retirement income, real estate can play a role in your financial future. And you don't need to buy a duplex tomorrow or have six figures in cash to begin.

Let's walk through how nurses can get into real estate investing, safely and smartly.

1. Why Real Estate?

Real estate offers something unique: the ability to build wealth over time, often with the help of other people's money (a.k.a. leverage). When done right, it provides cash flow, appreciation, tax advantages, and asset diversification.

But more importantly, it can provide **control.**

You don't set your hospital's 403(b) match. You don't control the stock market. But if you own a home or a rental property, you get to make the decisions: when to refinance, when to rent, when to sell, how to manage your expenses.

That kind of financial agency matters.

2. Real Estate Isn't All or Nothing

You don't have to go all-in and become a full-time investor. Real estate isn't binary. It lives on a spectrum:

- Living in your home = real estate involvement.
- Renting out a room = real estate income.
- Owning a rental property = active investing.
- Buying REITs (real estate investment trusts) = passive investing.

You can start small. You can stay small. You can grow at your pace.

3. House Hacking: The Nurse Starter Strategy

House hacking means using your primary residence to generate income. This could look like:

- Renting out a basement apartment
- Living in a duplex and renting out the other half
- Taking on a roommate or two

It's a way to reduce (or even eliminate) your housing costs while building equity. And it's often more financially accessible than buying a full-fledged investment property.

For example, Nurse Tasha bought a 3-bedroom condo. She lives in one room and rents the other two to travel nurses. Her mortgage is covered. She's building equity while paying nothing out-of-pocket for housing.

4. REITs: Real Estate for the Ultra-Busy Nurse

A REIT is a company that owns, operates, or finances income-producing real estate. You can buy shares of REITs just like you buy shares of stock. There are publicly traded REITs on platforms like Fidelity, Vanguard, and Schwab.

Pros:

- No landlord duties
- Liquid (can sell quickly)
- Diversified across properties

Cons:

- Less control
- Dividends taxed as ordinary income

But for a nurse who doesn't want midnight maintenance calls? REITs can be a simple entry point.

5. Short-Term Rentals: Airbnbs and the Nurse Hustle

Short-term rentals can offer strong cash flow, but they come with work: bookings, cleanings, guest communication, local laws.

This route can be great **if** you:

- Live in a tourist area
- Can automate systems (cleaners, smart locks, etc.)
- Have flexibility in your schedule (think PRN nurses)

Warning: burnout-prone nurses might want to think twice before adding Airbnb host to their resume unless it's highly automated.

6. Traditional Rentals: Long-Term Game, Long-Term Gain

Owning a single-family home or small multifamily and renting it out long-term can provide monthly income, equity growth, and tax advantages.

But it also comes with responsibilities:

- Tenant screening
- Maintenance
- Rent collection
- Legal compliance

You can self-manage or hire a property manager (usually 8-10% of monthly rent). Either way, it's important to run the numbers before buying:

- Gross Rent
- Mortgage (PITI: Principal, Interest, Taxes, Insurance)
- Maintenance/reserves
- Vacancy allowance (5-10%)

7. Partnerships: Team Up With Caution

You might find a friend or family member who wants to go in on a property together. This can work if:

- You have clear roles
- You document everything legally
- You treat it like a business

Never enter a partnership with verbal agreements. Always use a written operating agreement.

8. The Nurse Real Estate Checklist

Before you invest, ask yourself:

- Do I have an emergency fund (3-6 months)?
- Do I have high-interest debt?
- Am I maxing out retirement contributions (match at minimum)?
- Do I understand the market I'm buying in?
- Have I stress-tested my budget for vacancies or repairs?

Don't let Instagram fool you. Real estate success starts with strong financial foundations.

9. Tax Perks and Gotchas

Real estate comes with write-offs:

- Mortgage interest
- Property taxes
- Repairs
- Depreciation (on rentals)

But beware:

- Rental income is taxable
- Depreciation gets "recaptured" when you sell
- DIY mistakes can be costly

A good CPA who understands real estate is worth their weight in gold.

10. Real Nurse Stories

Nurse Camila bought a duplex near her hospital. She lives in one unit, rents the other, and saves $1,100 a month. She plans to repeat the process in a few years.

Nurse Jon tried Airbnb and burned out in six months. Now he invests in REITs and uses his time to mentor new grads instead of managing guests.

Nurse Mel and her partner bought a triplex out of state with a property manager. They split the down payment and have a written agreement. It cash flows $300/month per partner.

There is no one-size-fits-all strategy. Just like patient care, real estate requires critical thinking, not cookie-cutter advice.

11. Investing Without Losing Sleep

Real estate should support your life, not stress you out. Start small. Use a spreadsheet. Think like a nurse:

- Assess risk (location, tenant pool, local laws)
- Diagnose the numbers (rent minus expenses)
- Create a care plan (your investment strategy)
- Monitor vitals (cash flow, reserves, maintenance)

And always remember: the goal isn't just more money. It's **more options.**

12. Your Next Move

You don't need to rush into anything. But if real estate speaks to you:

- Start by learning. Books, podcasts, forums (like BiggerPockets).
- Open a dedicated savings account for a future down payment.
- Run sample numbers on local rentals to practice.
- Explore REITs to get exposure without ownership stress.

Financial independence isn't about becoming a landlord overnight. It's about using your nursing income to build wealth with intention.

Final Dose: Financially Empowered Nurses Invest Differently

You already know how to assess patients, manage chaos, and work under pressure. Those same skills transfer beautifully to real estate. But they work best when paired with education, preparation, and rest.

Start slow. Think long. Play smart.

And remember: you didn't become a nurse to be broke, tired, and scared of your future.

You became a nurse because you care. Let that same care extend to your finances.

Call to Act:

Make one financial move before your next shift. Just one. Open a REIT account, schedule a real estate webinar, or set aside $100 toward a house fund. Then do one more next week. That's how real estate investing for nurses really begins.

You've got the heart. Now build the portfolio to match.

Chapter 28: Credit Score Essentials – How to Build, Protect, and Leverage It

Let's talk credit—the kind that can quietly limit your future or unlock it with a key you didn't know you were holding.

You didn't get into nursing to master the financial system. You got into it to help people. To stabilize vitals. To offer comfort. To be there when no one else could be. But here's the truth: while you were saving lives, credit was silently shaping your own.

Your credit score isn't just a number. It's a gatekeeper. And too many nurses walk into adulthood with noble hearts—but no financial GPS.

This chapter is your map.

Why Your Credit Score Matters (Even If You're Not Buying a House Tomorrow)

Think of your credit score like your financial blood pressure—a silent but powerful indicator of your overall fiscal health.

A strong score can get you:

- Approved for loans with better rates
- Lower auto insurance premiums
- Easier apartment applications
- Higher credit card limits
- Favorable job background checks in some states

But a weak score? It can quietly cost you tens of thousands.

Here's the reality: Two nurses with the same salary and same job title might buy the same house. But the one with a 780 credit score will pay $20,000 less in interest over 30 years than the one with a 630 score.

Same life. Different financial trajectory.

Understanding Credit Score Ranges

Here's how credit scores typically break down:

- **300–579: Poor**
- You're considered high-risk. Expect rejections or sky-high interest rates.
- **580–669: Fair**
- You may get approved, but rates won't be ideal.
- **670–739: Good**
- You're seen as a responsible borrower. Most loans are in reach.
- **740–799: Very Good**
- Better-than-average score. You'll likely receive favorable terms.
- **800–850: Excellent**
- You're in elite territory. Lenders compete for your business.

Your goal? Not perfection. Just power. For most nurses, aiming for **700+** gives you access to better options across the board.

The Anatomy of a Credit Score

Here's what determines your score:

35% Payment History

Do you pay your bills on time? Every time? One late payment can follow you for seven years.

30% Credit Utilization

How much of your available credit are you using? Try to stay under 30%. Under 10% is even better.

15% Length of Credit History

Older is better. Keep long-standing accounts open.

10% New Credit

Too many applications at once? It looks like you're scrambling.

10% Credit Mix

Student loans, auto loans, credit cards, mortgages—it's good to show you can handle a variety.

Building or Rebuilding Credit From the Ground Up

Whether you're starting at 500 or 750, the principles are the same.

Start with a secured card

It's backed by a cash deposit. Use it for small purchases—gas, groceries—and pay in full.

Become an authorized user

Find someone you trust with a long, positive credit history. Their record helps boost yours.

Make every payment on time

Even your phone bill or utility bill can be reported.

Keep balances low

Ideally, don't use more than 10–30% of your limit.

Only open accounts when necessary

Every application triggers a hard inquiry.

Stay consistent

Don't try to "hack" your score. Just build steady, boring financial behavior.

Protecting Your Credit Like You Protect Your Patients

Nurses live in organized chaos. Don't let your credit profile fall through the cracks.

- **Freeze your credit** when not actively applying for loans. It prevents identity theft.
- **Check your credit reports annually** at AnnualCreditReport.com.
- **Dispute any errors**—names, balances, closed accounts that are listed as open.
- **Avoid co-signing** unless you're ready to own their debt.
- **Automate your bills**—especially on night shifts or during travel contracts.

Nurse-Specific Credit Landmines

Let's be real. Your job is exhausting. You're not just managing money—you're managing shifts, lives, and sleep deprivation.

- **Night shift fatigue** can cause missed payments. Set calendar reminders.
- **Travel nursing** often creates address mismatches. Keep credit profiles updated.
- **PRN income** may create cash flow gaps. Budget for the valleys, not just the peaks.
- **Scrub tech to RN transition** often involves new loans. Don't default to "I'll figure it out later."

Real-Life Nurse Credit Scenarios

Jasmine, 27 - ER Nurse

She had $5,000 in credit card debt. Was paying minimums. Her score hovered at 630. She switched to the avalanche method—paying off high-interest debt first. Within 8 months, her score jumped to 710.

Marco, 34 - ICU Travel Nurse

Missed a $52 urgent care bill. It went to collections. His score dropped 100 points. He now sets every bill to autopay—even for small balances.

Tina & James, 41 - Married OR Nurses

They wanted to buy a home but had two car loans and credit cards. They paused mortgage savings and focused on debt. After 6 months, their score jumped enough to land a lower mortgage rate—saving them $180/month.

Loans, Interest Rates, and the Long-Term Game

Think of loans like prescriptions.

- **Dosage = Interest Rate**
- The stronger your credit, the lower the dose (cost).
- **Duration = Term Length**
- A longer loan may reduce monthly costs but increase total interest.
- **Risk = Your Credit Score**

- The lower your score, the riskier you appear to lenders.

Examples:

- Auto loan with 750 score = 3.9% APR
- Auto loan with 600 score = 12.9% APR
- That difference? Thousands in interest.
- Refinance student loans? Aim for 700+.
- Buying a home? Lock in strong credit 12 months ahead.

Credit Prep Before Homeownership

If you're thinking about buying in the next year:

- **Pay on time**—every bill, every time.
- **Lower utilization**—below 10% if you can.
- **Avoid new credit cards**—even the ones that give you a free tote bag.
- **Dispute errors early.**
- **Save** for a down payment—at least 5%, ideally 20%.

Credit Myths Nurses Need to Let Go Of

- *"Carrying a balance builds credit."*
- Nope. Pay it off in full every month. Interest is a wealth killer.
- *"Checking my score hurts it."*
- Soft inquiries don't. Apps like Credit Karma are safe.
- *"My income boosts my score."*
- False. You can earn $30K with an 800 or $130K with a 580.

Action Plan: Nurse Edition

Step 1: Know your score

Check it monthly using Credit Karma, Experian, or your bank's tools.

Step 2: Set a 12-month credit goal

Write it down. 700? 750? Start with a number.

Step 3: Automate payments

Set it and forget it—even your $19.99 streaming subscriptions.

Step 4: Lower balances

Don't wait until the bill is due. Pay down balances mid-cycle to lower utilization.

Step 5: Monitor your reports

Check for errors every 4 months from one of the three bureaus.

Step 6: Don't let burnout sabotage your progress

Self-care includes financial care. Tired brains make expensive mistakes.

Closing Scrub-In

Before your next shift, check your credit score.

Not to panic. Not to obsess. But to own it.

Maybe you lower your balance by $50 this week. Maybe you finally dispute that old account. Maybe you automate that utility bill that always sneaks up on you.

That's progress.

And next week, you make another move. That's momentum.

Because you've worked too hard for your future to be held back by something as preventable as a low credit score.

You know how to save lives.

Now it's time to save money, interest, and long-term stress by managing your credit like the capable, powerful professional you are.

Let's scrub in.

Let's do this.

Chapter 29: Insurance Essentials for Nurses – Disability, Life, Auto, Home, Liability, and Umbrella Insurance

Let's break this down like you'd explain discharge instructions to a patient coming out of surgery: clearly, calmly, and with complete respect for their time, health, and safety. Except this time, the topic is your financial safety net—and we're not sending you home without understanding what protects your income, your family, and your future. You wouldn't skip a flu shot during an outbreak, so don't skip this chapter.

Why Insurance Matters for Nurses

Insurance is often seen as boring or confusing—but it's actually one of the most critical components of a strong financial foundation. For nurses, who often work long hours, juggle families, and face physical and emotional risks daily, insurance isn't a luxury. It's a lifeline.

You may not realize it, but every day you're exposed to scenarios that could impact your health, income, or ability to work. And guess what? You don't have to wait for a financial storm to start preparing your umbrella.

Let's walk through each type of insurance you should understand, consider, and potentially act on as a nurse.

1. Disability Insurance – Protecting Your Paycheck

What it is:

Disability insurance replaces a portion of your income if you can't work due to illness or injury. For nurses—who rely on their physical and mental capabilities to perform essential duties—this is arguably the most important insurance to own.

Why nurses need it:

Nursing can take a toll on your body. Back injuries, needlestick accidents, burnout, and chronic illness are real risks. If you couldn't work for 3 months—or 3 years—how would you cover your mortgage, car, and groceries?

Types:

- **Short-Term Disability (STD):** Covers you for a few weeks to 6 months.
- **Long-Term Disability (LTD):** Kicks in after STD and can last for years.

Example:

Jessica, a 34-year-old med-surg nurse, slipped a disc during a hectic shift. She couldn't stand for more than 20 minutes at a time and had to take a leave of absence. Because she had LTD through her employer and a personal policy that covered 60% of her income, she could still pay her bills and focus on healing—not hustling.

2. Life Insurance - Protecting the People You Love

What it is:

Life insurance pays out a lump sum to your chosen beneficiaries if you die. It's not for you—it's for your family.

Why nurses need it:

Even if you're young and healthy, life is unpredictable. If you have kids, a spouse, aging parents, or anyone who depends on your income—life insurance is a must.

Types:

- **Term Life Insurance:** Affordable, temporary coverage (e.g., 20 years).
- **Whole Life or Permanent Insurance:** More expensive, but lasts your lifetime and may build cash value.

Example:

Maria, a 40-year-old NICU nurse, and her husband each took out 20-year term policies worth $500,000 after having kids. When her husband passed away unexpectedly from a heart attack at 44, that policy allowed Maria to stay home for a year, pay off their mortgage, and avoid financial ruin.

3. Auto Insurance – More Than Just State Minimums

What it is:

Auto insurance covers accidents involving your vehicle—whether you're at fault, hit by another driver, or facing theft or weather damage.

Why nurses need it:

Shift work means driving tired, in the dark, or during rush hour. And if you live in a commuter-heavy city or rural area, car accidents aren't rare. One wreck can mean thousands of dollars in bills—or lawsuits.

Key coverages:

- **Liability (bodily injury + property damage)**
- **Comprehensive (weather, theft, fire)**
- **Collision (you hit someone or something)**
- **Uninsured/Underinsured Motorist**

Example:

Tasha, a 27-year-old ER nurse, was hit by a texting driver while heading to work. Her car was totaled. Thanks to her full coverage auto policy, she got a rental, her medical bills were covered, and her car loan was paid off.

4. Homeowners or Renters Insurance – Where You Lay Your Head Matters

What it is:

This protects your home and belongings in case of theft, fire, flood, or other disasters.

Why nurses need it:

Your schedule may mean you're away from home for 12+ hours. A kitchen fire or break-in while you're gone could ruin not just your stuff—but your savings.

Options:

- **Homeowners insurance:** For property owners.
- **Renters insurance:** For tenants. Cheap. Often $10–$20/month. Covers belongings and liability.

Example:

DeAndre, a float nurse, came home after a long shift to find his apartment flooded from the unit above. His renters insurance replaced his laptop, uniform wardrobe, and furniture—over $6,000 in damages.

5. Liability Insurance - The Extra Shield

What it is:

Personal liability coverage protects you if someone sues you for injury or damage.

Why nurses need it:

If someone trips in your apartment or your dog bites a neighbor, liability insurance (part of homeowners or renters) protects your assets.

Example:

Sasha's dog accidentally scratched a toddler at her backyard BBQ. The parents sued. Her homeowners insurance's liability clause covered legal fees and a settlement.

6. Umbrella Insurance - Big Coverage for Worst-Case Scenarios

What it is:

An extra layer of protection over and above your auto or home policies. Kicks in if damages exceed your primary coverage.

Why nurses need it:

If you have savings, investments, or own property, you're a financial target. A major accident or lawsuit could wipe out decades of earnings.

Example:

A nurse who accidentally hit a pedestrian while rushing to work was sued for $750,000. Her auto policy covered $300,000. Her umbrella policy covered the rest.

How to Review Your Insurance Portfolio Like a Pro

1. **Create an Insurance Checklist:**

- Disability
- Life
- Auto
- Home/renters
- Liability
- Umbrella

1. **Review Annually** (ideally around the same time every year—like your license renewal month).
2. **Bundle Where You Can:** Discounts often apply for combining auto/home or adding umbrella.
3. **Work with a Trusted Professional:** Preferably one who understands nurses' needs. Ask: "Have you worked with healthcare professionals before?"
4. **Never Assume Work Coverage Is Enough:**
5. Employer-provided disability or life insurance may be basic or end if you leave the job. Supplement it.
6. **Don't Let Fear or Confusion Paralyze You:**
7. Start with one policy. Build confidence. Then layer on.

Call to Act:

"Pick one insurance category this week. Just one. Get a quote. Read your current policy. Or ask a question. Don't wait until something happens to figure out if you're protected."

Final Word:

Being a nurse means you spend your days protecting others. Now it's time to protect yourself—your income, your health, your future. Insurance isn't just paperwork. It's a lifeline. You've worked too hard to build your life. Let's make sure one crisis doesn't undo it all.

You're the heartbeat of the healthcare system. Protect your own heartbeat, too.

Chapter 30: Entrepreneurship in Nursing – Starting a Side Business

You didn't go into nursing because it was easy. You chose it because it mattered. You showed up every day for your patients—and now, it's time to show up for yourself. Whether it's through legal nurse consulting, tutoring, launching a wellness brand, or building a per diem staffing agency, more and more nurses are exploring entrepreneurship as a pathway to both financial freedom and professional fulfillment. But before you throw your stethoscope at the status quo and leap into the unknown, let's talk money, mindset, logistics, and lifestyle.

Entrepreneurship can be smart. It can also be stressful. And this chapter exists to help you tell the difference—before you bet the house on an idea that needed more planning.

Let's scrub in.

Part I: Why Nurses Make Excellent Entrepreneurs

If you can manage a code blue, handle four patients on drips, or document while de-escalating a family member at 3:00 a.m., then you already have more business skills than you realize.

- **Critical thinking**? Check.
- **People management**? Check.
- **Resilience under pressure**? You practically invented it.
- **Ability to assess, plan, implement, and evaluate**? That's nursing 101—and it just so happens to be the same structure used to launch

and grow a business.

What most nurses lack isn't capacity. It's **clarity** and **confidence** when it comes to the financial and strategic side of things. That's what this chapter will walk you through.

Part II: Popular Side Business Ideas for Nurses

Let's get specific. Here are some side business ideas that nurses can start while still working their current job:

1. Legal Nurse Consulting

- **What It Is:** Helping attorneys interpret medical records and terminology in legal cases.
- **Startup Cost:** Moderate (may require certification, laptop, professional memberships).
- **Time Commitment:** Flexible; case-based.
- **Income Potential:** $100 to $300+ per hour.
- **Best For:** Detail-oriented nurses with strong documentation and analytical skills.

2. Nursing Education and Tutoring

- **What It Is:** Helping nursing students prepare for the NCLEX or clinicals.
- **Startup Cost:** Low to none (Zoom account, website, or social media).
- **Time Commitment:** Nights/weekends.
- **Income Potential:** $30 to $100 per hour.
- **Best For:** Nurses who love teaching and mentoring.

3. Per Diem Staffing Agency

- **What It Is:** Starting your own local staffing agency for facilities.
- **Startup Cost:** High (legal setup, insurance, recruiting, payroll).
- **Time Commitment:** High initially.
- **Income Potential:** Six figures or more.
- **Best For:** Nurses with leadership experience and business partners.

4. Health and Wellness Coaching

- **What It Is:** Guiding clients through lifestyle changes, weight loss, stress, or chronic disease management.
- **Startup Cost:** Moderate (certification often recommended).
- **Time Commitment:** Flexible.
- **Income Potential:** $50 to $150/hour or more with packages.
- **Best For:** Nurses passionate about prevention and lifestyle medicine.

5. IV Hydration or Aesthetic Nursing

- **What It Is:** Providing IV therapy, Botox, or wellness injections (state laws vary).
- **Startup Cost:** High (medical director, insurance, equipment, licensure).
- **Time Commitment:** Varies.
- **Income Potential:** High with consistent clientele.
- **Best For:** Nurses with entrepreneurial drive and local network.

6. Writing, Blogging, and Content Creation

- **What It Is:** Health content for companies, blogs, or your own brand.
- **Startup Cost:** Low.
- **Time Commitment:** Nights/weekends.
- **Income Potential:** $0 to $500+/article; passive income possible.

- **Best For:** Creative nurses who enjoy storytelling.

7. Speaking and Workshops

- **What It Is:** Educating other nurses or healthcare workers on wellness, leadership, or clinical skills.
- **Startup Cost:** Low to moderate.
- **Time Commitment:** Variable; great if you enjoy public speaking.
- **Income Potential:** $200 to $2,000+ per event.
- **Best For:** Nurses with a story and a message.

Part III: How to Choose the Right Business for You

Ask yourself:

- What am I naturally good at?
- What problem do I love solving?
- What kind of lifestyle do I want in 3, 5, or 10 years?
- What can I realistically manage outside of nursing?
- What am I willing to learn?

Remember: Not every idea has to scale to seven figures. Some side hustles are stepping stones. Others are safety nets. A few will turn into full-on empires.

Don't chase every trend. Choose the opportunity that complements your schedule, honors your energy, and grows your income without crushing your sanity.

Part IV: The Money Talk – Budgeting, Taxes, and Business Structure

1. Budget for Startup Costs

Every business has a price tag. It could be a few hundred dollars for a website and logo. Or several thousand for licensure, insurance, and equipment.

Action Step: Create a spreadsheet with expected costs, timeline, and how you'll fund it (savings, side job, business loan, etc.).

2. Understand Taxes

Once you earn more than $400 as a side gig, the IRS considers you self-employed.

- Keep track of **expenses**.
- Set aside **20% to 30%** of income for taxes.
- Consider hiring a **CPA** or using accounting software.

3. Choose a Business Entity

- **Sole Proprietor:** Easy start, no separate tax return.
- **LLC:** More protection, but costs vary by state.
- **S-Corp:** Tax-efficient if earning more than $50K/year.

Pro Tip: Open a separate business checking account to keep things clean.

Part V: The Emotional Rollercoaster

You'll be excited. Then scared. Then frustrated. Then proud. Then exhausted.

Welcome to entrepreneurship.

It will test you—and that's okay. Just like in nursing, confidence comes with reps.

So build slowly. Build with intention. And give yourself permission to rest when needed.

Burnout is not a business plan.

Part VI: Red Flags and Common Pitfalls

- Don't blow your savings chasing quick money.
- Don't sign contracts you don't understand.
- Don't join MLMs disguised as "health coaching."

- Don't undercharge for your expertise.
- Don't skip legal or tax advice to "save money."

Entrepreneurship is not just about ideas. It's about execution. Protect yourself and your money as fiercely as you protect your patients.

Part VII: Real Nurse Entrepreneurs – Stories That Inspire

Elena, RN, Legal Nurse Consultant

"I started by helping a lawyer friend translate medical records. Five years later, I consult full time and make twice what I did bedside."

Marcus, ICU Nurse & Tutor

"I tutor 5 NCLEX students a month on the side. It pays for my daughter's private school and keeps me connected to education."

Ava, Aesthetic Nurse

"I rent space in a medspa one weekend a month. It started as a side gig but now pays as much as my nursing job."

Part VIII: When to Quit Your Job (And When Not To)

You don't have to quit nursing to be an entrepreneur. But if you want to, make sure:

- Your business earns at least **75%** of your nursing income.
- You have **6+ months of expenses** saved.
- You've tested your offer and know your numbers.
- You're ready for inconsistent income (and still have health insurance).

Quitting your job prematurely turns a dream into a financial emergency. Be strategic.

Part IX: Your Entrepreneur Checklist

- Pick a problem to solve
- Validate your idea with real people
- Set a simple budget

- Choose your legal structure
- Get a business account
- Build a simple website or social presence
- Set your prices
- Track every dollar in and out
- Schedule time to work on your business
- Revisit your goals quarterly

Final Word: You're Not Just a Nurse

You're a problem solver.

You're a critical thinker.

You're a professional with a unique lens.

Don't let anyone—including yourself—tell you that your only path is punching in for a 12-hour shift.

You don't need to leave nursing.

But you deserve the **option**.

Build the option. Build the plan. Build the confidence.

Financial freedom isn't a fantasy. It's just a formula.

Now go make your side hustle make sense.

Call to Act:

Make one financial move before your next shift. Just one.

And do another next week.

Whether it's researching an LLC, setting up a business account, or brainstorming your offer—do something. Because the only thing worse than working yourself sick is staying stuck when you've got the skills, strength, and smarts to shift into abundance.

Final Note:

This chapter wasn't about quitting. It was about choosing.

You didn't become a nurse just to stay tired, broke, and boxed in.

This is your chance to scrub into your next identity.

Not just nurse.

Not just dreamer.

But **nurse entrepreneur**.

Welcome to the next level.

Chapter 31: Side Hustles for Nurses – Smart or Stressful?

You're already clocking twelve-hour shifts, charting through breaks, advocating for patients, and navigating the emotional intensity of the nursing profession. So the idea of adding *more* to your plate might feel ridiculous. But for many nurses, a side hustle isn't just about making extra money—it's about creating breathing room, building long-term wealth, paying down debt faster, or even exploring passions that nursing schedules haven't allowed.

But here's the reality: not every side hustle is smart, and many can absolutely lead you to burnout if you're not careful. This chapter will help you weigh the pros and cons, explore nurse-friendly side hustle ideas, evaluate time vs. return, and most importantly, figure out whether a side hustle helps or hinders your financial health and well-being.

Why Nurses Turn to Side Hustles

- To pay down student loans faster
- To boost savings or investment contributions
- To test new skills and passions
- To build a financial cushion between shifts
- To prepare for a career pivot
- To gain flexibility in scheduling

And let's be honest—sometimes it's to feel a little more in control.

When you're constantly reacting to patient needs, policies, and last-minute shift changes, there's something empowering about running a small business or earning money on your own terms.

The Pros of Nurse Side Hustles

- **Income diversification:** If your hospital cuts hours or if you need a break from bedside care, a side hustle can soften the financial blow.
- **Skill building:** Teaching, writing, coaching, or consulting as a nurse can grow skills that become part of your long-term career path.
- **Flexibility:** Many side hustles are remote or self-paced—ideal for your shifting schedule.
- **Confidence boost:** Earning income outside of your nursing job can remind you of your value beyond the badge.

The Cons of Nurse Side Hustles

- **Burnout risk:** You're already emotionally and physically stretched. Adding more can tip you into exhaustion.
- **Time theft:** Every hour you spend side hustling is an hour you don't rest, sleep, exercise, or spend with your family.
- **Tax complications:** If you earn more than $400 from a side hustle, the IRS will expect a self-employment tax filing. Be prepared.
- **Distraction from core goals:** Side hustles can feel productive while actually pulling energy from your main job, family, or financial plan.

Rules of Thumb Before Starting a Side Hustle

1. **Know Your "Why":** Are you trying to pay off debt, build savings, pivot careers, or fund fun purchases?
2. **Set a Time Cap:** Don't let the hustle creep into your rest or recovery.
3. **Prioritize Sleep:** If your hustle eats into sleep, it's not sustainable.
4. **Run the Math:** How much do you actually earn per hour after taxes, time, and stress?

5. **Build Systems, Not Just Hours:** Choose a hustle that eventually earns you more without requiring more time.

Smart Side Hustles for Nurses (With Examples)

1. **Health and Wellness Coaching**
2. You already understand anatomy, stress, and health behavior. Earning a coaching certificate can help you monetize those skills.
3. **Freelance Writing for Medical Blogs or CE Companies**
4. Write about nursing topics for continuing education companies, blogs, or health media outlets.
5. **Per Diem and PRN Work**
6. Pick up extra shifts at a second facility—but treat it like a business. Know the pay structure, taxes, and burnout risk.
7. **Online Course Creation**
8. Develop digital courses for nursing students or new grads (e.g., NCLEX prep, time management, stress tools).
9. **Speaking or Teaching**
10. Local nursing schools, community health organizations, and virtual conferences often need experienced nurses to speak.
11. **CPR/BLS Instructor Certification**
12. Teach CPR classes in your community. Schedule them on your terms.
13. **Medical Product Reviews or Influencer Work**
14. If you have a following, reviewing scrubs, shoes, or tools could bring in affiliate income or small sponsorships.
15. **Real Estate Investing (Slow Burn Strategy)**
16. Buy a duplex, rent out half, and live in the other. Or consider REITs (real estate investment trusts) for more passive exposure.
17. **Daycare or Pet Sitting on Your Days Off**
18. Use your people and caretaking skills in a new setting.
19. **IV Hydration or Aesthetics (With Proper Certification)**
20. Some nurses earn high income from IV hydration, Botox, or wellness pop-ups—just know the legal and financial structure first.

Case Study: Nurse Leah's Side Hustle Journey

Leah was a 32-year-old med-surg nurse who loved educating new hires. She started writing short NCLEX study guides on Etsy and slowly built an audience. Over time, she launched a small website, offered tutoring sessions on weekends, and created downloadable templates for nurses in their first year.

After two years, Leah made $1,500/month consistently—and reduced her shifts to part-time so she could manage her business. She didn't do it overnight, and she made plenty of mistakes, but her hustle helped her stay excited about nursing without burning out.

Burnout Prevention Plan for Nurse Side Hustlers

- Schedule *actual* off days
- Don't monetize *every* passion
- Watch for the signs: insomnia, irritability, dreading both jobs
- Set financial targets (e.g., pay off $10,000 in loans) and take a break when you reach them
- Give yourself permission to stop or pivot

Tax + Business Reminders

- Track all income and expenses
- Use separate bank accounts
- Learn what counts as a deduction (home office, mileage, internet?)
- Save 25-30% of income for taxes
- Consider forming an LLC if your income grows

Is a Side Hustle Right for You?

Only if it:

- Aligns with your energy and values
- Doesn't destroy your physical or emotional health
- Moves you closer to a life you want

If you're doing it just to keep up with everyone else, to escape your current job without a plan, or to prove something to someone else—pause.

Sometimes the best financial move isn't *more*. It's *better*.

Final Call to Act

Make one small financial move before your next shift. Whether it's brainstorming a passion project, researching a certification, or deleting a side hustle idea that doesn't serve you anymore—move forward with purpose, not pressure.

You didn't become a nurse just to work yourself into exhaustion.

You deserve options. You deserve control. And you deserve the financial literacy to design a life that honors your calling and your capacity.

Let your money start working as hard as you do.

Let it give you margin, not just more miles.

Let it remind you: your skills are valuable—on and off the floor.

Chapter 32: Financial Red Flags in the Nursing Community

You've handled codes, disasters, shortages, and pandemic shifts without flinching. But what about that DM you got promising you $10,000/month in passive income? Or that coworker who swears she made $6K last month selling leggings and shakes? Welcome to the shadowy side of finance in the nursing community—where burnout meets bad decisions and scammers know exactly who to target.

Let's be clear: none of this chapter is about shaming. It's about shielding. Because your license, your sanity, and your bank account are worth protecting. Nurses, for all their strength, often become easy prey for predatory financial products, scams, and get-rich-quick schemes—especially when money is tight, overtime is crushing, or hope feels in short supply.

Let's break it down.

1. MLMs: Multi-Level Marketing or Mostly Losing Money?

You've probably seen the social media posts:

- "I joined this wellness company and now I work from home in my scrubs!"
- "I made $1,000 in one week without quitting my shift!"

Sounds great. But let's look deeper.

MLMs (multi-level marketing companies) promise big earnings if you sell products AND recruit others to do the same. Think essential oils, skincare, supplements, weight loss tea, or trendy activewear. But what's usually left out is this: most participants lose money.

Red flags:

- You have to pay to join.
- You're encouraged to buy inventory you don't need.
- Most of your earnings come from recruiting—not actual sales.

Nurse Scenario:

Maria, an ER nurse, joined a shake-selling MLM. She made $1,200 in 3 months—but spent $2,000 on inventory. She didn't realize her upline earned commission on her purchases, not her profits. She got out. Others aren't so lucky.

2. Payday Loans: The Ultimate Trap

You work a brutal 12, your rent's due Friday, and your kid needs new shoes. Enter the payday lender: "Borrow $500, pay us back $575 in two weeks. Easy."

What's not easy? Escaping that cycle.

APR (annual percentage rates) on payday loans can exceed 400%. That $500 can cost you thousands if you roll it over again and again.

Better options:

- Emergency fund (start with just $500)
- Credit union personal loans
- Asking for an advance from your employer (some hospitals allow it)

Action Step: Call your HR and ask if they offer earned wage access programs. Some let you access a portion of your paycheck before payday.

3. Social Media Scams: Nurses with Targets on Their Scrubs

You post a proud graduation pic with your badge. Within days:

- A "nurse investor" slides into your DMs.

- Someone offers to "flip" your cash into crypto.
- A follower shares a "government grant for nurses" link.

If it sounds too good to be true, it is.

Common scams include:

- Fake investment flips ("send me $500, I'll turn it into $2,000")
- Impersonating government or HR departments
- Posing as travel nurse recruiters to steal personal info

Never do this:

- Share your Social Security number over email or text
- Send money via CashApp, Zelle, or Venmo to someone you don't know
- Click on sketchy links promising "instant grants"

4. Nurse-Centered Guilt Tactics

Scammers know how to weaponize your kindness:

- "Help a fellow nurse out—just sign up for this financial webinar."
- "Let's support each other by joining this group investment."

They know nurses are communal, loyal, and often exhausted. They use language like "support," "sisterhood," or "nurse empowerment" to lure you in. Be cautious. Community is beautiful—but not when it's financially weaponized.

5. Fake Certifications and CEUs

Another common trap? Programs that promise:

- "Double your income as a holistic nurse in 3 weeks!"
- "Get certified online and work from anywhere!"

Before paying for any course:

- Check your state BON (Board of Nursing) to confirm recognition
- See if the CEUs are accredited by ANCC or similar bodies
- Ask: will this certification actually increase my income?

6. Sketchy Real Estate Seminars

You're burned out. You're ready to quit the floor. A Facebook ad promises:

"Learn to retire from nursing in 2 years through real estate! Attend our free weekend seminar!"

Here's what happens:

- You attend.
- You're hyped.
- They upsell you into a $10,000+ coaching program.

Real estate can be a solid long-term wealth builder—but it's not instant, and it's not free. You don't need to pay thousands to start. A basic REIT or house hacking plan is more realistic.

7. Financial Abuse in Relationships

Sometimes the red flag isn't a company—it's a partner.

- They won't let you see joint accounts.
- They discourage you from saving independently.
- They take your full paycheck and give you an "allowance."

Financial abuse is real, subtle, and painful. If this feels familiar, seek help from a counselor or domestic violence advocate who understands financial control.

8. High-Fee Retirement Plans

Many hospitals offer 403(b) retirement plans—but not all are created equal.

Warning signs:

- High administrative or fund fees (over 1%)
- An advisor who pushes you into annuities or whole life insurance inside your 403(b)

Action Step: Ask HR for the plan documents. Use sites like Brightscope.com or Morningstar to compare fees.

9. Whole Life Insurance Pitched as "Savings"

You're told:

- "This is like a retirement account AND life insurance in one."
- "You'll never lose money."
- "It's what the wealthy do."

Except most nurses don't need it. Term life is cheaper and simpler. Whole life can work in rare cases—but not when you're still paying off student loans or building an emergency fund.

10. Comparison Pressure = Costly Moves

This one's sneaky. You see another nurse:

- Driving a new car
- Taking luxury vacations
- Buying a home with granite countertops

You think: "I work just as hard. I deserve that."

But you don't see their debt, stress, or silent spouse fights.

Comparison is a thief—of joy, peace, and your long-term wealth.

What To Do Instead

- Build a scam radar: If it's urgent, secretive, or promises fast money—it's a no.
- Practice "pause and verify": Sleep on it. Ask a financially savvy friend. Run it past a licensed advisor.
- Create an antifragile budget: One that bends when needed but won't

break you. Prioritize savings, debt, and long-term goals.
- Lean into education, not hype: If someone can't explain it simply—they probably don't understand it either.

Red Flags Recap Checklist

- You're being pressured to decide now
- You have to pay upfront to participate
- Returns or income seem unrealistically high
- You're encouraged to recruit others
- There's little to no transparency
- You feel guilted, shamed, or love-bombed into saying yes
- You couldn't clearly explain the deal to a fellow nurse in less than 30 seconds

Closing Reminder

You already deal with enough pressure. Your finances shouldn't be one more thing draining you. When in doubt—pause. When pressured—walk away. When confused—ask.

You are not "behind."

You are not "missing out."

You're just building something solid.

And that's what this book—and your future—is all about.

Call to Act:

Print this chapter. Highlight anything that made your stomach drop. Bring it to your next money huddle. And if you've already been scammed or shamed—breathe. Learn. Reclaim your power. Then move forward wiser, stronger, and financially bulletproof.

Chapter 33: Estate Planning – It's Not Just for the Elderly

Let's clear something up right away: estate planning isn't just for rich people, retirees, or the elderly. It's for everyone—especially nurses. Because nurses know better than most just how unpredictable life can be.

When you work 12-hour shifts, witness trauma firsthand, and care for patients through some of the hardest moments of their lives, you don't take tomorrow for granted. So why do so many nurses still put off estate planning?

Because it sounds like something you do when you're old.

Because no one taught you what an estate plan really is.

Because it feels like something that can wait.

But here's the truth: the earlier you start, the more control you have over your finances, your health decisions, your legacy—and your peace of mind.

So let's scrub in. This chapter is your clean, steady handoff into the world of estate planning. No legalese. No guilt trips. Just a warm, honest, and empowering conversation about what it means to protect yourself, your family, and everything you've worked for.

What Is Estate Planning, Really?

Estate planning is simply the act of putting legal and financial plans in place to ensure your money, property, healthcare wishes, and family are taken care of if you become incapacitated or pass away.

It includes things like:

- **Wills**
- **Beneficiary designations**
- **Powers of attorney**
- **Healthcare directives**
- **Trusts (optional but useful)**
- **Guardianship nominations**

It also includes keeping these documents up to date. Because estate planning isn't a one-and-done situation—it evolves as your life does.

And if you're thinking, "I'm just a nurse, I don't have much to pass on," pause right there. You absolutely do. You have your income, your retirement accounts, your car, your apartment, your insurance policies, your professional identity, and—most importantly—the people you love.

That's enough to plan for.

Why Nurses Especially Need an Estate Plan

You work hard. You see life up close and personal. You might be raising a family, supporting aging parents, or carrying significant student loan debt. You may even be the primary breadwinner.

Here are a few scenarios nurses often face that make estate planning critical:

- You co-own a house with your partner but aren't legally married. What happens to your share?
- You have children and want to name a guardian.

- You want to make sure your paycheck continues supporting someone you love if something happens to you.
- You want to designate who can make decisions for you if you're in a coma or incapacitated.
- You want to avoid family drama and financial chaos if you pass unexpectedly.

The Core Elements of an Estate Plan

1. **The Will**

A will is a legal document that lays out how you want your assets distributed after your death. It also lets you name guardians for your minor children.

Without a will, state laws decide who gets what. And it's not always who you would have chosen.

Things to include:

- Who inherits your home, car, savings, retirement accounts
- Who should care for your children
- Who will be your executor (the person who carries out your wishes)

2. **Beneficiary Designations**

Your 403(b), 401(k), life insurance policies, and some bank accounts let you name a beneficiary. That means the money bypasses probate and goes directly to the person you named.

This is huge. A lot of people do this once and forget it. If you got divorced, remarried, or had a child—you need to update your beneficiaries.

Don't let your ex get your retirement account because you forgot to make a change.

3. **Durable Power of Attorney**

This document gives someone legal power to handle your financial matters if you can't.

Imagine being in a car accident and unable to pay your bills, access your bank accounts, or sign tax documents. If no one has legal authority to act on your behalf, it can get messy fast.

Your power of attorney can:

- Pay your rent or mortgage
- Access your accounts to cover your bills
- File your taxes
- Talk to your financial advisor

Choose someone you deeply trust.

4. **Healthcare Power of Attorney & Directive**

Also called an advance directive or living will, this document spells out what kind of medical care you want if you can't speak for yourself.

Do you want to be on life support? What about a feeding tube? CPR?

And who gets to make decisions if you're unconscious?

You, as a nurse, have likely seen the chaos and pain families go through when this isn't in place. Spare your loved ones that stress.

Optional But Powerful: Trusts

If you have more complex financial needs—multiple properties, a special needs child, or blended family dynamics—a trust can give you more control over your assets and help avoid probate.

There are different types (revocable, irrevocable, special needs, etc.), but they all serve to:

- Keep your estate private
- Avoid probate
- Protect minor or financially irresponsible heirs
- Provide for disabled dependents without disqualifying them from benefits

The Financial Side of Estate Planning

This isn't just about death. It's about life.

It's about making sure your financial systems still run if you're out of commission.

Ask yourself:

- Who will handle your mortgage if you're in the ICU for a month?
- What happens to your paycheck, savings, and retirement accounts if you die?
- Who gets your car, jewelry, pets, and medical equipment?

Think about the debts you carry—student loans, credit cards, car notes. Some will be discharged at death. Some won't. Federal student loans usually disappear. Private ones might not.

Estate planning is how you prepare your loved ones for what comes next, whether that's recovery or the reading of your will.

Real-Life Scenarios

Scenario 1: The Single Nurse with a Sibling

Tina is 29. She rents a studio apartment, has a 403(b) through work, and drives a used car. Her only living family is her younger brother. She passes away unexpectedly in a crash.

She has no will, no named beneficiaries, and no power of attorney documents.

Her bank account is frozen. Her brother can't access her car or clean out her apartment. Her 403(b) goes to probate. Everything becomes a drawn-out, painful process.

With an estate plan, Tina could have:

- Named her brother as beneficiary on her 403(b)
- Given him durable power of attorney to manage her finances if she

were hospitalized

- Signed a simple will to state her wishes

Scenario 2: Married Nurse with Kids

James is 43, married with two children. He and his wife both work full-time. He handles their finances. When he collapses from a brain aneurysm and is hospitalized, his wife can't access their joint savings account or 403(b).

Without a durable power of attorney, she's blocked from handling bills, filing insurance, or even talking to the mortgage company.

With the right documents in place, James would have empowered his wife to manage their household seamlessly while he was recovering.

Common Misconceptions

1. I don't own enough to need a will.

Everyone owns something. A bank account. A car. Furniture. A favorite pair of sneakers. If you don't decide who gets it, the state will.

2. My spouse will automatically get everything.

Not necessarily. State laws vary. And without beneficiary designations, probate can be long and expensive.

3. I'm too young for estate planning.

If you're old enough to work, you're old enough to make a will.

How to Start

1. **Make a list of your assets.**
2. Bank accounts, retirement plans, vehicles, real estate, valuables.
3. **Review your beneficiaries.**
4. Go through every retirement account, life insurance policy, and bank account. Update them.
5. **Meet with an estate planning attorney.**
6. Even a 1-hour session can get your documents started.

7. **Create your will.**
8. You can use a lawyer or an online service—but make sure it's legal in your state.
9. **Complete powers of attorney and healthcare directives.**
10. Don't wait. You can revise later if needed.
11. **Tell someone where the documents are.**
12. Store them securely, but let a trusted person know where they are.

Action Steps

- Schedule a call with an estate planning attorney within the next month.
- Check all your beneficiary designations this week.
- Pick one day next week for a "nurse money huddle" to talk through your wishes with your partner or family.
- Set a calendar reminder to review your estate documents every January.
- Consider adding a letter of intent with your will—a personal note to your loved ones about how you want them to use your assets.

Final Word

Estate planning isn't about preparing for death. It's about protecting life—the life you built, the people you love, and the legacy you want to leave behind.

You already advocate for patients every day. Now it's time to advocate for yourself.

Don't wait until retirement. Don't wait until a diagnosis. Don't wait for the "right time."

Plan today, so you can live tomorrow with peace of mind.

Because you didn't become a nurse just to run on empty.

You became one to make things better—starting with yourself.

Call to Act:

Make one financial move before your next shift. Just one. And do another next week.

The only thing worse than working yourself sick is staying stuck when you've got the skills, strength, and smarts to shift into abundance.

Let your estate plan be your backup nurse—always there, ready to act when you can't.

You've got this.

Chapter 34: Teaching Your Kids About Money as a Nurse

Modeling Financial Literacy at Home

Let's be honest. As a nurse, you're probably used to solving everyone else's problems before your own. You help patients navigate life-threatening diagnoses, educate families under stress, and work back-to-back shifts with little thanks. But when it comes to teaching your own children about money? That can feel like a different kind of challenge. One that didn't come with a clinical handbook or CEU credit.

Here's the good news: you don't need to be a certified financial planner to model financial wellness for your kids. You just need to start where you are.

This chapter is about equipping your children with the financial knowledge you never got—and doing it in a way that works for your real life. Because the truth is, our kids are already watching. Every time you swipe your badge, pack a lunch instead of DoorDashing, or pay off a credit card, you're sending messages. The question is: what do you want those messages to be?

Why This Chapter Matters

Financial literacy isn't a one-time lesson. It's a culture. A lifestyle. A series of intentional moments that build the next generation of confident, capable, and self-aware adults. And as a nurse, you have a front-row seat to what can happen when people reach adulthood without these skills.

Too many nurses were never taught how to:

- Budget their first paycheck
- Understand interest rates
- Use credit responsibly
- Save for a rainy day
- Or talk about money without shame

So they learned by trial, error, and emergency.

Let's make sure your kids don't have to.

Start Early, Talk Often

Kids as young as 3 can start learning the value of money. But the conversation evolves. What you say to your kindergartener isn't what you say to your teenager. And that's okay. The goal is *ongoing exposure.*

Preschool (Ages 3–5):

- Let them play with pretend money.
- Give them small choices ("You can get this $5 toy or save for a $10 one next week.")
- Use a clear jar for saving—so they *see* money growing.

Elementary (Ages 6–11):

- Introduce chores with small allowances.
- Teach needs vs. wants ("Groceries are needs. That new video game? A want.")
- Have them save for a goal—a toy, outing, or book.

Middle School (Ages 12–14):

- Open a youth savings account.
- Let them earn money from neighbors (dog walking, babysitting, yard work).
- Start basic conversations about debit vs. credit, interest, and compound growth.

High School (Ages 15–18):

- Help them create their first budget.
- Consider a beginner credit card with you as a co-signer (teach credit score impact).
- Teach them to track expenses—from gas to fast food.
- Talk about student loans. Early and often.

Money Scripts & Mindsets: Break the Cycle

Every family has unspoken money beliefs. Maybe your parents never talked about money. Or maybe they constantly fought about it. Maybe they taught you that money was evil, greedy, or never enough.

Now, ask yourself: what beliefs are you passing on?

Are your kids hearing:

- "We're broke."
- "We can't afford anything nice."
- "Money doesn't grow on trees."

Or are they hearing:

- "We're prioritizing our savings right now."
- "Let's talk about the budget before we buy."
- "Let's set a savings goal together."

One creates fear. The other creates curiosity and empowerment.

Modeling the Right Moves

You can teach financial literacy by doing financial literacy. Let them *see* you:

- Pay bills on time
- Save for a vacation
- Say "no" to impulse purchases

- Set aside money for emergencies
- Talk calmly with your partner about money

It doesn't mean you need to have it all figured out. In fact, it's powerful to say, "I'm learning this too."

Smart Tools for Nurse Families

Use tech to your advantage. Apps like:

- **Greenlight** or **GoHenry**: Kids' debit cards that teach spending, saving, and giving.
- **YNAB (You Need A Budget)**: Helps older kids learn to budget their paycheck.
- **Acorns**: For teenagers to start investing with just a few dollars.

College Conversations

If your kids are college-bound, be real about student loans. Don't let the first time they hear "interest rate" be at their loan exit interview.

Things to cover:

- The total cost of attendance (not just tuition)
- Scholarships and grants
- Work-study options
- Borrowing only what they *need*
- Career ROI (Will the degree pay off financially?)

Allowance vs. Earning Model

Should you give your kids an allowance? Should they earn every dollar? There's no universal answer. But here are two effective models:

1. **The Commission Model**: Pay kids for chores and extra help. They earn their money, just like a job.
2. **The Hybrid Model**: Basic allowance for being part of the family. Extra pay for extra work.

Either way, teach them to split money into **spend**, **save**, and **give**.

Financial Pitfalls to Watch For

Even well-meaning parents can accidentally create poor habits:

- Bailing kids out every time they overspend
- Telling them to save but not letting them touch their savings
- Never letting them manage their own money
- Not modeling positive behavior (Do as I say, not as I do?)

Final Thoughts

Your nursing skills are saving lives. Your financial skills can build them.

You don't need a perfect budget, perfect credit score, or perfect life to teach your kids about money. You just need intention.

You show up for your shifts. Now show up for their financial future.

Start small. Stay consistent. Build wealth across generations.

Call to Act:

Have a money conversation with your child this week. Doesn't matter how old they are. Doesn't matter how messy your finances feel. Just start.

Because teaching your kids about money isn't just another parenting task. It's a legacy.

And you, nurse, are more than qualified to lead it.

Chapter 35: Taxes for Nurses – What to Know About Deductions and Filing

Let's talk taxes. Not in the dry, number-crunching, eyes-glazing-over kind of way. We're going to talk about taxes in a way that makes sense for *you* — a nurse who might work 12s, pick up overtime, float between units, or maybe travel to another state for a 13-week contract. Whether you're a floor nurse, an ICU warrior, a travel nurse on assignment, or doing part-time shifts while raising a family, the tax code doesn't pause for shift change. And not understanding it? That can cost you thousands.

So let's break it all down together.

Why Nurses Need to Know the Basics

As a nurse, your pay might include:

- Base pay
- Shift differentials (night/weekend/holiday)
- Overtime
- Per diem or PRN pay
- Travel stipends (housing, meals, mileage)
- Bonuses (sign-on, referral, retention)
- Contractor income (if you do consulting or pick up 1099 gigs)

Each of these is taxed *differently* — and understanding what goes where is the first step to keeping more of what you earn.

What You Need to File as a Nurse

You'll need:

- W-2s from any hospitals or health systems where you worked
- 1099s if you worked as a contractor or consultant (like teaching a CPR class or helping a clinic on the side)
- 1098-E if you're paying student loan interest
- Receipts or logs for tax-deductible expenses (more on that soon)
- Bank or brokerage statements if you had investment income
- HSA or FSA contribution forms if you used those accounts

Common Nurse Tax Deductions

Let's talk about what you *can* deduct — and what's just a myth.

1. **Scrubs and Uniforms?**

- *Maybe.* If your employer requires a specific uniform that can't be worn outside of work (like logo-branded scrubs), and you *don't* get reimbursed, that may be deductible. But if you wear generic scrubs you bought yourself, and your hospital doesn't have a strict policy, the IRS might not see that as deductible.

1. **Licensing and Continuing Education**

- These can often be written off if you're required to maintain licensure or certification to keep your job.
- Includes: state nursing licenses, BLS/ACLS/PALS renewal courses, CEUs, and sometimes even tuition for advanced degrees (if it qualifies as work-related).

1. **Union Dues or Professional Association Memberships**

- If you pay to be part of a nursing union or a group like the ANA, that may be deductible.

1. **Travel Nurse Expenses**

- Housing stipends and meal per diems can be tax-free if you qualify for a "tax home."
- Travel between contracts, temporary housing, and mileage may be partially deductible.
- Keep *meticulous records* — this is one area where the IRS loves to challenge deductions.

1. **Home Office (For 1099 Nurses or Side Hustlers)**

- If you work as an independent nurse contractor or run a health coaching business, a portion of your home expenses (rent, utilities, internet) could be deductible *if* you have a designated workspace.

Understanding Shift Differential and Overtime Taxes

Shift differential and overtime pay get taxed the same as your base pay. But here's what trips people up:

- If you worked a lot of OT during the holidays, you might see a much higher gross paycheck — and a *lot* more taken out in taxes.
- Why? Because payroll systems withhold based on what they *think* your annual salary is. If you made $3,000 one week, the system might assume you're earning $156,000/year and withhold taxes accordingly.
- This might mean you *overpay* taxes through the year, and then get a refund when you file. Or, it might mean you *underpay* if you have a side hustle or don't withhold enough on bonuses.

What If You're a Travel Nurse?

Travel nursing has unique tax perks *and* pitfalls.

- **Tax-Free Stipends:** If you maintain a tax home, stipends for housing, meals, and incidental expenses are often tax-free. This can save you thousands.
- **Double Housing Rules:** You need to prove that you duplicate expenses to maintain your tax home. Renting an apartment in your home city? Keep paying some amount monthly. Staying with a friend for free? That may disqualify your stipends from being tax-free.
- **State Taxes:** You may owe income taxes in multiple states if you work in several states during the year. This gets complicated fast, so work with a tax pro who understands travel nursing.

Tax Filing Tips for Nurses

1. **File Early (Especially If You Move Often)**

- Identity theft is a growing problem in the medical field. File before a scammer tries to file using your info.

1. **Consider a Tax Pro If You're a Travel or 1099 Nurse**

- A CPA who understands the complexities of nurse income can help you avoid audits and maximize deductions.

1. **Adjust Your Withholding if You Owe Every Year**

- If you keep getting hit with surprise tax bills, update your W-4 form with your employer to have more tax withheld.

1. **Use a Secure Portal for Documents**

- Whether you work with a CPA or file yourself, use a secure portal to upload your sensitive tax docs.

Side Hustles and Nurse Income Streams

If you run a side hustle as a nurse — think CPR instructor, health coaching, content creation, or contract work — you're now a *business owner*. Even if you don't feel like one.

That means:

- You may get a 1099-NEC instead of a W-2
- You're responsible for self-employment taxes
- You can deduct business expenses (supplies, marketing, mileage)
- You might qualify for a SEP IRA or Solo 401(k) to save for retirement *and* reduce taxes

Common Tax Mistakes Nurses Make

- **Not tracking CEU or license costs**
- **Forgetting to update address with employers (missed W-2s = filing late)**
- **Not withholding enough tax on bonuses or extra shifts**
- **Thinking tax software will catch everything (it won't)**

Real Life Nurse Tax Story: "I Got a $7,000 Bill I Wasn't Expecting"

A nurse named Amanda picked up several travel contracts in 2023. She also made some decent money selling wellness products on the side. When tax season came, she thought she was in the clear. But because she got multiple 1099s and didn't track her business expenses, she ended up owing over $7,000 in federal taxes.

She was devastated. But she learned:

- To save 25-30% of all 1099 income for taxes
- To work with a tax pro who knew the nurse hustle
- To keep receipts, mileage logs, and a separate business account

Now, Amanda's ahead of the game. You can be too.

Taxes Are a Tool — Not Just a Burden

Taxes can feel overwhelming. But once you understand the system, you can start using it to your advantage.

- Max out your HSA and reduce your taxable income
- Contribute to your 403(b) or IRA and plan for retirement
- Deduct professional expenses and keep more of your paycheck

The better you get at taxes, the more control you'll feel over your financial future.

Call to Action:

Make one money move before your next shift:

- Check your W-4 withholding
- Start a tax deduction folder
- Book a 30-minute call with a CPA
- Open a Roth IRA and start with $50

Then? Do another next week.

Nursing is tough. But you do hard things every day. Don't let taxes be the thing that steals your peace.

You've got this.

Final Note:

You didn't become a nurse to get buried under financial stress. You became a nurse to help people. This is about helping *yourself*. Knowing how the tax system works helps you work the system — instead of it working *you*.

Let this chapter be your shift toward clarity, calm, and control. Let's file smarter, save more, and step into abundance together.

Chapter 36: Investing in Yourself – Certifications, Coaching, and Education

Let's start here: You already know what it feels like to invest in other people. You pour into patients on every shift. You teach new hires how to chart faster, troubleshoot ventilators, or hold space for a grieving family. You are an investor in human dignity every single day.

But what does it look like to invest in *yourself*? What does it mean to use money, time, and energy to grow your own skillset, confidence, and earning power?

Let's talk about that.

This chapter isn't about burning yourself out with one more obligation. It's about choosing smart, high-leverage ways to grow. It's about understanding the return on investment (ROI) of that new certification, degree, or course. It's about knowing how to run the numbers, weigh the opportunity cost, and make a decision you can live with—financially and personally.

Because sometimes a $2,000 certification is worth every penny.

And sometimes it's just a fancy piece of paper gathering dust in your closet.

The Mindset Shift: Education As an Asset

Too often we treat education like a cost instead of an asset. But smart education—the kind that increases your income or improves your quality of life—is one of the most powerful investments you can make.

Let's say you pay $5,000 out of pocket for a nurse practitioner prep course that helps you pass boards on your first try and land a $25,000 salary bump.

That's a 400% return on investment in the first year alone.

Or let's say you pay $3,000 to work with a career coach who helps you negotiate better hours, find a more supportive employer, or pivot specialties without starting over. Maybe you don't increase your salary immediately, but you save your energy, time, and health—which leads to longevity in the profession and fewer financial missteps from burnout.

See the pattern?

The right investments in yourself multiply.

Types of Investments Nurses Make in Themselves

Let's break down some common categories:

1. **Certifications**: ACLS, PALS, CCRN, CEN, CNOR, etc.
2. **Advanced Degrees**: BSN, MSN, DNP, CRNA, NP, CNM, etc.
3. **Continuing Education Units (CEUs)**
4. **Career Coaching or Mentorship**
5. **Public Speaking, Leadership, or Management Courses**
6. **Nursing Conferences and Networking Events**
7. **Side Business Education** (e.g. health coaching, wellness products)
8. **Technology/EMR Certifications**
9. **Financial Literacy and Money Coaching**
10. **Mental Health and Resilience Training**

Each comes with different price tags, time commitments, and potential payoffs. Your job is to match the *right* investment to your *current* season of life.

ROI: How to Evaluate Return on Investment for Nurses

Before you swipe your credit card or apply for that new program, ask:

- Will this increase my income in the next 1–3 years?
- Will this reduce my burnout or improve my work/life balance?
- Can I use this to pivot into a more stable or rewarding specialty?
- How long will it take to break even on the cost?
- What is the total financial investment (tuition, time off work, travel,

supplies)?

And this big one:

- Am I doing this out of pressure and panic—or strategy and empowerment?

Investments made out of fear rarely pay off. Investments made with a plan usually do.

Real-Life Nurse Scenarios

- *Alex, 27, ICU RN*: Paid $325 for CCRN prep, passed on first try, negotiated a $2/hr raise = +$4,000/year
- *Maria, 41, Med-Surg*: Enrolled in an MSN leadership program, took out a $30,000 loan, but pivoted into a salaried nurse educator job with no more night shifts and better benefits.
- *Sean, 33, Travel RN*: Paid $1,800 to attend a national nursing conference, made a contact who later helped him land a high-paying crisis response contract.

Red Flags and When to Say No

Not every program is worth your time or money. Watch out for:

- Overpriced programs promising huge income with no experience
- Predatory schools or for-profit colleges
- Unaccredited certifications that no employer values
- Vague promises without clear curriculum or support
- MLMs dressed up as "certifications"

Remember: The goal is *freedom*, not more financial entanglement.

Creative and Low-Cost Alternatives

- Free webinars hosted by reputable associations

- CEUs provided through your employer or union
- Podcasts, YouTube, and open-access journals
- Online courses on Coursera, Udemy, or Khan Academy
- Local nurse mentor groups or Facebook communities

Action Steps

1. Make a list of certifications or degrees that interest you
2. Research average salary differences before and after earning them
3. Call or email nurses who've done it and ask if it was worth it
4. Ask HR or management about tuition reimbursement or professional development funds
5. Calculate how long it would take to break even based on your post-certification income
6. Make a short list: One investment you could make this year, one in the next 3 years

Final Word

Investing in yourself is a sign of self-respect. It says, "I believe in my future, my capacity, and my worth."

But don't mistake hustle for progress. Not every degree or certification will move the needle.

Smart investments take into account your time, your energy, your values, and your real-life goals. Don't just chase titles. Build a career—and a financial future—that fits who you are and where you want to go.

Let that be your North Star.

Now take one small step before your next shift.

You've got this.

And your future self will thank you for it.

Part V: Mid-Career Moves and Nurse Leadership – Synopsis

By the time nurses reach their 30s, 40s, and 50s, many have already weathered years of 12-hour shifts, career pivots, and personal sacrifices. This phase isn't about survival anymore—it's about strategy. *Part V: Mid-Career Moves and Nurse Leadership* helps nurses move from burnout to building, from reactive to proactive, and from doing the work to directing their wealth.

This section is for the seasoned ICU nurse wondering how to make her income last, the floor nurse exploring a leadership or advanced practice role, and the nurse manager who's mentoring younger staff while secretly questioning their own financial plan. Whether you're thinking about returning to school, running your unit more efficiently, preparing for your kids' college tuition, or just wanting a more sustainable work-life balance—this section meets you exactly where you are.

We'll explore how to:

- Evaluate the ROI of certifications, graduate degrees, and career transitions
- Understand pensions, vesting schedules, and the real value of long-term benefits
- Manage money in dual-income healthcare households (or as the breadwinner)
- Decide whether to pursue nurse leadership, education, or entrepreneur-

ship

- Protect your time, energy, and wealth as your responsibilities grow
- Use your mid-career earnings window to build serious financial momentum
- Become a mentor and model for younger nurses—without losing yourself in the process

You've spent years giving. Now it's time to make sure that what you're building actually works for *you*. Part V helps you leverage your wisdom, stabilize your financial foundation, and take ownership of your next chapter—not just in your career, but in your whole life.

This isn't just about climbing the clinical ladder. It's about using your mid-career power to step into purpose, impact, and financial peace.

Chapter 37: Nurse Managers, Educators, and Leaders – What Changes Financially?

You didn't move into nurse leadership for the glory. You did it for the impact. Maybe you were tired of clocking in and out without having a say. Maybe you saw broken systems and thought, *"I could fix that."* Maybe you wanted a new challenge—something to stretch your skills beyond the bedside.

But here's what no one tells you when you step into management, education, or leadership roles:

Your badge changes.

Your stress changes.

Your money changes.

And not always in the ways you expect.

This chapter is your honest, no-fluff guide to understanding the financial realities of becoming a nurse manager, unit director, clinical educator, or nurse executive. Because climbing the career ladder in nursing isn't just about promotions. It's about understanding trade-offs, recalibrating your wealth-building plan, and making sure that leadership is lifting your life—not draining it.

1. The Myth of "More Money, Less Worry"

Leadership roles in nursing often come with a higher salary on paper. But a bigger paycheck doesn't automatically translate into financial ease. You may earn more, but you may also:

- Lose shift differentials (nights, weekends, holidays)
- Be ineligible for overtime pay (especially if salaried)
- Have less predictable hours (emails, meetings, crises outside of your shift)
- Face higher tax liability if you cross into a new bracket

Real-Life Example:

Jessica, an experienced ER nurse, stepped into a nurse manager role thinking the $20K pay increase would finally give her breathing room. But without her night shift differential and with extra childcare needs due to longer hours, she found herself more stressed financially—not less.

Key Takeaway:

Before accepting a promotion, compare your new *net* pay—after taxes, lost differentials, and any extra expenses like commuting, childcare, or work attire. Then decide if the role aligns with your financial goals **and** your life.

2. Salary vs. Hourly Pay: Know What You're Trading

When you go from hourly to salaried, you trade time for responsibility. This can be empowering—or exhausting.

Hourly Roles:

- You're paid for your time
- Overtime = more money
- Easy to track earnings

Salaried Roles:

- You're paid for your role—not your hours
- Overtime may not be paid
- More meetings, projects, and "after-hours" demands

If your salaried job expects 50-60 hours a week, that "raise" might actually be a pay *cut* on an hourly basis.

Action Step:

Do the math. Divide your annual salary by the real number of hours you expect to work weekly. Then compare that hourly rate to your previous role. Numbers don't lie—even if your title gets fancier.

3. Retirement Contributions May Change

Many leadership roles include access to additional retirement perks:

- 401(a) contributions (employer-funded)
- Higher match percentages
- Eligibility for profit-sharing or bonuses

But—this only matters if you actually *contribute.* As your pay increases, bump your contributions to 403(b), 401(k), or 457(b) plans to match. Aim to save at least 15-20% of your gross income for retirement.

Pro Tip:

If your employer matches 5% of your salary and your new salary is $90,000, that's $4,500 a year. But if you don't contribute, you don't get the match. That's like refusing free money.

4. Benefits That Become Bigger Deals

With a leadership role, revisit:

- **Disability insurance** – You're paid more now. Protect that income.
- **Life insurance** – Consider increasing coverage, especially if others depend on you.
- **Health savings** – Max out HSAs or FSAs to manage rising healthcare costs.

Also check your eligibility for:

- Tuition reimbursement (if pursuing DNP, EdD, MBA)
- Leadership development stipends or conferences
- Sabbaticals or professional leave

5. Taxes: New Brackets, New Responsibilities

Higher income can bump you into new tax brackets. That's not a bad thing—it just means part of your income is taxed at a higher rate.

Watch for:

- Higher federal withholding
- Loss of some tax credits
- The need to pay estimated taxes (especially if earning bonuses or consulting)

Action Step:

Meet with a CPA or tax advisor the same year you step into a leadership role. Don't wait until April to discover a surprise bill.

6. Student Loans: Can You Pay More? Should You?

If leadership boosts your income, reassess your student loan strategy.

- Should you switch from income-driven repayment to aggressive payoff?
- Will your higher salary disqualify you from forgiveness programs?
- Can you refinance at a lower rate?

Warning:

Leaving a nonprofit hospital to become a higher-paid educator at a for-profit institution may disqualify you from PSLF (Public Service Loan Forgiveness).

Action Step:

Call your loan servicer and explore new payment options that reflect your new salary and goals.

7. Time Is Now Money (More Than Ever)

Leadership eats up time in ways you don't expect:

- Evening phone calls
- Email management on days off

- Staff coverage during call-outs
- Preparing for meetings on weekends

Cost of Leadership Time:

You may now *pay* others to free up your time:

- House cleaning
- Meal prep
- Babysitting or pet care

That's okay. In fact, it can be wise. Just build it into your budget.

Empowering Reminder:

Delegating tasks isn't laziness. It's leadership. Protect your bandwidth.

8. Educators and Faculty Roles: Passion vs. Pay

If you move into nursing education—whether clinical, academic, or administrative—you may take a pay cut compared to bedside or management roles.

Why Nurses Still Choose It:

- Love for mentoring
- Better work-life balance
- Burnout from bedside or politics
- Desire to shape future nurses

But Financially, Be Ready For:

- Lower base salaries
- Fewer bonuses or differentials
- Tenure tracks that take time

Tip:

If you move into education, plan for additional income streams:

- Speaking gigs
- NCLEX tutoring
- Adjunct faculty work
- Publishing or consulting

9. Nurse Executives – Big Title, Big Pay, Big Pressure

Chief Nursing Officers (CNOs) and Directors of Nursing often earn six figures—but those roles come with:

- Budget responsibility
- Union negotiations
- Legal exposure
- Teamwide morale issues

If you pursue an executive path:

- Build an emergency fund with 6-12 months of expenses
- Consider an executive coach
- Protect yourself with personal umbrella liability insurance
- Diversify your income and skills—so you're never stuck

10. You're Now the Mentor. Model Financial Wellness.

One of the greatest gifts of leadership is *influence*. Use your role to:

- Normalize financial conversations among staff
- Teach the power of saving early
- Recommend resources and financial advisors
- Break generational silence about money

You might be the first person your staff sees practicing:

- Weekly money check-ins
- Saying no to burnout-inducing shifts

- Planning for retirement before 65

Be the leader who leaves not just a legacy of policies—but one of peace, empowerment, and financial dignity.

End of Chapter Call to Act:

Make one financial move before your next shift. Just one.

- Review your new paycheck and match it to your budget.
- Increase your retirement contributions by 1%.
- Book a meeting with HR to clarify your benefits.
- Research financial advisors who understand nurses.

And do another next week.

The only thing worse than working yourself sick is staying stuck when you've got the skills, strength, and smarts to shift into abundance.

Final Note:

This isn't just about your salary, your benefits, or your badge.

It's about dignity.

It's about freedom.

It's about creating the financial lift to say *no* to burnout—and *yes* to rest, legacy, and security.

You didn't become a nurse leader just to run on empty.

You became one to leave something better behind. Now make sure that includes your financial life, too.

Chapter 38: Should You Go Back to School Again? — Cost-Benefit of DNP, MBA, or Education-Focused Degrees

Let's have a real conversation, You're thinking about going back to school—again. Maybe it's for the DNP. Maybe an MBA. Maybe you want to teach the next generation of nurses or shift into leadership. But you're also staring down student loans, tired feet, 12-hour shifts, and the voice in your head whispering, "Can I really do this again?"

This chapter is for the ambitious nurse. The curious nurse. The burned-out but still-believes-in-the-mission nurse. It's also for the skeptical one, wondering if another degree is just a flashy nameplate or a real ticket to wealth, stability, and freedom.

So let's break it down. Dollars. Time. Lifestyle. Return on investment. Real-world scenarios. And your heart, because this isn't just about tuition. It's about your energy, your calling, and your future.

The Degrees on the Table

Let's clarify what we're talking about.

- **DNP (Doctor of Nursing Practice)**: A terminal clinical practice degree. Common for advanced practice nurses and leadership roles.
- **MBA (Master of Business Administration)**: For nurses heading into administration, entrepreneurship, or health system management.

- **MSN in Education**: For the nurse educator route—professors, clinical instructors, or simulation lab specialists.
- **Post-Master's Certificates**: Often used to pivot specialties or roles.

These aren't easy credentials. They require time, money, and emotional bandwidth. So let's dive into the factors that actually matter.

Section 1: What's the Financial Cost?

Tuition Breakdown:

- **DNP**: $30,000 to $90,000 depending on the program.
- **MBA**: $25,000 to $100,000 depending on part-time, online, or executive formats.
- **MSN (Education track)**: $20,000 to $60,000.

That's just tuition. Add books, lost work hours, childcare, and stress-related Thai food.

How to Lower the Cost:

- Employer tuition reimbursement
- Scholarships for underrepresented nurses or second-career students
- Public Service Loan Forgiveness if you stay in nonprofit systems
- Tax deductions for work-related education

Questions to Ask Yourself:

- Do I have student loans already?
- Will I need to reduce hours or quit work?
- What is my time worth?
- Will my salary increase immediately, eventually, or not at all?

Section 2: What's the Payoff?

Let's look at average salaries:

- **RN (BSN)**: $75,000–90,000
- **Nurse Practitioner**: $100,000–115,000
- **DNP in leadership**: $115,000–130,000
- **Nurse Educator**: $65,000–85,000 (adjunct or academic faculty)
- **Nurse with MBA (Director/Executive roles)**: $110,000 to $180,000+

Here's the catch: just getting the degree doesn't guarantee the job. It opens the door. You still have to walk through it—network, apply, get hired, and often relocate or accept more responsibility.

That's why we measure ROI not just in salary but in:

- Flexibility
- Schedule control
- Work-life balance
- Career fulfillment
- Professional longevity

Section 3: Pros and Cons Breakdown

DNP

- Pros: Clinical autonomy, ability to lead, impact systems.
- Cons: High cost, not always linked to a salary bump, long time to completion.

MBA

- Pros: Broad options—business, entrepreneurship, healthcare admin.

- Cons: Can be expensive and not nursing-specific; requires translating skills.

MSN (Education)

- Pros: Lower cost, passion-driven, high need in academia.
- Cons: Lower pay, often adjunct/part-time roles, burnout from dual teaching and clinical loads.

Section 4: Real-Life Scenarios

Alicia, 29, ICU RN: Wants more control, less night shift. Chooses DNP-FNP track with tuition reimbursement. Graduates with $25K in loans but doubles her autonomy. Now works in an NP-run urgent care with full control of her schedule.

Marcus, 42, Charge Nurse: Tired of floor politics. Gets an MBA with a healthcare emphasis. Lands a director of nursing ops role in a system clinic. Salary jumps from $98K to $150K. Time now filled with spreadsheets, but he loves it.

Teresa, 51, NICU Nurse: Wants to teach. Completes an MSN in education part-time. Adjuncts two nights a week while working per diem. Loves mentoring the next generation and slowly building a second career.

Section 5: What Do You Want Your Life to Feel Like?

Seriously. Stop here.

Do you want to:

- Lead?
- Educate?
- Change systems?
- Work less?
- Make more?

- Start your own practice?

Education should move you toward that feeling—not just a fancy title. Ask what success looks like on a random Tuesday. Then ask if this degree brings you closer to that version of yourself.

Section 6: Hidden Costs No One Talks About

- **Clinical hours and preceptorship stress**
- **Missed family time or burnout from juggling both roles**
- **Licensing delays and credentialing hoops**
- **Emotional debt**: Feeling "behind" peers, guilt about taking on more loans

Also: many programs expect unpaid internships or capstone projects. These aren't free.

Section 7: The Case for Waiting (or Not Going at All)

You don't *have* to go back to school to:

- Make more money
- Feel fulfilled
- Be respected
- Change your schedule

You can also:

- Start a consulting side hustle
- Move into education or case management without a new degree
- Invest in coaching or certifications for less than $2K

Sometimes the smartest move is learning on the job and leveling up through experience.

Section 8: If You Decide to Go Back

Your Financial Checklist:

- Get a tuition reimbursement agreement in writing
- Estimate full cost of attendance (COA)
- Apply for scholarships (start with nursing orgs and state funding)
- Compare loan terms and forgiveness eligibility
- Budget monthly for childcare, gas, study materials, lost shifts
- Build a 3-month emergency fund BEFORE school starts

Action Steps:

- Interview 3 nurses who finished the degree you're considering
- Ask your current employer how many people in that role have the degree
- Try shadowing someone with that title for a week
- Explore ROI calculators online for nurse degrees

Section 9: When It's Absolutely Worth It

You should absolutely consider going back to school if:

- You need it to practice (NP, CRNA)
- Your job requires it for promotion
- You feel a deep call to teach, lead, or innovate
- You've researched the financial impact and can pay without drowning

Final Thoughts

Don't confuse motion with meaning.

Another degree might be your path to freedom. Or it might be an expensive detour if you're running from burnout or pressure.

You already have value. You already have skills.

A degree should *amplify* what you bring to the table—not validate it.

Ask:

- Is this degree a key that unlocks a locked door?
- Or is it just a shinier key to a door that was already open?

Call to Act:

Make one move this week:

- Reach out to a DNP, MBA, or MSN you respect and ask, "Was it worth it?"
- Run the numbers. Get real with the cost.
- Write your 3-year life vision.

And then ask:

Does this degree get me there? Or do I just need better boundaries and a raise?

You're not behind.

You're a nurse with options.

And that's the most powerful degree of all.

Chapter 39: Financial Planning for Dual-Nurse Households

It might sound like a dream team: two nurses in one household, both bringing in stable paychecks, often with strong benefits. But if you've ever tried to coordinate shift schedules, juggle retirement plans from two different hospital systems, and figure out who's got the better health insurance plan, you know the reality is a little more complex.

This chapter is for every couple navigating life as a dual-nurse household. Whether you're just moving in together, newly married, or deep in the trenches of mortgage payments and college planning for your kids, we're going to talk about how to maximize your financial lives without maxing out your stress levels.

Let's walk through what changes when there are two scrubs in the laundry basket and two incomes in the household—and how you can build wealth, set boundaries, and create a strong financial future together.

The Blessing and Burden of Two Nursing Incomes

When both partners are nurses, it can feel like a built-in financial buffer. You know each other's grind. You both understand shift work, burnout, the importance of benefits. But without a shared financial game plan, two incomes can disappear just as fast as one.

Let's look at why dual-income households (especially in nursing) sometimes feel financially squeezed, and how to flip that script.

Challenge #1: Lifestyle Creep

Two full-time nursing incomes can bring in $120K to $200K+ annually depending on roles and regions. But more income often leads to more spending—without more saving.

Fix It: Commit to living on one income and saving the second. Or set a cap on lifestyle upgrades (car payments, vacations) until savings targets are hit. This creates breathing room in your budget.

Challenge #2: Shift Misalignment = Childcare Mayhem

Different units. Different hospitals. Different shifts. This logistical dance can lead to last-minute babysitting costs or fatigue-fueled overspending.

Fix It: Map out your overlapping shifts and plan childcare with military-level precision. Consider a shared online calendar. Batch-cook meals. Automate bills. Eliminate decision fatigue.

Challenge #3: Separate vs. Shared Accounts

Some couples merge everything. Others keep it all separate. Most land somewhere in between.

Fix It: Agree on a system: yours, mine, ours. The goal isn't control—it's clarity. Decide what expenses are joint, how savings are handled, and how to navigate if one nurse goes part-time or back to school.

Challenge #4: Too Many Retirement Accounts, Not Enough Strategy

A 403(b) here. A 401(k) there. Maybe one of you has a pension. Are you duplicating efforts or covering your bases?

Fix It: Sit down (or hire someone to help) and look at all accounts together. Are you both in high-fee funds? Are you taking advantage of Roth options? Could one partner's plan be better for both?

Coordinating Benefits: Which One's Better?

Every open enrollment season, dual-nurse couples have a decision to make: Do you each stick with your own employer benefits—or go with one plan as a family?

Health Insurance

- **Compare deductibles, premiums, and networks.** A lower monthly premium isn't always better if it means higher out-of-pocket costs.
- **Run scenarios.** What would delivery of a baby cost on Plan A vs. Plan B? How about an emergency surgery?

- **Tip:** If one of you has access to an HSA-eligible high-deductible plan and the other doesn't, that could be a tax-advantaged option for the household.

Life Insurance

- You both need it, especially if you have children or a mortgage. Check if employer-provided coverage is portable (many aren't if you leave).
- Consider term policies outside of work—so you're covered even if one of you changes jobs.

Disability Insurance

- Nurses are physically vulnerable to injuries. Dual coverage helps ensure one person doesn't have to carry all the weight if the other becomes disabled.
- Read the fine print. Many employer plans cover only a percentage of base pay—not overtime or differentials.

Paid Time Off (PTO) and Leave Policies

- One partner may have better parental leave or PTO accrual. Use it strategically during family planning, surgeries, or sabbaticals.

Budgeting as a Nurse Couple

You know how chaotic nursing shifts can be. Now imagine applying that chaos to money without a system.

Create a Joint Financial Dashboard

- List all income sources, retirement accounts, debts, and insurance policies.
- Use a shared app or spreadsheet to track monthly expenses.
- Designate a monthly financial huddle—15 minutes over coffee or

wine—to check in.

Set Household Rules of Engagement

- "No major purchases without a 24-hour cooling-off period."
- "We contribute 10% of each paycheck to savings, no matter what."
- "Every year, we check credit reports together."

These rules aren't rigid—they're reassuring. They help you avoid money fights when both of you are too exhausted to think straight.

Coordinating Retirement Goals

If both partners contribute to retirement, great. But are your contributions aligned?

- **Make sure you're not over-concentrated** in one type of fund or one market sector.
- **Use one partner's match first.** If one employer matches 6% and the other only 3%, prioritize the higher match.
- **Tax diversification matters.** One Roth, one pre-tax 403(b), a joint taxable brokerage account—diversifying account types gives you flexibility in retirement.

Emergency Planning for Dual-Nurse Families

Two working nurses often means minimal overlap in downtime. That makes it even more critical to have a plan for emergencies.

- **Create a shared ICE (in case of emergency) document.** Include passwords, policies, emergency contacts, and instructions if one of you is hospitalized.
- **Build a joint emergency fund.** Aim for 3–6 months of combined expenses—not just one person's.
- **Consider backup childcare.** Who steps in if both of you are pulled into overtime? Have a rotation of trusted contacts.

Real-Life Scenarios: Nurse Couple Case Studies

Case 1: Married ICU + ER Nurses in Their 30s

They both make $90K, no kids yet, but want to start trying next year. He's contributing to a 403(b) with a 5% match. She's maxing a Roth IRA but not using her employer match.

Opportunity: Shift her to at least get the full match. Start an HSA if eligible. Consider disability insurance policies outside of work in case one becomes pregnant or injured.

Case 2: Nurse Educator + Travel Nurse

She's staff at a local university hospital, making $110K with a pension. He's on the road, making $180K but with no benefits.

Opportunity: She could add him to her insurance. They can build a massive HSA and Roth pipeline by using her benefits and his high income. Also, stash his income aggressively toward early retirement or investment property.

Case 3: Retired Nurse + Working Spouse

He retired at 60. She's still working night shifts at 58. They're unsure when she should step back.

Opportunity: Model their monthly expenses without her income. Run Social Security scenarios. Downsize home or explore long-term care planning.

Money Conversations You Must Have

- "What are our top 3 financial goals this year?"
- "Are we saving enough for retirement—or just earning a lot and spending it all?"
- "What would we do if one of us burned out or needed a break?"
- "What happens if one of us passes away? Are we covered?"
- "Do we both understand our investments and insurance, or is one of us flying blind?"

These conversations don't have to be scary. They can be grounding. You already do hard things every day. Talking about money shouldn't be harder than managing a code.

Call to Act

Make one financial move before your next shift. Just one. Sit down with your partner. Pull up your bank statements. Look at your retirement accounts. Ask one another, "Are we building together—or just surviving?"

The only thing worse than working yourselves sick is doing it with no financial security to show for it.

Don't let money be the stressor that finally breaks your stride. Let it be the structure that supports you. The tool that lifts you. The quiet plan that frees you to focus on the life and love you've built together.

Final Word

Two nurses. One household. Infinite possibilities.

You already know how to care for others. Now it's time to care for your future. Together.

Chapter 40: Owning Property, Starting a Business, or Becoming an Investor

When to Expand Your Financial Life Beyond Your Paycheck

Let's begin this chapter with something honest: you don't have to be rich to build wealth.

But you do have to think beyond your paycheck.

Many nurses spend their entire careers showing up, giving everything to others, collecting a solid income—and then retiring with too little to show for it financially. They ran full-speed for years, but their money never got the same direction or momentum. Why? Because they never shifted from being an income earner to a wealth builder.

This chapter is your pivot.

Whether you're a 28-year-old nurse just starting to get traction or a 55-year-old RN wondering if you waited too long, the answer is the same: It's never too early, and it's never too late.

Let's talk about how to step beyond your hospital paycheck and explore the three big wealth-building doors available to you:

1. Owning Property
2. Starting a Business
3. Becoming an Investor

Owning Property

Why Property Ownership Matters

Property ownership is one of the most time-tested paths to wealth. It creates equity, stability, tax benefits, and the potential for passive income. But here's the key: property ownership is powerful *if* you do it wisely.

Primary Residence vs. Investment Property

Primary Residence: This is the home you live in. Owning your own home can be a great hedge against rent increases and a solid way to build long-term equity. But it can also be a money pit if you buy more than you can afford.

Investment Property: This is a property you rent to others for profit. It can provide ongoing cash flow, tax deductions, and appreciation. But it also comes with landlord responsibilities, vacancies, and repair costs.

House Hacking for Nurses

One beginner-friendly real estate strategy is called *house hacking*. Here's how it works: you buy a duplex, triplex, or even a single-family home with a basement apartment. You live in one unit and rent the other. The rental income helps cover your mortgage. This allows you to build equity while your tenant helps pay the bills.

It's an excellent strategy for a nurse starting out who doesn't mind being a live-in landlord or having roommates. It also works well for travel nurses who want to keep a home base.

Real Estate Rules of Thumb

- Don't buy until you've saved 10% to 20% for a down payment.
- Keep your monthly housing costs (including taxes and insurance) under 30% of your gross income.
- Run the numbers like it's a business. If renting it wouldn't cover the mortgage, reconsider.
- Always have an emergency fund for unexpected repairs.

What to Watch Out For

- Overpaying in a hot market.
- Taking on too much debt too early.
- Becoming a landlord without researching the legal and logistical responsibilities.

Starting a Business

You might be thinking, "I'm a nurse, not a CEO."

But let's reframe that.

If you've ever managed a 12-hour shift, precepted a new nurse, juggled medications and documentation under stress, and still had compassion left for your patients—you're already running a business. The product has just been your labor.

What if you packaged your experience in a way that builds something beyond your hourly wage?

Nurse-Owned Business Ideas

- **Legal Nurse Consultant**: Use your clinical expertise to help law firms with medical cases.
- **Nurse Health Coach**: Provide wellness coaching and disease prevention services.

- **Medical Writing or Blogging**: Create health content for websites, magazines, or your own platform.
- **Online Courses or Tutoring**: Teach NCLEX prep, continuing ed, or clinical skills to other nurses.
- **IV Hydration or Aesthetics Business**: For nurses in states that allow these services, these can be high-margin and in demand.
- **Speaking, Podcasting, or Coaching**: Turn your passion into a platform that educates and earns.

Business Models That Work for Nurses

1. **Side Hustles**: Low-risk, flexible, and can be scaled up over time.
2. **LLCs and Solo Practices**: Offer legal protection and tax advantages.
3. **Franchises**: Provide a system and support but require upfront investment.

Pros and Cons

Pros:

- More control over your time and income
- Scalable income potential
- Creative and professional freedom

Cons:

- No guaranteed paycheck
- Startup costs and business risk
- Can be time-consuming or stressful

Action Steps

- Write down your top 3 marketable skills outside the bedside.
- Brainstorm how you could package those into a product or service.
- Talk to a CPA or business attorney about setting up an LLC.
- Start small. Test before you invest heavily.

Becoming an Investor

There's a big difference between *working for money* and *having money work for you.*

Investing is how you build wealth without trading more time for more money. You earn while you sleep, not just while you chart.

Start with the Basics

Index Funds: Low-cost, diversified, and great for hands-off investors. They follow the overall stock market or specific sectors.

IRAs and 403(b) Plans: These tax-advantaged retirement accounts grow your money over decades and reduce your tax burden now or later.

Brokerage Accounts: For investments outside retirement. More flexible, but more tax exposure.

Nurse-Friendly Investment Options

- **Target-Date Funds**: Automatically adjust your investment mix as you get closer to retirement.
- **Dividend Stocks**: Provide ongoing income.
- **REITs (Real Estate Investment Trusts)**: A way to invest in property without being a landlord.
- **Robo-Advisors**: Great for busy nurses who want investing to be automatic and low maintenance.

Avoid These Mistakes

- Chasing hype (meme stocks, crypto fads)
- Day trading without research or experience
- Putting all your savings in one stock or sector
- Borrowing to invest (especially early on)

Rules of Thumb

- Invest 15% of your income if you can—start with 5% and grow.
- Make investing automatic every payday.
- Don't try to time the market—time *in* the market matters more.

Real-Life Example Scenarios

Erica, 33, Med-Surg Nurse: Rents a small apartment, contributes 6% to her 403(b), and just inherited $20,000. She's deciding between starting an Etsy shop for nursing gear or using the money as a down payment on a small duplex. She runs the numbers and chooses the duplex—planning to live in one unit and rent the other.

Devon and Lisa, Dual-Nurse Couple, Mid-40s: They each have pensions and are maxing out their retirement accounts. They decide to open a consulting business for nurse staffing and use their vacation time to attend conferences and market their services. It takes 2 years to grow but becomes a six-figure business.

Carlos, 59, ER Nurse Manager: Wants to semi-retire in five years. He meets with a financial advisor and begins investing in dividend-paying ETFs and converting some of his 403(b) to a Roth IRA annually to lower future taxes.

Action Checklist

1. **Know your numbers.** What's your net worth? What are your monthly expenses?
2. **Clarify your goal.** Are you aiming for passive income, more time, or a creative outlet?
3. **Pick one path to start.** Don't try to start a business, flip a house, and become a crypto investor all at once.
4. **Automate where possible.** Set your investments and savings to auto-draft.
5. **Get help.** Consider a fee-only financial advisor, CPA, or mentor in your chosen area.

Final Thought

If your paycheck is the only tool in your financial toolbox, you'll always be limited by your shift count.

But if you add equity, ownership, and investing to the mix, your income gets momentum.

You don't have to do it all at once. But you *do* have to start.

So ask yourself:

- What legacy do I want to build?
- What skills do I have that the world needs?
- What investments will support me when I'm ready to retire—or just rest?

Then make one move before your next shift.

Just one.

Because you're not just a nurse. You're the CEO of your future.

And it's time to chart a new path forward.

Part VI: Protecting and Preserving Your Wealth

By the time most nurses reach mid- to late-career, they've put in the hours, weathered the storms, and built something meaningful—financially and professionally. But here's the truth no one says loud enough: *earning money is only half the equation.* If you don't protect it, preserve it, and plan for what's next, you could be left working shift after shift just to stay afloat—even when you don't have to.

This part of the book helps nurses *guard what they've built.*

We dive deep into the critical, often overlooked elements of financial stability: insurance coverage (not just the bare minimum), estate planning that actually works, teaching your kids how to avoid your money mistakes, and smart tax strategies that let your money breathe, not burn.

You'll also learn how to say "yes" to financial growth opportunities—like property ownership, starting a side business, or investing—*without saying yes to unnecessary risk or burnout.*

Whether you're a staff nurse thinking about your family's future, a nurse manager approaching retirement, or a dual-nurse household trying to plan for long-term peace of mind, this section is your steady guide. We're not here to overwhelm you with financial jargon. We're here to *give you structure, power, and control*—so you can protect your income, your legacy, and your sanity.

Because money shouldn't just get you through the next shift—it should buy you *freedom*, options, and the ability to step back when you're ready.

This is the part where you *build the fence, reinforce the foundation,* and *secure the future you've been working toward all these years.*

Chapter 41: Lifestyle Creep – Don't Let Your Income Disappear

You didn't survive nursing school, make it through orientation, and grind through years of double shifts just to feel broke with every raise. Yet that's the exact cycle many nurses find themselves in. You get a bump in pay, and somehow… it vanishes. A better title, a better shift, maybe even a better department—but your checking account still feels like it's in the ER, on life support.

This is lifestyle creep. And this chapter is your code blue intervention.

What Is Lifestyle Creep?

Lifestyle creep is when your expenses rise with your income. You start making more money, so you start spending more. Maybe it starts small: You upgrade from fast food to delivery apps. You trade your economy car for a luxury lease. Suddenly, you're justifying every purchase with, "I work hard, I deserve it."

Let's be clear: *You do deserve good things.* But there's a big difference between *celebrating milestones* and *sabotaging your future.*

Lifestyle creep feels good in the moment but often comes at the expense of long-term financial health. Instead of building savings, investments, or retirement security, you're locked into a cycle of working just to pay for the stuff you bought because you were working.

The Nurse-Specific Version

Nurses are especially vulnerable to lifestyle creep. Here's why:

- **Overtime and shift differentials** can make paychecks look deceptively large.
- **Peer pressure from coworkers** who lease new cars or go on vacations can set new "norms."
- **Compensation for burnout** (retail therapy, expensive self-care) becomes routine.
- **Inconsistent schedules** make it easy to justify last-minute food delivery, childcare splurges, or travel.
- **Working holidays and nights** might lead to higher pay, but also to higher stress spending.

Real Talk: Examples

- *Maya,* an ICU nurse, went from $65K to $90K in three years. She upgraded her apartment, bought a new SUV, and started weekly massages. Five years in, she still has no emergency fund.
- *Jordan* and *Ashley,* both RNs, are a dual-income couple making over $200K. They live paycheck to paycheck, thanks to two car payments, private school tuition, and monthly "just because" Amazon orders.
- *Tamika,* a night-shift med-surg nurse, used every raise to increase her shopping budget. She justifies it as stress relief. But when she broke her ankle and had to miss work, she had no savings.

These aren't failures of character. These are financial habits that snuck in while no one was looking.

Why Lifestyle Creep Happens

- **Emotional fatigue:** After 12-hour shifts and staffing crises, retail therapy can feel like survival.
- **No clear goals:** If you don't have financial goals, lifestyle creep will set them for you.
- **No boundaries with money:** If every raise leads to a new bill, you're not building freedom.
- **Social media pressure:** Instagram isn't real life, but your wallet doesn't always know that.
- **Guilt:** Nurses give so much to others, they often feel guilty putting money aside for themselves—so they spend it instead of saving it.

The Cost of "I Deserve It"

- The difference between spending $300 vs. $2,000 a month on lifestyle upgrades is $20,400 a year.
- That's more than enough to max out a Roth IRA *and* contribute to your 403(b).
- It could be the difference between retiring at 60 vs. 70.

Diagnosing Your Own Creep

Ask yourself:

- Has your savings rate increased with your income?
- Are you carrying more debt now than you were two years ago?
- Do you regularly say, "I'll start saving next month"?
- Do you feel like your lifestyle changes are running on autopilot?

If you answered yes to even one of these, it's time for a reset.

Treatment Plan: How to Avoid Lifestyle Creep

1. Automate Your Raises

Every time you get a raise, send half of it straight into savings or investments. Pretend you never saw it. Build wealth before your spending expands.

2. Create a "Lifestyle Cap"

Decide in advance how much you *want* to spend each month. Anything above that goes toward debt, investing, or savings.

3. Define Your "Enough"

Write down what *enough* looks like to you. That might mean a reliable car, weekly groceries, and one vacation a year. Stick to it.

4. Build a Value-Based Budget

Instead of cutting coffee, focus on spending in alignment with your values. If your top priority is family time, invest in that—and trim what doesn't serve it.

5. Take Social Media Breaks

If lifestyle envy triggers you, pause the scroll. Spend that time reviewing your budget or making a money move.

6. Conduct a Spending Audit

Print three months of bank statements. Highlight every expense that didn't bring lasting value. That's your creep. That's your opportunity.

7. Create a Delay Rule

Implement a 24-hour or 7-day wait rule before making non-essential purchases. This slows emotional spending.

8. Talk With a Financial Coach or Advisor

Let someone help you set goals, create systems, and keep you accountable.

What Happens When You Beat Lifestyle Creep

- You have margin.
- You sleep better.
- You can take time off without panic.

- You retire earlier.
- You make work optional.

A Final Note

Lifestyle creep isn't about not enjoying life. It's about making sure your income doesn't get hijacked by automatic spending. You deserve more than just stuff. You deserve freedom, peace of mind, and options.

So the next time that raise hits? Before you click "add to cart" or test-drive something new, pause. Breathe. Automate. Then *celebrate* the fact that you're a nurse who knows exactly where her money is going—and what it's building.

Because the only thing better than a pay raise is *keeping* what you earn and turning it into a future you actually want.

Call to Act:

Before your next shift, automate 10% of your paycheck to a high-yield savings account. Just one move. Then next week, schedule a 30-minute money review. You earned your money. Now make sure you *own* it.

This isn't about deprivation. This is about design. Financially fit nurses don't just survive shifts. They *build lives they don't need to escape from.*

Chapter 42: Nurse-Specific Retirement Planning – Shift-Based Pensions, Retirement Age, and Social Security Timing

Retirement isn't a far-off dream. It's a shift you're working toward every day—whether you realize it or not. For nurses, who are constantly giving of themselves physically, mentally, and emotionally, retirement planning is more than a savings account or a pension benefit—it's a strategy to regain time, autonomy, and health.

This chapter is your scrub-in moment for your financial future. We're going to cover everything from how pensions actually work, to why shift work can make or break your retirement age, to how Social Security timing impacts your check (and your choices).

Let's get to it—no whiteboards, no jargon. Just real talk, real strategies, and a real plan to make sure you don't spend 30 years saving lives and then feel broke or stuck when it's time to live your own.

PART I: UNDERSTANDING RETIREMENT OPTIONS FOR NURSES

1. Pensions – The "Old School" Benefit
2. Some hospital systems and government entities still offer pensions, but they are becoming rarer. If you have one, you're sitting on a potentially valuable asset—but it comes with rules.

Pros:

- Guaranteed lifetime income (depending on the plan)
- Not subject to market risk
- Can provide survivor benefits for a spouse

Cons:

- Lack of control over investment growth
- Often requires 20+ years of service
- May reduce flexibility for job changes

Action Step:

Call your HR department and request your pension benefit statement. Ask: "What is my vesting status, estimated monthly benefit, and projected retirement age?"

1. 403(b) Plans – The Hospital-Side 401(k)
2. A 403(b) is a tax-advantaged retirement account for nonprofit and healthcare workers. Contributions are made pre-tax (unless you choose Roth), and employers often offer a match.

Why it matters:

If your employer offers a 3% match, and you're not contributing at least 3%, you are literally turning down free money.

Compare this to:

A shift differential that gives you $2/hr extra—that's $4,160 a year pre-tax. A 3% 403(b) match on a $70,000 salary? That's $2,100 annually—and it grows tax-deferred.

Action Step:

Log into your 403(b) account or contact your provider. Make sure you're contributing enough to get the full match—and check whether you're in a traditional or Roth 403(b).

1. Roth IRAs – Flexibility and Tax-Free Growth
2. Roth IRAs are funded with after-tax dollars, but the growth and withdrawals in retirement are tax-free.

Why nurses love them:

- Great for younger nurses or those in lower tax brackets
- Allows tax diversification in retirement
- You can withdraw contributions (not earnings) penalty-free

Contribution limit (as of 2024): $6,500 annually (under 50), $7,500 (50+)

Action Step:

Open a Roth IRA online (Fidelity, Vanguard, Schwab) and automate monthly transfers. Even $100/month makes a difference when you do it consistently.

PART II: RETIREMENT TIMING AND SHIFT WORK

You know how grueling night shifts, 12-hour days, and back-to-backs are. But have you ever thought about how they shorten your working runway?

Burnout = Early Exit = Less Time to Save

Let's talk real numbers:

If you plan to work until 67 but mentally tap out at 59, that's 8 years of missed income and retirement contributions.

Example:

Let's say Nurse A contributes $500/month from age 30 to 59. That's 29 years of saving.

Nurse B contributes $500/month from age 30 to 67. That's 37 years.

With an average 7% return:

- Nurse A ends with: ~$566,000
- Nurse B ends with: ~$944,000

That's a $378,000 difference just from hanging on 8 more years.

Action Step:

Start reverse-engineering your exit age. What's your burnout point? What does your budget need to look like to allow flexibility in your 50s?

PART III: SOCIAL SECURITY FOR NURSES

Social Security may not make you rich—but it will be a major part of your income.

Key ages:

- 62: You can start collecting, but receive a 25-30% reduction
- 66-67: Full retirement age (depending on birth year)
- 70: Maximum benefit age (you get ~8% more per year you delay past full retirement age)

Big Nurse Mistake: Taking Social Security too early because you're tired and broke.

Why that's costly:

If your full retirement benefit is $2,000/month at age 67, taking it at 62 gives you ~$1,400. That's $600/month or $7,200/year less—for life.

How do you know when to take it?

Ask:

- Do you have other retirement income?
- Are you healthy and expected to live past 80?
- Are you still working?

Action Step:

Create a "My Social Security" account at ssa.gov. Run estimates for 62, 67, and 70. Factor it into your retirement income plan.

PART IV: RETIREMENT STRATEGIES FOR DIFFERENT TYPES OF NURSES

1. Staff Nurse on a W-2

- Max out your 403(b) if matched
- Consider opening a Roth IRA or a brokerage account for flexibility
- Don't rely on pension alone

1. Per Diem Nurse

- No benefits? You need to create your own retirement plan
- Open a Traditional or Roth IRA
- Consider a Solo 401(k) if you have side income

1. Travel Nurse

- Use your high income wisely
- Save aggressively during high-earning years
- Be disciplined with spending—housing stipends are not forever

PART V: HEALTHCARE IN RETIREMENT

Nurses know how expensive care is. But when you're the patient, the bill hits different.

Options:

- Medicare (starts at 65)
- Employer retiree health coverage (rare now)
- Health Savings Accounts (HSAs)

If you have a high-deductible health plan, an HSA lets you:

- Save pre-tax money
- Grow it tax-deferred
- Withdraw tax-free for medical expenses

Triple tax-advantaged. Use it now, or save it for medical costs in retirement.

Action Step:

If you have an HSA option, contribute—even a small amount. Don't use it for cold medicine now if you can afford not to. Let it grow.

PART VI: THE NURSE RETIREMENT CHECKLIST

☐ Know your pension (if applicable)

☐ Max your 403(b) match

☐ Open and contribute to a Roth IRA

☐ Estimate your retirement age and income gap

☐ Check your Social Security benefits

☐ Build a realistic exit plan that factors in burnout and health

☐ Don't rely on just one source of income

☐ Create a monthly post-retirement budget

☐ Have an estate plan (yes, even if you're single)

☐ Stay financially fit—don't coast just because you're "almost there"

Final Words:

Retirement isn't just about leaving work. It's about buying back your time, peace, and purpose. Nurses spend their careers showing up for others—retirement is your chance to show up for yourself.

But it won't just happen.

You've got to plan for it.

Make one financial move before your next shift. Just one.

And do another next week.

You've got the strength, the smarts, and the strategy to retire with dignity—not just fatigue.

Keep going. You're closer than you think.

Chapter 43: Burnout Recovery and Career Changes – When to Pivot

Let's start with a truth that doesn't get spoken enough in nurse lounges, unit meetings, or HR memos:

Sometimes, the thing you need most isn't a new job.

It's a break.

A reset.

A chance to breathe.

But for most nurses, that thought comes with a wave of anxiety. Because when you rely on your income to survive—to pay your mortgage, care for your kids, and keep the lights on—the idea of stepping back feels impossible.

That's what this chapter is about: giving you the structure, the numbers, and the plan to take care of yourself without torching your finances in the process. Whether you're contemplating a leave, pivoting to a new role, going back to school, or leaving the bedside for good, this is your financial blueprint.

Let's get clear. Let's get calm. Let's get real.

Burnout Is Real — And Expensive

The World Health Organization classifies burnout as an occupational phenomenon characterized by:

- Emotional exhaustion

- Depersonalization (feeling detached from your work or patients)
- Reduced personal accomplishment

For nurses, it shows up in long shifts, short staffing, unrelenting alarms, missed meals, aching feet, and emotional whiplash from code blues to patient loss to family education to charting nightmares—often in a single shift.

The financial cost?

- Increased sick days
- Missed shifts (and lost differentials)
- Health costs from stress-related conditions
- Mistakes that could risk your license

Planning your exit or break from burnout is not a luxury.

It's survival.

Step 1: Take Your Emotional Vital Signs

Before we dive into budgets or timelines, assess your emotional state like you would a patient intake:

- Are you crying before shifts?
- Snapping at patients or family?
- Dreaming of walking out mid-shift?
- Feeling numb?

These are symptoms. They deserve attention, not shame.

If you're here, reading this, it means you want out *without going broke.* And that's possible. But you need a steady head to make bold moves.

Step 2: Define the Pivot You Need

There are different levels of burnout recovery:

1. **A Break**

- Short-term unpaid leave
- Sabbatical (if employer offers it)
- Temporary PRN work only

1. **A Shift in Role**

- Lateral move to less intense department
- Ambulatory or clinic setting
- Nurse educator, case manager, telehealth

1. **A Total Exit from Bedside**

- New career path
- Going back to school
- Starting a business

1. **A Hard Stop**

- Quitting without another job
- Full medical leave

Each pivot requires a different financial runway.

Let's build yours.

Step 3: Know Your Numbers Like You Know Your Vitals

To plan a burnout recovery strategy, you need:

- **Your fixed monthly expenses** (mortgage, car, insurance)
- **Your variable expenses** (groceries, gas, fun)
- **Your current take-home pay**
- **Your savings**
- **Any side income or partner income**
- **How many months of expenses you can currently cover without working**

Build a simple spreadsheet or use an app. Be honest.

If your numbers say you can take 6 months off, *now you have power.*

If your numbers say you need 6 more months of saving first, *you have a mission.*

Step 4: Build a Financial Burnout Buffer

A good target? 3–6 months of essential expenses saved before you pivot.

If that sounds impossible, try:

- Temporarily cutting all non-essentials
- Working one extra shift a week (short-term)
- Selling unused items
- Banking all PRN income
- Pausing retirement contributions to build cash

Once you hit that buffer, your nervous system will feel it. Your brain knows you're safer.

That's when the real planning begins.

Step 5: Benefits Check — What Do You Lose If You Leave?

Before changing roles or quitting:

- **Health Insurance**: Will you be COBRA eligible? Covered under a partner? Need ACA?
- **Retirement**: Are you vested in your employer's 403(b)? Should you roll it over?
- **PTO**: Will it be paid out?
- **Life & Disability Insurance**: Will these lapse if you leave?

Use your HR portal or schedule a benefits call.

Step 6: Explore Non-Bedside Roles That Still Use Your License

If you want to stay in nursing but get out of the stress spiral, consider:

- Case management
- Nurse educator
- Health IT or informatics
- Legal nurse consulting
- Risk management
- Public health
- School nursing
- Clinical documentation improvement (CDI)
- Telephonic triage
- Wellness coaching
- Research nurse coordinator

These jobs still value your clinical background—without the 12-hour floor chaos.

Step 7: Evaluate Going Back to School (Carefully)

A new credential could open new doors—or it could pile on more debt.

Do the math:

- Cost of tuition
- Years to pay it off
- Expected salary increase
- Current burnout level

Sometimes, switching jobs beats enrolling in grad school. Sometimes, school is the step forward. But always calculate *return on investment*.

Step 8: Talk to a Financial Planner Who Gets Nurses

A good planner can:

- Help you model different exit plans
- Check your benefits and risk gaps
- Guide retirement rollover
- Set up cash-flow from savings

Not all advisors understand shift work, PRN income, or nurse-specific benefits. Find one who does. Ask:

"Have you worked with other nurses in career transition?"

Step 9: Communicate With Your Household

Don't do this alone.

If you have a spouse, partner, or dependents, loop them in. Transparency builds trust and helps plan support:

- Can your partner take on more for a while?

- Will you downsize or pause vacations?
- Do kids understand mom/dad is changing paths?

This is part of your *whole-health care plan.*

Step 10: Create Your Exit Plan Like a Discharge Plan

Build a real checklist.

60-90 Days Before Leave or Pivot:

- Recheck savings
- Understand COBRA or ACA timeline
- Finish major shifts or projects

30 Days Before:

- Notify manager or HR (if appropriate)
- Write resume and prep interviews
- Move forward on license transfers (if needed)

Day Of Exit:

- Download pay stubs and HR documents
- Keep a copy of credentials and CEUs
- Reflect. Breathe. Celebrate.

Post-Pivot:

- Track spending weekly
- Maintain health insurance coverage
- Keep professional licenses current

Real-Life Stories: Nurse Burnout Pivots

Lana, 37: Burned out ICU nurse. Saved $12K, took 4 months off, returned as a school nurse with 20% less pay but 80% less stress.

Jorge, 42: Med-surg charge nurse. Used PTO, then FMLA. Got counseling. Pivoted to telehealth triage. Now makes similar pay from home.

Kendra, 29: PRN float pool nurse. Realized she hated clinical work. Started freelance health writing on the side. Now full-time copywriter for a hospital system.

Their common theme?

They planned first. Then jumped.

Pitfalls to Avoid

- **Quitting without a budget**
- **Going back to school without ROI math**
- **Assuming your employer will pay out PTO or keep insurance**
- **Relying on credit cards during burnout**
- **Thinking you'll never return to nursing** (you might—on new terms)

You deserve options, not panic.

You Are More Than Your Job

Let's say this together:

My health matters more than my hospital.

Being a nurse is noble. But you are allowed to rest. To shift. To reinvent.

This chapter was not about walking away from purpose.

It was about reclaiming your power to choose how you use your gifts—and when.

The finances? Those can be figured out.

But first: believe you're worth the plan.

Final Call to Act:

Make one move this week:

- Open a savings account labeled "Burnout Pivot Fund"
- Book a financial planner consult
- Talk to HR about PTO cash-out
- Apply to one non-bedside job
- Journal how your body feels before every shift

Then, do another next week.

You're not stuck. You're in transition.

And transitions are powerful when they're done on purpose.

Your chart is in your hands now.

Let's write a better care plan—for *you*.

Chapter 44: Divorce, Death, and Disability – Financial Preparedness for the Unexpected

Let's start with a truth that nurses already understand better than most: life can change in an instant.

You can walk into a shift expecting a normal day and end up in the middle of a trauma case you didn't see coming. Same thing happens outside the hospital: relationships break down, diagnoses come out of nowhere, and tragedy doesn't always give notice. Financially, the same rules apply. That's why planning for the unexpected isn't paranoia—it's protection. And as a nurse, you're already trained to plan for worst-case scenarios. Now let's apply that skill set to your finances.

This chapter is about crisis-proofing your money. We'll talk about what every nurse should have in place before a divorce, death, or disability hits—because by the time a crisis shows up, it's too late to start planning.

Section 1: The Three D's That Can Derail You

Let's define what we're really talking about:

- **Divorce:** The financial and emotional unraveling of a shared life. Can lead to asset division, child support, spousal support, housing disruptions, and even career compromises.
- **Death:** The loss of a spouse, parent, or anyone whose income or presence impacted your household. If there's no will, insurance, or savings, grief can quickly turn into chaos.

- **Disability:** The most overlooked and most common financial blindside. Getting hurt, sick, or too burned out to work isn't theoretical. It happens—especially in high-stress, high-physicality professions like nursing.

Why You Must Plan for All Three:

Because statistically, one of them *will* affect you.

And because planning ahead doesn't just protect your wallet—it protects your mental health. It gives you one less thing to panic about when everything else is already falling apart.

Section 2: Legal Documents You Need NOW (Not Later)

Let's be blunt: every adult should have basic estate planning documents, especially nurses. Here are the non-negotiables:

- **Will:** States who gets your stuff, guardianship for kids, and who handles your estate.
- **Living Will / Advance Directive:** Lays out your wishes for medical care if you're incapacitated.
- **Healthcare Power of Attorney:** Appoints someone you trust to make medical decisions if you can't.
- **Durable Power of Attorney for Finances:** Allows someone to manage your bills, accounts, and financial decisions if you're unable.
- **Beneficiary Designations:** These override your will. Keep them updated on:
- 403(b)/401(k)
- Life insurance
- Pensions
- Bank accounts with Payable-On-Death (POD) status

Pro Tip: Review these documents every 2 years or after any major life change (marriage, divorce, kids, move, new job).

Section 3: Insurance as Your Financial Trauma Kit

Insurance isn't fun. But it's the only thing that stands between your loved ones and financial collapse if something goes wrong.

Here are the types you MUST have:

- **Life Insurance:** Especially if someone depends on your income. Choose term life insurance over whole life for affordability.
- Example: A healthy 30-year-old nurse can often get $500,000 of term life coverage for under $30/month.
- **Disability Insurance:** Covers your income if you're too hurt or sick to work.
- There's short-term (a few months) and long-term (years or until retirement).
- If your employer doesn't offer it, get it privately. Nurses are in a high-risk category due to the physical demands of the job.
- **Auto Insurance with Uninsured Motorist Coverage:** Especially important if you drive to multiple job sites or travel for work.
- **Umbrella Insurance:** Adds extra liability protection in case someone sues you. Helpful if you own property, a business, or have assets worth protecting.

Section 4: Divorce-Proofing Your Finances (Even If You're Happy Right Now)

Nobody gets married thinking they'll split up. But as a nurse, you've seen firsthand how quickly situations can unravel.

Here's how to make sure you don't get financially wrecked:

- **Have Your Own Bank Account:** Joint accounts are fine—but keep a separate one too. Just in case.
- **Know Where Everything Is:** Passwords, account numbers, insurance policies, mortgage docs—if you don't know where it is, you can't protect it.
- **Prenups and Postnups Aren't Just for Celebs:** If you're entering marriage with debt, property, or kids from another relationship, talk to a lawyer.

- **Stay Involved:** Don't let your partner run all the finances. Be part of the budget. Know your household numbers.

Section 5: What to Do If the Worst Happens

Let's say you didn't prepare. Or maybe you did, but life came harder than expected.

Here's what to do first in each situation:

After Divorce:

1. Update beneficiaries immediately.
2. Separate joint accounts.
3. Re-run your budget and adjust your savings/investments.
4. Refinance any jointly held debt.
5. Get a financial therapist or advisor if needed. Divorce is emotional and financial.

After Death:

1. Request multiple copies of the death certificate.
2. Contact the employer for any final paycheck, pension, or life insurance.
3. Notify Social Security and insurance companies.
4. Contact an estate attorney, even if there's a will.
5. Give yourself time. Don't rush into big financial decisions during grief.

After Disability:

1. File for short- or long-term disability immediately.
2. Contact your employer's HR and benefits department.
3. Reassess your monthly budget.
4. Explore side income if you're able.
5. If permanent, consider meeting with a disability planner.

Section 6: Building a Crisis-Proof Budget

Here's a basic monthly framework every nurse should use:

- 50% Needs (rent, groceries, transportation)
- 20% Savings (retirement, emergency fund)
- 30% Wants (yes, even self-care counts)

Now add the Crisis Layer:

- Emergency Fund = 3-6 months of expenses (ideally 9+ if you're single or have dependents)
- Sinking Funds = Cash set aside for predictable one-off events: car repairs, holiday travel, back-to-school costs.
- Crisis Fund = A separate stash for divorce/legal fees, time off for grief, or sudden medical costs.

Section 7: Don't Forget the Emotional Toll

Money is logical. But crises are emotional.

The goal here isn't to remove pain. It's to prevent panic.

When you have financial systems in place, you give yourself permission to fall apart emotionally without your entire life falling apart practically.

That's the gift of preparation.

A Final Story

Meet Renee. A 42-year-old ER nurse, single mom of two, who lost her partner suddenly in a car accident.

Because they hadn't finalized a will and weren't married, she had no legal access to his life insurance, and she had to fight for everything. She went from stable to scrambling in under a week.

Now meet Lauren. A 38-year-old NICU nurse who'd seen enough in the hospital to know she needed a plan. She had a will, life insurance, an emergency fund, and powers of attorney set up by age 30. When she was diagnosed with breast cancer at 39, she didn't worry about money once.

Lauren focused on healing.

That's the difference.

Call to Act:

Make one move this week:

- Set up a power of attorney.
- Get a term life insurance quote.
- Check your beneficiary designations.
- Create a folder labeled "Crisis Plan" and start filling it.

One step. One shift. One act of protection.

You protect lives every shift.

Now protect yours.

Final Note:

This isn't about being paranoid. It's about being prepared.

You don't have to have all the answers.

You just have to take the first step.

Your future self, your family, and your peace of mind will thank you.

Chapter 45: Charitable Giving and Legacy Planning for Nurses – How to Give Back While Still Securing Your Own Future

There's something beautifully unique about the nursing profession. Nurses spend their days giving—time, energy, compassion, and expertise. But when it comes to giving money, the questions get trickier. Can I afford to donate? Should I start a scholarship fund? Will giving now hurt my retirement later?

This chapter is about learning how to give with both heart and strategy. Because giving back doesn't have to mean giving yourself away. You can build a life where generosity and financial strength go hand in hand. Let's talk about what legacy really means for nurses, how to give meaningfully without sabotaging your future, and what tools can help you leave a mark long after your final shift.

Why This Chapter Matters

Nurses give everything on the floor—but many hesitate to give financially. It's not because they don't want to. It's because they don't know if they *can.* This chapter helps you:

- Think clearly about charitable giving and legacy planning

- Learn the financial tools available (like donor-advised funds, charitable trusts, and bequests)
- Understand the tax benefits of smart giving
- Set giving goals without neglecting your retirement, emergency fund, or student loans
- Model generosity to your kids, coworkers, and community

You don't have to wait until you're wealthy to be a philanthropist. You just need a plan.

Part 1: Why Nurses Want to Give Back

The Heart of the Profession

Nursing attracts people who care deeply about others. It's more than a job—it's a calling. So it makes sense that many nurses look for ways to give beyond the bedside. Some want to support patient families, contribute to causes they care about, or give to schools that helped launch their careers. Others want to help fellow nurses through grants or scholarships.

But Then Real Life Happens

- You're paying off $100,000 in student loans.
- You're helping your own kids pay for college.
- You're working extra shifts just to keep up with bills.

So you tell yourself you'll give back "someday"—after the debt is paid off, after the kids graduate, after you retire. But here's the truth: You don't have to wait until your life is perfect to give. You just have to structure your giving in a way that fits where you are now.

Part 2: Start Where You Are

What Do You Want Your Legacy to Be?

Let's be clear—legacy isn't just about money. It's about impact. It's about what you leave behind: financially, emotionally, and spiritually. Here are questions to reflect on:

- Who helped *you* when you were struggling?
- What cause stirs your soul?
- Is there a specific person, place, or community you want to bless?
- Do you want to give now or later—or both?

Legacy planning starts with vision. The logistics come next.

Rule of Thumb: 1% Now, More Later

Even if you feel stretched, consider giving 1% of your income to a cause that matters to you. If you earn $80,000, that's $800 a year—or about $67 a month. That might be one night of takeout or a few Starbucks runs. That money could help feed a family, support a fellow nurse in crisis, or keep a nonprofit afloat.

You can always give more later—but start flexing your generosity muscle now.

Part 3: How to Give While Still Building Wealth

Action Step: Don't Give from Your Emergency Fund

Your giving plan should not compete with your financial survival. Cover the basics first:

1. **Emergency fund (3–6 months of expenses)**

2. **Debt repayment plan**
3. **Retirement contributions**
4. **Health and disability insurance**

Once those are rolling, you can:

- Automate small monthly donations
- Use donor-advised funds to grow your giving
- Allocate a portion of a raise or bonus to charity

Give from Surplus, Not Scarcity

Think about:

- **Rounding up** your monthly bills and donating the difference
- Donating a **tax refund** or **incentive check**
- Contributing from your **side hustle** income

When you plan your giving, it becomes sustainable.

Part 4: Smart Giving Tools

Donor-Advised Funds (DAFs)

Think of a DAF like a mini foundation you can manage with a few clicks. You contribute to the fund, take a tax deduction immediately, and then give to charities over time.

Why nurses like it:

- It simplifies your recordkeeping
- You can grow the money tax-free
- You can give when *you* are ready, not when the tax year ends

Charitable Bequests

Leave money to a cause in your will. Simple. Powerful. Legacy defined.

You can also:

- Name a charity as a **beneficiary** of a life insurance policy or retirement account
- Set up a **charitable remainder trust** if you want to donate assets but still get income from them in retirement

Talk to a financial advisor and estate planning attorney to find what fits.

Qualified Charitable Distributions (QCDs)

If you're over 70½, you can donate directly from your IRA to a qualified nonprofit and avoid paying income tax on that distribution. It counts toward your Required Minimum Distribution (RMD) and reduces taxable income.

Smart giving = smart tax planning.

Part 5: Ways Nurses Give Back

- **Scholarships for nursing students**
- **Annual giving to hospitals** or patient funds
- **Volunteering medical services overseas** (can be a tax write-off)
- **Faith-based giving** to a church or mission
- **Funding a local clinic** or nonprofit
- **Creating a legacy award** through your professional association

Part 6: How to Talk to Family About It

Sometimes family doesn't understand why you give when you're still paying off loans. Here's what to say:

- "We give because it reminds us of what matters most."
- "It's a core value—like saving or investing."
- "We're planning for our future *and* helping others."

Be clear that giving is part of your plan—not a reckless decision.

Part 7: Giving Without Regret

Give with intention, not guilt.
Ask yourself:

- Can I afford this without jeopardizing my needs?
- Does this align with my values?
- Am I giving out of love or pressure?

Boundaries are part of generosity. Give wisely, not reactively.

Part 8: Your Legacy Beyond Money

You can also leave a legacy by:

- Mentoring younger nurses
- Writing a letter to your kids about what money means to you
- Recording stories from your nursing journey
- Teaching financial literacy to new nurses
- Advocating for policy changes in healthcare

Legacy isn't about the size of your bank account. It's about the footprint you leave behind.

Part 9: Real Nurse, Real Story

A 52-year-old trauma nurse created a scholarship for single moms entering nursing school. She started with $1,000 a year. After five years, she added the charity to her will. Today, she funds two full scholarships annually—and mentors both students. Her name is remembered by people she'll never meet. That's legacy.

Final Call to Act

Make one giving decision this week. Just one. Maybe it's:

- Setting up a $25 monthly donation
- Calling an attorney to add a bequest to your will
- Researching donor-advised funds
- Talking to your spouse about the causes you care about

And make another next month.

You don't have to choose between generosity and security. You can have both. Your legacy as a nurse isn't just the lives you save—it's the good you set in motion.

Remember: Financial literacy isn't just about building wealth.

It's about deciding what you want your wealth to do.

It's about purpose.

And purpose never expires.

Chapter 46: Financial Advisors – How to Choose the Right One

You know how to triage a patient, stabilize a code, and advocate for your patients like your life depends on it. But when it comes to picking a financial advisor? Many nurses feel like they're walking into a room without a diagnosis or a plan.

Let's change that.

Let's demystify the world of financial advisors so you can walk in with clarity, confidence, and a clipboard of questions ready.

Because here's the truth: the right advisor can help you build wealth, reduce stress, and avoid costly mistakes. The wrong one? They can cost you thousands and leave you disillusioned.

So let's break this down in nurse-to-nurse language—clean, clear, and no jargon.

What Does a Financial Advisor Actually Do?

Think of a good financial advisor like a seasoned charge nurse. They don't do everything for you—they help you assess your situation, prioritize what matters, delegate tasks, and make confident decisions.

A financial advisor helps with:

- Retirement planning
- Investment management
- Debt payoff strategies
- Insurance analysis

- Tax planning
- Education savings
- Estate planning
- Budgeting and cash flow

But not all advisors offer all services. Some just manage investments. Others help you plan your entire financial life. That's why asking the right questions is crucial.

Fee-Only vs. Commission-Based vs. Fee-Based: What It Means

Here's where many nurses get tripped up. The way an advisor gets paid affects their advice—just like a med rep pushing a new drug might not always be giving the whole picture.

- **Fee-Only**: These advisors only get paid by YOU. No commissions. No hidden product kickbacks. They're typically fiduciaries (more on that in a second). This model is transparent, aligned with your interests, and clean.
- **Commission-Based**: These folks get paid when they sell you something—insurance, annuities, mutual funds. This creates potential conflicts of interest. They may still offer decent advice, but you need to ask tough questions.
- **Fee-Based**: A hybrid. They charge you fees AND may receive commissions. You'll need to ask what they get paid for, and how.

What's a Fiduciary—And Why Should You Care?

In simple terms, a fiduciary is legally obligated to put YOUR interests ahead of theirs. Imagine a nurse manager who always advocates for the patient—even when it's inconvenient. That's what you want in an advisor.

Not all advisors are fiduciaries. Some follow a "suitability" standard—meaning the investment just has to be "okay," not best.

Ask: **"Are you a fiduciary 100% of the time—and can you put that in writing?"**

What to Look for in a Financial Advisor as a Nurse

- **Understands shift work** and fluctuating income
- **Knows 403(b) plans**, pensions, and public service loan forgiveness
- **Understands burnout**, second jobs, and career pivots
- Can explain complex things in plain English
- Encourages education, not intimidation

Questions to Ask in the First Meeting

1. Are you a fiduciary 100% of the time?
2. How are you compensated?
3. What licenses or certifications do you have? (Look for CFP®, CFA, or CPA)
4. Do you specialize in working with nurses or healthcare professionals?
5. What services are included in your fee?
6. How often will we meet?
7. How do you handle investment management—actively or passively?
8. Will you help with taxes, insurance, or estate planning?
9. What's your investment philosophy?
10. Can I see a sample financial plan?

Red Flags to Watch Out For

- Pushy sales tactics or pressure to buy now
- Vague answers about compensation
- Overpromising returns
- Complex products like annuities with long surrender periods (without full explanation)
- Lack of transparency

If it feels like a sales pitch and not a patient consult—walk away.

How Much Should You Pay?

It varies:

- **Flat fee planning**: $1,000–$3,000/year
- **Assets under management (AUM)**: ~1.5% of your investments
- **Hourly consulting**: $150–$500/hour

Fee-only advisors may offer a monthly subscription model (e.g. $200/month). You don't have to be wealthy to get good advice.

What If You Can't Afford an Advisor Yet?

Start with education:

- Read books like *The Simple Path to Wealth* or *Your Money or Your Life*
- Use budgeting tools like YNAB or Monarch
- Follow fee-only advisors on social media
- Use your workplace EAP to meet with a financial counselor

Real Nurse, Real Story

Teresa, 42, had been working as an ER nurse for 20 years. She was making over $100K/year but had no retirement plan, was drowning in student loans, and had three credit cards she never paid off in full. A friend referred her to a fiduciary CFP who specialized in working with nurses.

They built a plan that prioritized:

- Student loan forgiveness through PSLF
- Starting a Roth IRA
- Adjusting her 403(b) investments
- Creating a debt snowball plan

Two years later, she was maxing out her Roth, had eliminated two credit cards, and finally felt in control.

Empowered Nurses Ask Questions

You would never start a shift without a report. Don't start a financial relationship without asking for one.

Final Prescription

- Get clarity on what you want from an advisor: Investment help? Debt strategy? Retirement planning?
- Interview 2–3 advisors before choosing one.
- Always ask about fiduciary status and fees.
- Trust your gut. If something feels off, it probably is.
- You don't need to be perfect—you just need to be informed.

Your Next Move

Make one financial move before your next shift. Just one.

And do another next week.

The only thing worse than working yourself sick is staying stuck when you've got the skills, strength, and smarts to shift into abundance.

You stabilize others for a living. Now it's time to stabilize yourself—with the right financial partner by your side.

Let this be the year you scrub into your financial life—and take charge with confidence.

Chapter 47: Financial Therapy and Breaking Money Shame – Why It's Okay to Ask for Help and Reset Your Relationship with Money

Let's start here: Money is emotional. It just is.

You can know every dosage calculation, every lab value, every CPR protocol by heart—but when it comes to opening a bill or logging into your bank account, your heart rate spikes and you want to hit "Escape."

And that reaction is more common than you think.

As nurses, we are trained to handle pressure, crisis, and complexity. But very few of us are taught how to sit with the emotions that come up around money—especially when that money story is shaped by scarcity, shame, trauma, or just plain exhaustion.

This chapter is about financial therapy.

It's about releasing the guilt. Unlearning the silence. And knowing that asking for help isn't weakness—it's wisdom.

What Is Financial Shame and Where Does It Come From?

Money shame isn't about not having enough. It's about the belief that *you* are not enough because of your finances.

- "I should be further along."
- "I make good money—why can't I manage it?"

- "I don't want anyone to know how much debt I'm in."
- "I'm too embarrassed to ask for help."

These thoughts don't come out of nowhere. They're layered in from years of messages:

- The family that didn't talk about money at all.
- The partner who criticized your spending.
- The financial aid forms you filled out alone as a teen.
- The Instagram feed that makes you feel like everyone else is thriving.
- The voice in your head that whispers, *"You should know this by now."*

Financial shame thrives in silence.

But like any wound, once you bring it into the light, it begins to heal.

The Power of Financial Therapy

Financial therapy is exactly what it sounds like: a space to explore the thoughts, feelings, and behaviors around money that are shaping your life.

Just like emotional therapy helps people work through trauma, relationships, and mindset patterns, financial therapy helps you:

- Identify harmful money beliefs
- Replace shame with strategy
- Develop self-compassion around financial mistakes
- Create behavior change that sticks

It's not just budgeting. It's not just spreadsheets.

It's inner work that frees you to step into financial clarity with courage.

For many nurses, financial therapy starts with admitting:

- "I'm burned out and I don't know if I can keep doing this job."
- "I make six figures and still live paycheck to paycheck."
- "My parents relied on me to help financially, and now I'm drowning."

There is *no shame* in any of this. There is only your next right step.

Understanding Your Money Story

Everyone has a money story.

It's the set of beliefs, habits, and emotional associations you carry with you. Most of it is unconscious—until you start paying attention.

Let's unpack a few common money stories nurses carry:

1. **The Provider Script**
2. "I have to take care of everyone else first."
3. You sacrifice for others, delay your own needs, and often overextend. Burnout isn't just physical—it's financial.
4. **The Survivor Script**
5. "I didn't grow up with money, so I don't know how to keep it."
6. You work hard, but as soon as money comes in, it disappears. You may avoid investing or saving out of fear.
7. **The Deserving Script**
8. "I work hard, so I should treat myself."
9. You spend as a way to self-soothe—but the cycle leaves you stuck and stressed.
10. **The Expert Script**
11. "I should know better."
12. You're educated, respected, and organized at work—so when you feel financially messy, it hits hard. You hide it, instead of seeking help.

Becoming aware of your money story is the first step toward rewriting it.

You Are Not Your Bank Balance

Say it with me:

> *"My financial worth does not define my personal worth."*

You are allowed to have made mistakes. You are allowed to have debt. You are allowed to start over. You are allowed to need help.

Let's take that pressure off your shoulders. You've carried enough already.

What Financial Healing Looks Like

1. **Naming the Pain**
2. Write down the beliefs you carry about money. Where did they come from? Whose voice is that?
3. **Replacing Shame with Curiosity**
4. Instead of asking, *"Why am I so bad with money?"* try:

- "What was I taught about money growing up?"
- "What do I want to teach my kids differently?"
- "What would financial peace look like for me?"

1. **Normalizing Support**
2. You wouldn't shame a patient for asking for help. Why do it to yourself?

- Talk to a financial advisor.
- Find a money coach.
- Journal or work with a therapist trained in financial wellness.
- Join a support group.

1. **Creating Safety Nets**
2. Part of healing is creating structure. That means:

- Automating savings
- Setting up emergency funds
- Getting disability insurance
- Naming beneficiaries

Structure creates calm.

Real Nurse, Real Story

Tanya was a 37-year-old ER nurse making $108K a year. She had nothing in savings, was $13K in credit card debt, and avoided checking her accounts because of how ashamed she felt.

She told herself:

- "I work too hard to be broke."
- "I'm just bad with money."
- "My brother is the smart one with money, not me."

Then one day, she hit pause. She found a financial coach through her hospital's EAP. She started weekly money dates with herself. She tracked spending without guilt. She cried after paying off her first $1,000 of debt.

She didn't fix everything overnight. But she got her power back.

And so can you.

Action Steps to Break Money Shame

1. **Write a Money Confession Letter**
2. Be honest. Get it out. You never have to send it. But name what's been holding you.
3. **Sẹt a No-Judgment Budget Review**
4. Print out last month's bank statements. Highlight what brought you joy. What didn't? Adjust accordingly.
5. **Start a Weekly Money Huddle**
6. 30 minutes. Set the mood. Light a candle. Play music. Review your numbers with kindness, not criticism.
7. **Create a Financial First-Aid Kit**

- $1,000 emergency savings
- Disability insurance
- A go-to advisor or coach
- A trusted friend to talk to

1. **Read One Chapter a Week**
2. Make this book your safe place. Revisit sections. Highlight what speaks to you. Talk it out with a friend.

You Deserve to Feel Safe with Money

You deserve rest.

You deserve clarity.

You deserve support.

You don't have to hustle your way into peace.

You can *heal* your way there.

You have helped people breathe again, eat again, walk again.

Now it's your turn.

To breathe.

To be seen.

To be supported.

To begin.

Make One Financial Move Before Your Next Shift

Just one.

- Text a friend and ask if they want to read this chapter with you.
- Look up a local financial coach.
- Set a reminder for your first money huddle.

And then do another next week.

Because you're not stuck.

Because you're stronger than you feel.

Because the healing starts now.

You didn't become a nurse to live paycheck to paycheck in silence.

You became a nurse because you knew you could handle hard things.

Now it's time to handle money with the same heart, honesty, and humanity you bring to every patient.

You've got this.

Let's rewrite the story together.

Part VII: The Exit Plan – Retirement and Beyond

This final section of *Financial Literacy For Nurses* is about more than just leaving the profession—it's about exiting with grace, power, and a plan. Whether you're five years from retirement or just starting to wonder what life looks like after bedside care, this section guides you through the financial, emotional, and practical transitions of your nursing career's final chapters.

Here, we cover how to prepare your finances for retirement in a nurse-specific way—accounting for pensions, shift differentials, variable hours, and healthcare costs. We explore how Social Security fits into the picture, when to draw from your accounts, and how to avoid the common tax pitfalls that trip up many retirees.

But we don't stop at numbers. We talk legacy. We talk meaning. We help you navigate what it looks like to give back, protect your loved ones, and build a financial story that outlives your last shift. This section is about more than retirement—it's about closing one chapter and opening another with confidence.

You've poured into others your entire career. Now, it's time to make sure you're poured into too.

Topics in this section include:

- Lifestyle creep in your final earning years
- Nurse-specific retirement planning

- Burnout recovery and when to pivot
- Divorce, death, and disability readiness
- Charitable giving and legacy planning
- Choosing the right financial advisor
- Financial therapy and breaking money shame

This is your permission to slow down, reassess, and rebuild—not from fear, but from intention. Because exiting the career doesn't mean exiting your power. It means stepping into a new role: financial author of the life you still get to write.

Chapter 48: Retirement Budgeting – What Will Life Cost When You're Done Working?

The Transition from Earning to Withdrawing

Retirement isn't the end of your financial story—it's the next chapter. And it's one you deserve to write with intention, strength, and clarity. If you've spent decades charting vital signs and stabilizing patients, now it's time to stabilize your own financial life as you prepare for a new kind of shift—one where rest, legacy, and freedom take center stage.

But freedom costs money.

And the biggest mistake many nurses make is underestimating what retirement will cost—and overestimating how far their current savings will stretch. This chapter walks through that gap. It's not here to scare you; it's here to wake you up, map it out, and give you a plan.

You've done hard things before. Retirement planning is no different. Let's break it down.

SECTION 1: Why Retirement Budgeting Matters (Even If You're Not Retiring Soon)

You might be thinking: "I'm not retiring for 10, 15, maybe 20 years. Why stress now?"

Here's why:

- Every dollar you *don't* prepare for today is a dollar you may have to *borrow* from your future self.
- Compound interest only works if you give it time.
- Healthcare costs are rising faster than most people plan for.
- Life doesn't magically become cheaper when you stop working.

The truth is, retirement isn't just about not working. It's about:

- Managing fixed income instead of variable overtime.
- Preparing for new expenses (hello, Medicare premiums, out-of-pocket meds, and grandkid spoiling).
- Shifting your identity from earner to steward.

So yes, it matters now. Because by the time you're ready to punch out for the last time, you want to do it on your terms—not because your body gave out before your finances gave you permission.

SECTION 2: What Retirement Really Costs (And Why It's More Than You Think)

Let's go line by line and talk about what life will likely cost you when you're no longer collecting a regular paycheck.

1. Housing

Even if your mortgage is paid off, you're not done. You'll still face:

- Property taxes (which can increase over time)

- Home maintenance and repairs (that 25-year-old roof won't replace itself)
- HOA fees (if you downsize to a condo)
- Utilities, landscaping, and possible accessibility renovations (walk-in showers, ramps, etc.)

If you're renting? Factor in annual rent increases.

Real-life scenario: A retired nurse in Texas thought she was set because her home was paid off—but rising property taxes and a failing HVAC system drained her emergency fund within two years. Plan for ownership, not just occupancy.

2. Healthcare

Even with Medicare, you'll pay out-of-pocket for:

- Part B premiums
- Part D prescription plans
- Medigap or Medicare Advantage (depending on the route you choose)
- Dental, vision, and hearing (not typically covered)
- Long-term care (which can average $4,000–$8,000 per month, depending on location)

And that's if you're relatively healthy.

3. Food and Groceries

You may eat out less, but inflation affects grocery budgets too. Add in any dietary needs (gluten-free, diabetic-friendly options, supplements), and this number may surprise you.

4. Travel and Leisure

Remember all those things you wanted to do when you retired? Cruises. Road trips. Visiting the grandkids. Seeing Ireland. Even local hobbies (golf, gardening, pottery) can add up.

Don't punish yourself by omitting these from your budget. Plan for them. They're part of why you worked so hard in the first place.

5. Family Support

Many retired nurses continue to help:

- Adult children with student loans or childcare
- Aging parents with home care costs
- Grandchildren with education expenses

Give generously—but don't give until you jeopardize your own stability.

6. Taxes

Just because you stop working doesn't mean Uncle Sam stops charging. You may owe taxes on:

- Traditional 401(k)/403(b) withdrawals
- Pension income
- Social Security (yes, it can be taxable!)
- Capital gains if you sell property or investments

This often catches retirees off guard. Your tax bracket in retirement might not be as low as you thought.

SECTION 3: Building Your Trial Retirement Budget

Before you actually retire, test your future budget.

Step 1: Estimate your post-retirement monthly expenses.

Use real numbers, not wishful thinking. Go category by category:

- Housing (property taxes, maintenance, insurance)
- Food (groceries + occasional meals out)
- Healthcare (premiums, co-pays, supplements)
- Travel (big trips + day-to-day activities)
- Utilities
- Subscriptions and memberships
- Hobbies
- Gifts + donations

Step 2: Estimate your monthly income.
This could include:

- Social Security (use SSA.gov to get your personalized estimate)
- Pension (ask HR for your projected amount)
- Retirement accounts (calculate safe withdrawal rates)
- Annuities, rental income, or part-time work

Step 3: Subtract expenses from income.
What do you get?

- If you're in the green, great! Test living off that amount for 3-6 months before retiring.
- If you're in the red, now is the time to adjust—not later when the paycheck stops.

You don't need a crystal ball to budget retirement. You need awareness, a calculator, and a bit of courage.

Chapter 49: Downsizing, Relocating, or Aging in Place

Real Estate and Lifestyle Options in Retirement

When you retire from nursing, you're not just walking away from long shifts, emotional intensity, and institutional hallways. You're stepping into an entirely new stage of life that requires intentional decisions—especially about where and how you live.

The lifestyle that carried you through your nursing career may not be the one that serves you best in retirement. The big house with stairs might become a maintenance burden. The familiar neighborhood may feel too far from family, too quiet, or too expensive. You might want warmer weather, lower taxes, or just a change of pace.

That leads us to three major pathways nurses often consider:

1. **Downsizing**
2. **Relocating**
3. **Aging in Place**

Each comes with financial, emotional, and practical trade-offs.

This chapter is your deep dive into those decisions. Whether you're 5 years from retirement or already packing boxes, we'll walk through what to consider, what to avoid, and how to align your housing choice with your financial future.

SECTION 1: The Case for Downsizing

What Does Downsizing Mean?

Downsizing isn't just about square footage. It's about simplifying. It might mean:

- Moving from a four-bedroom home to a two-bedroom condo
- Trading the suburbs for an apartment near public transit
- Letting go of a mortgage in favor of a paid-off smaller home

For nurses, especially those who spent years accumulating equity in a family home, downsizing can unlock serious financial benefits—and emotional clarity.

Pros of Downsizing

- **Lower monthly expenses**: Utilities, insurance, property taxes, and upkeep typically drop
- **Equity release**: Selling a larger home may free up cash to invest or pad your retirement accounts
- **Less maintenance**: Fewer rooms mean fewer responsibilities
- **More lifestyle flexibility**: Travel more, clean less

Cons of Downsizing

- **Emotional attachment**: Leaving a family home can feel like grief
- **Moving costs**: Realtor fees, movers, closing costs, new furniture—it adds up
- **HOA fees**: Condos and retirement communities may carry monthly fees
- **Storage challenges**: You'll likely have to part with belongings

Real Nurse Scenario

"I sold my 3,000-square-foot house and moved into a two-bedroom cottage in a 55+ community. My heating bill was cut in half. And for the first time, I had money left over at the end of the month. But I cried the day I left our old kitchen. So many memories."

SECTION 2: The Relocation Question

Retiring in place isn't your only option. Many nurses consider moving to another city, state, or even country. Some want to be closer to grandchildren. Others seek better weather, lower cost of living, or improved healthcare access.

Common Relocation Goals:

- **Tax savings**: States like Florida, Texas, and Nevada have no income tax
- **Cost-of-living shifts**: Moving from California to North Carolina might cut expenses in half
- **Healthcare access**: Some areas have stronger Medicare-accepting systems
- **Social proximity**: Living near adult kids or friends can improve quality of life

Key Factors to Evaluate

- **State taxes on pensions or Social Security**
- **Healthcare networks nearby**
- **Cost of housing and groceries**
- **Weather/climate considerations**
- **Safety and walkability**
- **Cultural or lifestyle fit**

Renting Before Buying

If you're seriously considering a move, try renting in that location for 6-12 months before buying. Your retirement dollars go further when you know what you're getting into.

SECTION 3: Aging in Place

Many nurses say: "I'm not leaving my home. I want to retire and stay right here."

That's a valid and often beautiful goal. But aging in place well means planning ahead.

Key Questions:

- Is your home accessible now? What will it take to make it so?
- Are there bedrooms and full bathrooms on the first floor?
- Can you afford a home health aide if needed?
- Are you within reach of grocery stores, pharmacies, and healthcare?

Costs to Consider

- Home retrofits (stair lifts, ramps, wider doorways, shower bars)
- Security systems or remote monitoring
- Transportation if you can't drive
- In-home care, cleaning, or food delivery

Social Considerations

Isolation is a hidden cost of aging in place. Nurses are used to team-based environments. Retiring into silence can impact mental health.

Plan for:

- Community centers
- Churches or faith groups
- Volunteering opportunities
- Family check-ins

SECTION 4: Run the Numbers – A Financial Comparison

Let's look at a simplified example. Assume you're a retired nurse with a paid-off home worth $400,000.

Option 1: Stay Put

- Property tax: $4,000/year
- Maintenance/repairs: $3,500/year
- Utilities: $2,400/year
- Total: $9,900/year

Option 2: Downsize to Condo

- HOA fees: $2,400/year
- Property tax: $2,000/year
- Utilities: $1,500/year
- Total: $5,900/year

Equity unlocked from home sale: $250,000 (after fees and downsizing costs)

That equity could be invested to generate $10,000–$12,000/year in income (at 4% withdrawal).

SECTION 5: The Emotional Side of the Decision

Money matters, but so does your heart.

- What does "home" mean to you?
- Who do you want nearby?
- Will you feel free or lonely in a new space?
- What kind of neighborhood do you imagine growing old in?

Nurses often carry decades of emotional labor. Don't discount how it feels to rest somewhere that brings you peace.

Talk with family. Visit prospective neighborhoods. Ask other retirees what they'd do differently.

SECTION 6: Financial Planning Tips for Real Estate Changes in Retirement

1. **Talk to a financial advisor before selling your home.** Understand capital gains rules, tax timing, and how the proceeds affect benefits.
2. **Update your estate plan.** Changing property ownership? Add it to your will or trust.
3. **Review insurance coverage.** Condo living means different liabilities than a single-family home.
4. **Don't rush.** Retiring doesn't mean you have to move immediately. Try it in stages.
5. **Create a "housing horizon" plan.** Where do you want to live at 65, 75, and 85?

A Clear Call to Act

Before your next shift or your next cup of coffee:

- Write down your current housing costs.
- List what you love about where you live now.
- List what frustrates you or may become a burden later.
- Choose one option to research: downsizing, relocating, or aging in place.

Knowledge builds power. And power builds peace.

The only thing worse than running on fumes is retiring without a housing plan that fits your future.

Final Note:

You spent a lifetime helping others feel safe. Now it's your turn.

Whether you end up in a cozy condo, a lakeside cabin, a city loft, or the same house you raised your babies in—make sure it works for your finances, your health, and your peace of mind.

You don't have to have all the answers now. But the more you ask the right questions today, the more freedom you'll have tomorrow.

This is your retirement. And this is your next safe place to land.

Let's make sure it's one you choose on purpose.

Chapter 50: Nurses and Wealth – Your Legacy, Your Story

The Final Shift: Closing the Book with Power and Purpose

This isn't just the final chapter of the book—it's the first chapter of the rest of your life. And whether you read this cover to cover, skipped around, or bookmarked chapters for later, you showed up for yourself. That matters.

You didn't pick up a financial literacy book for nurses because you were bored. You picked it up because deep down, you know something bigger is calling you. Financial freedom. Peace of mind. Confidence with money. A life where you're not just surviving the next shift, but building something lasting.

And that brings us here—this moment, this chapter—where we zoom out.

It's time to talk about legacy.

What Does It Mean to "Retire Well" as a Nurse?

For nurses, retirement isn't just about 401(k)s, pension balances, or Social Security checks. It's about finally getting to live a life where your time, energy, and wisdom are fully your own.

You've spent a career caring for others. You've juggled shifts, worked holidays, missed family events, and put your patients' lives ahead of your own sleep and sanity. So what does it look like to step back and say: I did my part. And now it's time to rest, enjoy, and give on my own terms?

Retiring well as a nurse means:

- **Owning your story.** Every dollar you've earned tells a tale of grit and sacrifice. Honor that.
- **Designing your days.** Want to travel? Start a garden? Mentor younger nurses? Now is your chance.
- **Protecting your future.** Set up estate plans, reduce tax burdens, and make sure your wishes are known.
- **Giving with intention.** Whether it's to your kids, church, favorite nursing program, or a scholarship fund—you decide what impact your money makes.

Wealth Isn't About Luxury—It's About Leverage

When nurses hear the word "wealth," some cringe. That's for CEOs, they think—not for me. But wealth, when viewed through the right lens, is not about yachts and designer clothes.

It's about options.

It's about security.

It's about not having to say "yes" to every shift because you're afraid of what happens if you don't.

It's about leaving something behind—not just in memory, but in motion.

Let's talk about what that looks like.

Define Your Wealth on Your Own Terms

Every nurse's version of a wealthy life is different. Some want a quiet cabin by the lake. Others want to spoil their grandkids or launch a nonprofit for underserved communities. Some just want to know they can cover their prescriptions, their groceries, and the occasional cruise without fear.

The first step is to write your definition. Literally. Here's your prompt:

"I'll feel financially wealthy when I can _______________________ ____."

Fill that in. Post it somewhere visible. Make every financial decision—from budgeting to investing—with that sentence as your guide.

How to Leave a Legacy Without Losing Your Mind

You don't need to be a millionaire to leave a legacy. Here's what matters:

- **Have a will.** Make sure what you've built goes where you want it to.
- **Set beneficiaries.** Update them annually. Check your 403(b), IRA, and insurance policies.
- **Use Roth IRAs and trusts strategically.** Tax-free distributions can bless your loved ones.
- **Tell your story.** Your legacy isn't just assets. It's lessons. Write them down.
- **Mentor others.** Pass down knowledge. Help someone else avoid the same money pitfalls.

The Emotional Side of "Enough"

Nurses are notorious for giving everything they have—until there's nothing left. So in retirement, it can be hard to switch from giver to receiver, or from worker to at-rest.

Some questions to ask yourself:

- Do I feel guilty spending money on myself?
- Am I afraid of outliving my savings?
- Do I worry that I didn't "do enough" to deserve peace?

Here's the truth: you've already done more than enough. Financial wellness in retirement isn't about perfection. It's about planning, adjusting, and giving yourself grace.

You wouldn't shame a patient for being in recovery. Don't shame yourself for learning, growing, and reclaiming your future.

Ending This Book—But Beginning a New Chapter

This book wasn't about forcing you into one right way to handle your money. It was about giving you tools, language, and confidence. About reminding you that nurses—yes, *you*—deserve clarity, comfort, and control over their finances.

Your career might've started with a stethoscope, a badge, and a pair of scrubs. But it doesn't have to end in uncertainty.

It can end in peace.

It can end in strength.

It can end with a clear plan—and a proud heart.

Or better yet: it doesn't *end* at all.

Because your wealth—financial, emotional, and spiritual—will ripple long after you've taken off your badge for the last time.

One Last Call to Action

Before you close this book, I want you to do three things:

1. **Write your definition of wealth.** Post it where you can see it.
2. **Make one financial move this week.** Just one. Update a beneficiary. Book time with an advisor. Open a Roth IRA.
3. **Talk to someone you love about money.** Your child. Your partner. Your fellow nurse. Open the door.

You're not just a nurse.

You're a builder of wealth.

You're a keeper of legacy.

You are powerful.

Thank you for reading. Thank you for showing up for yourself. Now go live your story—and write the next chapter your way.

The badge may come off, but the impact never does.

Disclaimer

Important Notice About This Book

This book, *Financial Literacy For Nurses,* was written to educate, empower, and encourage nurses—from brand-new RN graduates to seasoned nurse managers and retiring nurse practitioners—to take control of their financial lives with clarity and confidence. The insights shared throughout these pages reflect the author's personal journey, professional expertise, and decades spent advising high-performing professionals in healthcare, wealth education, and retirement planning.

That said, it's important to understand the following:

Educational Purpose Only

The content in this book is provided for **educational purposes only**. It's here to help you understand financial principles, recognize common pitfalls nurses face, and begin designing a care plan for your own long-term financial wellness—whether you're managing student loan payments as a new grad or reviewing pension options after a 30-year career.

However, **this is not personal advice**.

Every nurse has a different story: income, shift schedule, family dynamic, tax situation, retirement plan access, risk tolerance, and life goals. That means no single chapter in this book can—or should—replace the tailored guidance of a financial professional who understands your full financial picture.

What works for one nurse may be totally inappropriate—or even harmful—for another.

Before making any major decisions related to investing, insurance, legal documents, or taxes, please consult with a licensed financial advisor, CPA, attorney, or insurance specialist.

No Legal Advice

This book does **not provide legal advice** and should not be used in place of professional counsel. Whether you are:

- Creating a will, trust, or advanced directive
- Starting a side business or private practice
- Reviewing an employment contract or benefit package
- Naming beneficiaries or establishing power of attorney

...you should speak with a qualified attorney in your state. Every legal matter carries nuance, and your financial security deserves personalized attention—not a one-size-fits-all checklist.

No Investment or Financial Advice

While this book explores investing, retirement strategies, and money management tools relevant to nurses, it does so from an **educational lens** only.

It is **not investment advice**, and it does **not recommend specific securities, portfolios, or products**.

Never make investment decisions solely based on the content in this book. Always speak with a fiduciary financial planner or licensed investment advisor to ensure that your strategy aligns with your career stage, goals, time horizon, and tax profile.

Financial wellness is a process—not a product. Don't "wing it." Build your plan with structure and support.

No Tax or Accounting Advice

This book is **not written by a CPA** and is **not a tax manual**.

While it includes financial topics relevant to nurses—such as:

- Tax-deferred vs. Roth retirement accounts
- HSA and FSA strategies
- Self-employment taxes for 1099 or travel nurses
- State-specific income issues for compact license holders

...these topics are for educational purposes only. Tax law changes frequently, and your personal income, state of residence, deductions, and filing status all impact your outcome.

Consult a qualified tax professional before filing, making IRA conversions, setting up a business entity, or taking deductions.

No Guarantees

There are no guarantees in the ICU—and there are no guarantees in personal finance.

Reading this book won't promise you wealth, debt freedom, or a stress-free retirement. Results depend on your decisions, consistency, habits, behavior, and sometimes just the unpredictability of life.

This book offers structure, mindset, and a financial framework—but **not a magic cure**.

Use it like you'd use a nursing care plan: as a guide. Not a substitute for thinking critically and personalizing your approach.

Limitation of Liability

By reading this book, you agree that the author, Pat Brown, MBA, and associated platforms including *FinancialLiteracyForNurses.com* and other related educational brands, are **not liable for any financial, legal, tax, or**

investment decisions you make based on the content herein.

We are not responsible for losses, penalties, missed opportunities, or financial outcomes resulting from the use or misuse of this information.

A Reminder to Build Your Financial Team

One of the core messages of this book is this:

You don't have to go it alone.

Just like no good nurse works solo on a critical code, no one should try to manage complex finances without a support team.

If you don't already have a trusted financial advisor, estate planning attorney, insurance expert, or CPA—this is your invitation to start building your care team.

Interview them. Ask questions. Look for people who serve with integrity, explain clearly, and understand the realities of a nurse's career, income, and retirement path.

You've cared for everyone else. Now it's time to care for your financial future.

Let This Be the Start of Smarter Conversations

This book won't solve every problem overnight. But it can help you ask better questions, advocate for yourself, and make financial decisions with **structure instead of stress**.

When you understand your money, you stop feeling ashamed or confused.

You stop guessing.

You stop deferring.

You stop burning out financially just to survive another shift.

You start planning.

You start protecting.

You start building a life—and legacy—you can be proud of.

So take a deep breath.

Take notes.

Ask for help when you need it.

And most of all—keep going.

You've handled codes, conflict, and crisis.
You can handle your money, too.
Let's get to work.

Financial Calendar for Nurses

Stay Ahead of Burnout, Bills, and Big Goals—All Year Long

This calendar isn't just about taxes—it's about staying ahead of the chaos. Whether you're a first-year nurse adjusting to night shifts and student loan payments, a mid-career nurse balancing a mortgage and 401(k) contributions, or a seasoned nurse leader planning for retirement, knowing when to act financially can make all the difference.

Nurses rely on systems, protocols, and handoffs. You don't start a shift without checking the MAR, updating the whiteboard, or reviewing your patients. Why should your finances be any different?

Here's your month-by-month money check-in—to help you stay organized, protected, and on track all year long.

January – Start the Year Like a Fresh Chart

- **New Tax Year Begins** – Wipe the slate. New budget. New goals. New plan.
- Review your paycheck: Benefits, withholdings, and contributions.
- Set up or refresh your household budget. Track fixed costs (rent, student loans), variables (eating out, childcare), and savings goals (403(b), Roth IRA, HSA).
- **Update W-4 withholding** if your life changed last year—new job, marriage, kids, or per diem work.
- **Rule of Thumb:** Save 25%–30% of any per diem, contract, or 1099 income for taxes.
- **Jan 15** – Estimated tax payment due (if you worked agency or 1099 shifts in Q4).

- **Jan 31** – Deadline to receive W-2s, 1099s, and other tax docs.
- **Pro Tip:** Create a digital folder called "2024 Taxes – Nurse" and drop files in as you go.

February – Organize and Prepare

- Gather your tax documents: especially if you worked multiple jobs, travel assignments, or agency shifts.
- Know Your Tax Forms:
- **W-2** – Traditional hospital/clinic employment.
- **1099-NEC** – Per diem or agency work.
- **Schedule C** – If you freelance as a CPR instructor, write CEU content, or do nursing consulting.
- **Schedule E** – If you rent out a room, AirBnB, or own property.
- Finalize any side hustle bookkeeping.
- Organize business receipts for write-offs: scrubs, CEUs, work mileage, certifications, licenses.

March – Business Entity & Hustle Review

- **March 15** – Deadline to file taxes for S-Corps or partnerships (if you run your own wellness practice, LLC for speaking, or private nursing service).
- Forms to Know: **1120-S** for S-corps.
- Review your side income: Is it worth setting up an LLC or solo 401(k)? Do you need professional liability insurance?

April – The Tax Final Countdown

- **April 15 – Federal Tax Day**
- File your taxes or request an extension with Form 4868.
- First quarter estimated tax payment due if applicable.
- **Last day to contribute** to:

- Roth or Traditional IRA (for prior year)
- HSA (for prior year tax benefits)
- **Even if you can't pay the full bill, still file.** Late filing penalties are worse than late payment penalties.

May – Mid-Year Money Checkup

- Review spending year-to-date: Has lifestyle creep snuck in?
- Check progress toward:
- Roth IRA contributions
- Maxing out 403(b)/401(k) contributions
- HSA savings (if eligible)
- Revisit your goals. Are you moving toward financial peace or away from it?
- Schedule a "nurse money huddle"—with your advisor, spouse, or solo.

June – Second Quarter Tune-Up

- **June 15** – Second estimated tax payment due if applicable.
- Are you setting enough aside from side income?
- Plan for summer spending—vacations, camps, travel—without derailing savings goals.

July – Reset and Rebalance

- Review:
- Your emergency fund (3–6 months of expenses).
- Investment allocations: Do you need to rebalance your 403(b) or Roth IRA?
- Risk exposure: Are you invested too aggressively—or not enough?
- Check your coverage:
- Long-term disability insurance
- Term life insurance (vs. whole life)

- Umbrella liability coverage
- Loss of license insurance (if relevant in your role or specialty)

August – Credit, Debt, and Career Planning

- Pull your **free credit report** from AnnualCreditReport.com.
- Review student loan progress or refinancing options.
- Check your mortgage, car loan, or any other major debt.
- Consider rewards cards for nurses who travel or have high job expenses.
- Update your resume and CEU log—whether you're looking or not.

September – Strategic Year-End Planning Begins

- **September 15** – Third quarter estimated tax payment due.
- Review:
- Year-to-date income and deductions
- Charitable giving plans
- Roth conversions if you're in a low-income year
- Business write-offs if you own a side hustle or consulting gig
- Consider adjusting contributions or income timing before year-end.

October – Extension & Enrollment Season

- **October 15** – Final day to file if you requested a tax extension.
- **October 1** – FAFSA opens if you're supporting kids or grandkids in college.
- Begin reviewing health insurance for open enrollment (especially if switching jobs or turning 65).
- Compare 403(b) matches, HSA vs. FSA, dependent care, etc.

November – Year-End Tax Strategy Session

- Meet with your advisor or CPA to discuss:
- Required Minimum Distributions (RMDs) if 73+
- Roth conversions
- Tax-loss harvesting in brokerage accounts
- Final charitable giving plans
- Section 179 deductions (if you've made business purchases like equipment or tech)
- Consider "bunching" medical expenses, donations, or deductions.

December – Land the Plane Smoothly

- **December 31** – Deadline for many tax moves.
- Last chance for:
- Maxing out 403(b), Roth IRA, Solo 401(k), or SEP IRA
- HSA contributions
- Charitable donations
- Using FSA dollars before they

Financial Glossary for Nurses

Asset – Anything you own that holds value, such as cash, stocks, property, or investments. Assets are your fuel tanks—they power your financial journey.

Liability – Money you owe to others, including loans, mortgages, and credit card debt. Think of liabilities as drag on your shift—manageable, but they'll slow you down if left unchecked.

Net Worth – The difference between what you own (assets) and what you owe (liabilities). This is your personal vitals chart—it shows how healthy your finances really are.

Budget – A monthly or weekly plan for how you spend, save, and invest. This is your care plan for money—without it, you're working without orders.

Emergency Fund – Savings set aside specifically for financial turbulence—such as job loss, medical expenses, or family emergencies. Aim for at least 3–6 months of expenses.

Compound Interest – Interest that earns interest over time. It's the autopilot of wealth building—quiet, steady, and powerful.

Diversification – Spreading investments across different asset classes (stocks, bonds, real estate) to reduce risk. Think of it as not putting all your shifts in one unit.

Roth IRA – A retirement account funded with after-tax dollars. Withdrawals in retirement are tax-free, making it ideal if you expect higher taxes later in life.

Brokerage Account – A flexible investment account to buy and sell stocks, ETFs, bonds, and more. Great for mid- to long-term financial goals.

ETF (Exchange-Traded Fund) – A bundle of investments traded like a stock, offering diversification and low fees. Like owning a whole hospital wing instead of one room.

Inflation – The rise in prices over time, which reduces the buying power of your money. Today's $1 might feel like $0.85 in a few years.

Credit Score – A number that measures how responsible you are with credit. It affects your borrowing power and interest rates.

Interest Rate – The cost of borrowing or the earnings on your savings/investments, expressed as a percentage.

Risk Tolerance – Your emotional and financial ability to endure investment ups and downs. Important when building your portfolio.

Stock – A share in a company. Stockholders benefit from value increases and possibly dividends.

Bond – A loan you give to a company or government, in return for regular interest and repayment.

Capital Gain – The profit from selling an asset for more than you paid. Long-term gains are usually taxed more favorably.

Liability Insurance – Protects you if you're legally responsible for injury or damage to others.

Term Life Insurance – Covers you for a set period (e.g., 20 years). Good for income protection while raising kids or paying off a mortgage.

Financial Literacy – The ability to understand and use financial knowledge to make informed decisions.

Accounting Terms for Nurses with Side Hustles

Income – Money earned through your job, side gigs, rental properties, or investments.

Expenses – All the costs related to daily life or side work: rent, scrubs, licensing fees, supplies.

Profit – What's left after subtracting expenses from income. Profit is what keeps your side hustle healthy.

Loss – When expenses exceed income. Normal in new businesses, but should be tracked.

Cash Flow – Money moving in and out of your accounts. Like your IV drip—you want steady flow.

Invoice – A request for payment for services. Useful for tutoring, CEU writing, or consulting gigs.

Receipts – Proof of purchase. Save for taxes, audits, and bookkeeping.

Write-Off – Deductible business expenses (e.g., laptop, scrubs, continuing education).

Deduction – Expenses that lower your taxable income, like retirement contributions or student loan interest.

Depreciation – A way to account for wear and tear on big purchases over time.

Revenue – Total income before subtracting expenses.

Net Income – What's left after all expenses and taxes. This is your real bottom line.

Gross Income – Total earnings before any deductions.

Audit – A review of your financial records, usually by the IRS.

Chart of Accounts – Categories for organizing your income and expenses.

Bookkeeping – Recording all your income and expenses. Do it regularly.

Taxable Income – The portion of your income that the IRS uses to calculate your taxes.

Form 1099 – For contract work (e.g., staffing agency or education gigs).

Form W-9 – Used to give your tax info to clients/employers.

Schedule C – Used to report income and expenses from self-employment.

Questions to Ask Financial Professionals

For Financial Advisors:

- Are you a fiduciary 100% of the time?
- How are you paid (fee-only, commission, hourly)?

- Do you have experience working with healthcare professionals?
- Can you help with irregular income or part-time work?
- Will you coordinate with my CPA and estate attorney?

For CPAs:

- Are you familiar with nurse-specific deductions (scrubs, license, CEUs)?
- Can you help with 1099 income from side work?
- Do you offer tax planning or just filing?
- Can you help with multi-state income or travel nurse taxes?

For Attorneys:

- Can you help with employment contract reviews?
- Do you offer estate planning (wills, POA, trusts)?
- Can you help start an LLC or nonprofit for a nurse-led initiative?

For Business Partners:

- What are your goals for this project?
- How will decisions and profits be shared?
- Who is contributing what?
- What's the exit strategy if one person wants to leave?

This glossary was created to empower nurses. Whether you're on the floor, managing a side hustle, or planning for retirement, you deserve plain language, clear terms, and confidence in your financial toolkit.

Final Word: From the Breakroom to Retirement – Let's Chart Your Course

This book exists because financial education is a powerful tool—especially for nurses.

It can unlock freedom, protect your legacy, and give you the confidence to take control of your future, both in and out of scrubs. But just like in nursing—and in life—long-term success isn't about luck. It's about consistency, preparation, critical thinking, and knowing when to call for backup.

Use this book as a **guide**, not a rule book. Let it spark your curiosity and inspire your next financial move. But don't let it replace the wisdom of licensed, credentialed professionals when it matters most.

You wouldn't respond to a critical patient without checking vitals, reviewing history, and calling in your team. So why would you treat your finances any differently?

Be proactive. Stay informed. Ask questions before making major financial decisions. And most importantly—know that you are not alone.

Need Help? Start Here.

Reach out to a team that understands what it means to care for others—and how to care for your wealth with the same level of skill, structure, and intention.

Contact:

Pat Brown, MBA

Financial literacy advocate and advisor to nurses and healthcare professionals nationwide

info@financialliteracyfornurses.com

www.financialliteracyfornurses.com

Subscribe to the newsletter for nurse-focused financial guidance—delivered with clarity, compassion, and zero jargon. It's like patient education—but for your paycheck, your retirement, and your peace of mind.

Final Word to Every Nurse Who Flipped These Pages:

These tools weren't meant to sit on a shelf.

They were created to help you make confident, informed decisions—from your first nursing paycheck to your final shift.

Revisit this book. Highlight it. Dog-ear it. Share it with a nursing student, a colleague, a friend. Use it as your **financial care plan**. Use it like you'd use a protocol—something reliable, something you can turn to when the pressure's on.

Because the best decisions are made before the code is called.

And your financial journey deserves just as much planning as your next shift.

Your future self—the one who has **freedom**, **options**, and **peace of mind**—will thank you.

Chart your course.

Own your legacy.

And never again let money be the one thing that holds you back.

Scrubs on. Wallet ready.

Let's go.

How to Vet Financial Professionals Like You Vet Patient Protocols

Scrubs On. Questions Out.

You've trained for thousands of hours. You trust clinical protocols. You double-check MARs, lean on your care team, and rely on surgeons, anesthesiologists, and pharmacists to help every shift run safe and smooth.

Your financial life deserves that same level of teamwork and diligence.

Choosing the right financial professionals—whether it's a financial advisor, CPA, or both—can shape your financial future more than any market move or benefit package. The wrong fit could cost you years of progress, hidden fees, or missed opportunities. The right team? It can save you thousands, help you avoid burnout-level stress, and give you clarity—even in the middle of life's financial "code blues."

So let's treat this like you would a new hire on your unit. Vet them. Ask questions. See how they think, what they value, and whether they're the kind of professional who brings calm to the chaos.

Here are **30 must-ask questions** to help you evaluate your financial care team before you trust them with your money, your goals, or your future.

Questions to Ask a Financial Advisor

General Fit and Philosophy

1. Are you a fiduciary 100% of the time—and can you put that in writing?
2. How are you compensated—fee-only, commission-based, or fee-based?
3. Do you specialize in working with nurses, healthcare professionals, or high-stress shift workers?
4. What licenses and certifications do you hold (CFP®, CFA, MBA, ChFC, etc.)?
5. What's your core investment philosophy—and how does that align with someone who works 12s and has income variability?
6. How will you personalize my financial plan based on my hospital system, union, pension, and benefit options?
7. What types of clients do you typically serve—single professionals, dual-income families, early retirees?
8. Do you have an account minimum to work with you?
9. Can we meet virtually, or do you only offer in-person appointments?
10. How do you stay up to date on issues that affect healthcare workers financially?

Services and Support

1. What services do you provide beyond investment management—do you advise on insurance, taxes, or estate planning?
2. Will you help me review my hospital benefits package, 403(b), and healthcare plan annually?
3. How often will we meet to review my plan—and how do you track progress?
4. What planning software or tools do you use, and will I have access to them?
5. Can you help me build a monthly spending plan that works with shift

differentials and side income?

6. Will you help me navigate loan forgiveness programs like PSLF or repayment strategies for student debt?
7. Do you coordinate with my CPA or estate attorney if needed?
8. How do you define financial success for your clients—what metrics do you use?
9. If I decide to leave, are there exit fees, surrender charges, or costs to transfer my investments?
10. Will I work directly with you or be handed off to junior staff?

Questions to Ask a CPA or Tax Advisor

Tax Planning & Filing

1. Do you have experience working with nurses or others in healthcare who have irregular income, bonuses, differentials, or travel pay?
2. Do you offer both tax prep and proactive, year-round planning?
3. How do you charge—flat fee, hourly, or ongoing retainer?
4. Can you help me optimize strategies for income from multiple sources (W-2, 1099, rental, or contract nursing)?
5. Will you estimate how much I should be setting aside for quarterly tax payments if I do travel, consulting, or PRN work?
6. Are you familiar with nurse-specific issues like per diem, union dues, continuing education, and uniform deductions?
7. Can you advise on charitable giving, donor-advised funds, or tax-smart donations?
8. If I'm audited, do you provide representation or support through the process?
9. Can you guide me on retirement withdrawal strategies and required minimum distributions later in life?
10. How do you stay current with tax law changes that impact healthcare workers, retirees, and high-income professionals?

A Few Reminders From the Breakroom:

Don't be afraid to ask these questions directly.

You're hiring someone to help protect your financial life—just like you'd protect your patient's care plan.

A great advisor or CPA will welcome your questions. They're not there to impress you with jargon. They're there to serve with clarity, confidence, and compassion.

Ask for a discovery call. Take notes. Compare answers.

And remember—**you're not just hiring someone for today. You're choosing a financial partner for your future.**

One More Thing

Every nurse knows what happens when assumptions go unchecked.

The wrong dose. The missed allergy. The unspoken concern.

The same is true for your money.

- Don't assume credentials = clarity.
- Don't assume confidence = competence.
- Don't assume "professional" = personal fit.

Ask. Verify. Trust your gut. Then decide.

Because this is your money.

Your well-being.

Your legacy.

Your future.

Treat it with the same intentionality, empathy, and diligence you bring to every patient, every chart, every shift.

Should You Work With a Financial Advisor?

What Nurses Need to Know Before Bringing in a Professional

As a nurse, you're trained to follow protocols, read vitals under pressure, and stay focused even in chaotic environments. Your job demands precision, compassion, adaptability—and you bring those same strengths into your personal life.

So when it comes to managing your money, here's the question:

Should you go it alone—or bring in professional support?

The truth? **Working with a financial advisor can be life-changing**—especially for nurses navigating long shifts, unpredictable income, student loans, retirement decisions, and limited time to manage it all.

But just like evaluating a treatment plan, ordering labs, or calling in a consult—you've got to weigh the pros and cons.

Let's break it down.

Pros of Working With a Financial Advisor

1. **Comprehensive Expertise**

A qualified advisor isn't just focused on investments. They bring insight across key areas:

- Retirement planning (403(b), pension decisions, Roth IRAs)

- Insurance (disability, life, long-term care)
- Debt payoff strategies
- Education savings plans
- Tax-smart investing
- Estate planning

If you're juggling shift work, aging parents, college-bound kids, or burnout, an advisor helps you build a strategy that holds up under real life—not just textbook scenarios.

2. **Saves Time and Reduces Mental Load**

Let's be honest—after a 12-hour shift, the last thing most nurses want to do is dig into insurance policies or rebalance a portfolio. A financial advisor helps take the weight off your shoulders by managing the big picture while you focus on your family, your career, or your next moment of rest.

3. **Objective, Calming Guidance**

Even the most level-headed nurse can panic when the market drops or life throws a curveball. A good advisor acts like your financial charge nurse—calm, experienced, and able to zoom out when emotions creep in. They help you stay grounded and avoid costly mistakes.

4. **Accountability and Follow-Through**

Knowing what to do isn't the hard part—doing it consistently is. An advisor provides structure. They help make sure your plan actually gets executed:

- Updating beneficiaries
- Tracking savings goals
- Rebalancing investments
- Reviewing your progress each year
- Preparing you for retirement and long-term goals

It's like having a standing huddle for your finances.

5. **Customized Planning for the Nurse Life**

You don't work a 9-to-5 job. You deal with shift differentials, PRN gigs, union benefits, preceptorships, side income, and sometimes unpredictable burnout. A great advisor builds your financial plan around your life—not just generic assumptions.

Whether you're a 28-year-old nurse paying off student loans or a 59-year-old nurse manager eyeing early retirement, the right advisor helps you navigate your next move with confidence.

Cons of Working With a Financial Advisor

1. **Cost**

Most advisors charge a percentage of the assets they manage (often 0.5%–1%), a flat fee, or hourly rates. If you're just getting started financially, it can feel like one more expense. That said, the cost may be worth it if it prevents bigger mistakes—or helps you build wealth faster.

2. **Not All Advisors Are Created Equal**

Some advisors are fiduciaries—legally required to act in your best interest. Others are just brokers who may earn commissions on insurance or investments. It's up to you to vet them. Ask questions. Read the fine print. If something feels unclear, press for transparency.

3. **You Still Need to Be Involved**

An advisor can guide the plan—but you're still in charge. You'll need to participate in the big decisions around:

- Retirement timing
- Real estate or relocation
- Insurance choices
- Budgeting and spending
- Legacy planning

Delegation is smart. Disengaging completely? Not so much.

4. **Risk of Cookie-Cutter Advice**

If your advisor isn't asking about your shift schedule, union benefits, 403(b) plan, PSLF eligibility, or burnout risk, they're not customizing the plan. Nurses live complex lives—and your finances deserve nuance and detail.

5. **You Might Not Need One—Yet**

If you're financially literate, love managing your accounts, and have relatively simple needs—401(k), Roth IRA, emergency fund—you may be fine DIY-ing for now. But as life grows more complex (marriage, home buying, aging parents), having a professional becomes a powerful advantage.

So... Should You Work With a Financial Advisor?

Start by asking yourself a few honest questions:

- Do I have the time, discipline, and tools to manage my money well, consistently?
- Am I confident about my investing, insurance, and tax strategies?
- Do I understand how my hospital benefits, 403(b), pension, and Social Security fit together?
- Am I prepared for financial curveballs like job loss, illness, or early retirement?
- Would working with someone I trust reduce my stress and help me avoid mistakes?

If you answered "**no**" to one or more, it may be time to bring someone onto your care team.

Final Word: Advisors Aren't Just for the Wealthy

You don't have to be rich to work with a financial advisor.

You just need to want structure. Clarity. Strategy.

You need to want *peace of mind*—and a professional who respects what you've built, honors your goals, and knows how to help you grow it.

The best advisors don't sell products. They deliver plans.

They ask better questions.

They hold you accountable.

They walk beside you—through every season, every shift, and every decision.

You've spent your career caring for others. You deserve someone who will help care for your financial future.

Don't fly solo if you don't want to.

Bring in a trusted co-pilot.

And let your money start working as hard as you do.

Because your retirement shouldn't be a gamble.

It should be a plan.

Made in the USA
Monee, IL
04 November 2026

67386750R00213